VISUAL INTERFACE DESIGN FOR DIGITAL CULTURAL HERITAGE

We would like to dedicate this book to our other co-authors.

Visual Interface Design for Digital Cultural Heritage

A Guide to Rich-Prospect Browsing

STAN RUECKER, MILENA RADZIKOWSKA
AND STÉFAN SINCLAIR
University of Alberta, Mount Royal University and McMaster University, Canada

LONDON AND NEW YORK

First published 2011 by Ashgate Publishing

Published 2016 by Routledge
2 Park Square, Milton Park, Abingdon, Oxfordshire OX14 4RN
711 Third Avenue, New York, NY 10017

First issued in paperback 2016

Routledge is an imprint of the Taylor and Francis Group, an informa business

British Library Cataloguing in Publication Data
Ruecker, Stan.
Visuali nterface designf ordi gital cultural heritage :a gui det or ich-prospect browsing.
1. Web-based user interfaces – Design. 2. Cultural property – Electronic information resources – Management. 3. Electronic information resource searching.
I. Title II. Radzikowska, Milena. III. Sinclair, Stéfan.
005.4'37–dc22

Library of Congress Cataloging-in-Publication Data
Ruecker, Stan.
Visual interface design for digital cultural heritage : a guide to rich-prospect browsing / by Stan Ruecker, Milena Radzikowska, and Stéfan Sinclair.
p. cm.
Includes bibliographical references and index.
ISBN 978-1-4094-0422-4 (alk. paper)—ISBN 978-1-4094-0423-1 (ebook)
1. Browsers (Computer programs) 2. Electronic information resource searching.
3. User interfaces (Computer systems)—Design. 4. Humanities—Digital libraries.
I. Radzikowska, Milena. II. Sinclair, Stéfan. III. Title.
ZA4230.R84 2011
025.04252—dc22

2010053667

ISBN 13: 978-1-138-25030-7 (pbk)
ISBN 13: 978-1-4094-0422-4 (hbk)

Contents

List of Figures

Chapter 1
Introduction to Rich-Prospect Interfaces

> In the early stages of a new technology, people tend to think that its purpose is merely to replace and improve on something they already know. The promise of the new is thought to be quantitative: the new thing will do the old job faster, more efficiently, and more cheaply. Tools, however, are perceptual agents. A new tool is not just a bigger lever and a more secure fulcrum, rather a new way of conceptualising the world.
>
> (McCarty 1991)

In this book, we discuss our efforts, as designers, programmers, and scholars in the humanities, to explore some theories we have about how we can improve people's experience in working with digital collections and documents. As authors, we represent collectively a variety of educational backgrounds and research experiences in visual communication design, literary studies, digital humanities, and computer science, and we routinely work with others who bring deeper skills in these areas as well as complementary skills in other areas. We believe that the approach that we take and the results we achieve benefit from our multidisciplinary perspectives and that our work will be relevant to colleagues working in several fields.

Our strategy has been to create prototypes that reify (and refine) our theories, in consultation with the intended users of the tools. The task is complex and open-ended, since the theories could be instantiated for testing in a variety of ways. Morever, the responses of users trying out the systems are influenced by any number of factors that may or may not derive directly from the tools. There are also diverse opinions about the best ways to consult people, ranging from controlled psychometric experiments in labs, which produce comparative statistics, to thinkaloud protocols and screen captures, which provide potentially richer qualitative data about fewer people, to *in situ* observational studies or documentary reports of people living with new technologies in their homes and workplaces.

Different research communities also espouse different standards with respect to appropriate numbers and kinds of participants, the nature of the introductory information participants receive, and the types of tasks or questions that yield the most useful results. From our perspective, we think it is important to recognise that we are primarily interested in formative rather than summative studies, meaning that we hope to learn what we can, then move on to the next iteration of a prototype or to the next project (this is in contrast to other objectives, such as understanding a user community or conducting an in-depth study of a production-level tool). We are also working with digital artifacts that are amenable to our revision. Although large summative studies performed under carefully controlled conditions remain the primary interest of many publication venues, we believe that the core work consists of reifying a theory by creating an object that can be studied and revised, and in order to do that, a series of small studies is often more than sufficient. As David Sless (2004) has said, if you are someone who has built a staircase and are interested in finding out if any of the stairs creak, how many participants do you need to walk up the stairs?

In total, we have produced well over two dozen experimental prototypes, for nearly that many different communities of people and kinds of data, and we have used a wide range of existing methods for finding out if we are actually improving people's experience in working with digital materials. Links to many of these prototypes can be found at the following URLS:

- humviz.org
- monkproject.org
- inke.org
- voyeurtools.org

Where it seemed appropriate or necessary, we have also worked on developing new research methods for studying prototype digital humanities tools (Chapter 3).

Our starting point – some 10 years ago – was the idea that retrieval systems, or search engines, are often provided to users when dedicated browsing technologies would be more congenial for the user. From a tool provider perspective, this is not surprising since search interfaces (such as the Google single box model) tend to be much easier and faster to design and develop than meaningful browsing interfaces. The danger is that the user may not realise that a more nuanced way of exploring a dataset is possible and that the dataset remains needlessly mysterious.

For people who are looking for a well-defined target document, search interfaces, based on more or less sophisticated retrieval engines, are a good solution. However, users looking for an understanding of an entire collection and how the various components comprising it interact are not well served by retrieval interfaces. The limitations of a retrieval interface become even more apparent when potentially useful information is available in the relationships between items – how they group, for instance, or whether they are sequenced in some particular way, or if they happen to be a component in some more complicated structure such as a tree or a pattern of relationships. Often this information is stored in ways that are invisible to the user, being contained, for example, in structural and semantic markup, links and anchors, relational fields, and other forms of metadata.

Valuable research has already been done to expand the range of tools and perceptual advantages available to people accessing electronic materials. The literature is impressive and constantly growing, with thousands of papers published annually by scholars at research centers like MIT, UIUC, IBM, HCIL Maryland, Carnegie Mellon, and elsewhere. We owe a tremendous intellectual debt to colleagues in the areas of human–computer interaction, visual communication design, user experience studies, library and information studies, and digital humanities. We have attempted to recognise some of that important work in this book where appropriate, without attempting to exhaustively contextualise the relevant fields. Our perspective here is what we call *experimental prototype design* where we try to allow the design and HCI literature (among others) to inform the process of iteratively developing prototypes (we don't share the same priorities as, say, developers of a widely used online store). In any case, more work remains to be done in the area of tool development in the digital humanities, especially as the number and sophistication of research projects continue to increase.

One of our fundamental beliefs is that providing the user with a wealth of well-designed visual information is better than attempting to artificially or arbitrarily restrict the amount of information provided, especially if certain features of the visual display can be easily controlled by the person using the system (and if those controls presented in an intuitive way). We have been trying to understand the conditions under which this approach is generally useful, but within localised contexts, given the necessity of working with specific people undertaking particular kinds of work with a given type of digital materials. We have also tried to learn which features of the visual display are most important to put under user control. Finally, we have been attempting to expand the range of forms that control can take.

Rich-Prospect Browsing

In many of our experimental interfaces, the home page displays a visual representation of every item in a given collection, combined with tools for manipulating the display. We call these kinds of interfaces "rich-prospect browsers," using a term first suggested in conversation by the designer Jorge Frascara (1999). Rich-prospect browsers embody the following list of principles:

- The primary page or screen should show a meaningful representation of every item in the collection (these might consist of photos, graphical objects, or pieces of text; however, for brevity, rather than saying "meaningful representation of every item in the collection," we'll often opt for the word "image" as shorthand).
- The user should be able to adjust various controls in order to reorganise these images.
- Each item or image should link to more data.
- The available metadata about the images should determine the tools available, so that, for example, metadata that could produce groups should be used for grouping, and metadata about associations should allow the user to see network diagrams.
- Where possible, more than one image should be available, so that the user can choose among alternatives (Ruecker and Liepert 2004).
- The visual organisation of the images should bear meaning that is apparent

to the user.
- The user should be able to mark the images somehow, so that it is possible to keep track of images even when they are reorganised in the display (Giacometti et al. 2008).

Rich-prospect browsers have the benefit of providing the user with a visual basis for understanding what is available in a collection. This kind of visual knowledge is particularly suitable for many collections of digital cultural objects, where a meaningful image of each item is readily available, and users may not be aware of everything that is in the collection, making searching more difficult. However, our research timeline does not typically involve the creation or digitisation stage. Although there have been some exceptions, in general, we take as our starting point the existence of a digital collection, which usually includes some metadata.

In attempting to develop our list of principles above, and in the process of assessing the degree to which they are valid, we have created a wide range of prototypes. The flagship group consists of a family of eight or nine rich-prospect showcase browsers, each one of which allows people to browse through a different kind of material. For instance, there is a browser for a collection of biodiversity projects in the city of Edmonton (Figure 1.1), another of researcher profiles at Mount Royal University in Calgary, and a third showcasing some of Edmonton's historic buildings. As a means of introducing the concept of rich-prospect browsing with reference to some specific details, we will use the biodiversity project browser as an example. Carried out in conjunction with the City of Edmonton and the 2009 conference of the International Council for Local Environmental Initiatives (ICLEI), the biodiversity browser was a means of showcasing approximately 60 environmental projects in the Edmonton city region.

The showcase browsers implement a type of faceted browsing (Spiteri 1998) and each relies on the metadata that are specific to the collection, so that for biodiversity projects, the user can group by any of the following criteria, or by any combination:

- project type
- ecological areas
- status
- project lead
- what groups are involved
- biodiversity threats
- methods

To return briefly to the subject of "images" in rich-prospect browsing, note that it is not necessarily straightforward to represent something as complex as a biodiversity project with a picture or graphical object. Some projects have taken a photo of a representative landscape. Others have chosen to identify themselves with a logotype. Ideally, the representations should be meaningful for the users, but

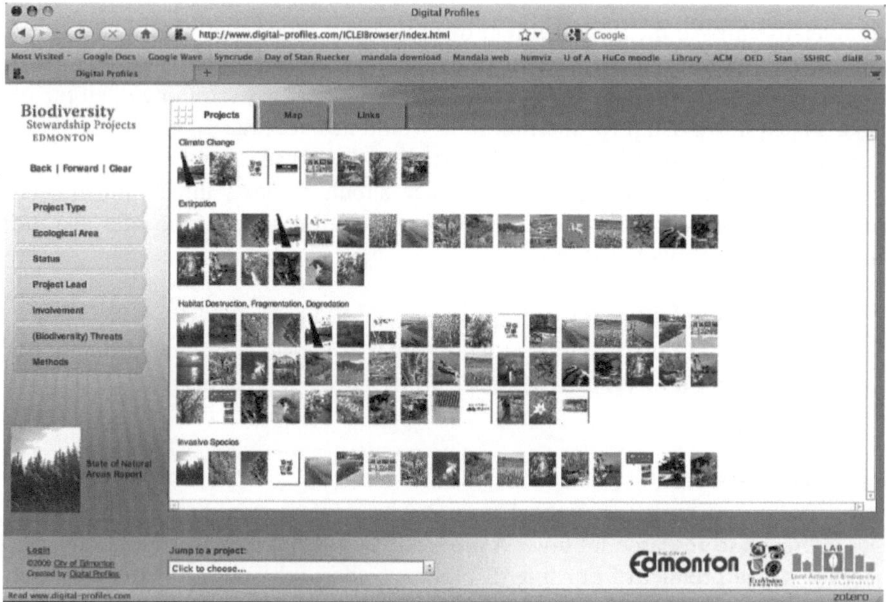

Figure 1.1 Biodiversity stewardship projects of Edmonton[1]

one of our studies (Giacometti et al. 2008) suggests that putting the representation under user control is not as important as it might at first seem. People seem to be able to treat the representations as signifiers for the items they access.

Note too that in cases where a project falls into more than one category, the image gets duplicated, since the goal is not to have a set of mutually exclusive categories, but rather, to allow the user to see within each category what projects are included (obviously, the less duplication of images possible, the better). Returning to the ungrouped display removes the duplicates, which only appear when necessary to display a particular grouping.

Using the Biodiversity browser, people with no knowledge of the projects being done in Edmonton can quickly get a sense of their range and scope. They can recognise with a few button clicks what groups are involved in supporting the projects, what kinds of biodiversity threats are being confronted, and who is leading the work. They can see at the push of one button, and without leaving the screen, the relative proportion of projects within each category. Furthermore, they can begin to understand (or at least speculate) how the people who created the metadata for the collection construed the material. For example, in terms of

1 The buttons on the left are toggles that allow the user to group the projects. More than one grouping criteria can be applied at the same time. Here all groups are shown, but the user can focus on one group by clicking the header, at which point the others minimise (without entirely disappearing) to the bottom of the screen. Design by Michael Lewcio.

biodiversity threats, the largest group of projects in Edmonton deal with habitat destruction, fragmentation, and degradation – a category that sits alongside climate change, extirpation, and invasive species. A person examining the topic of biodiversity stewardship for the first time would not necessarily guess that these were the kinds of threats that would be listed, or that these were the terms used.

In general, any prospect-based interface should address three fundamental questions for the user; these questions relate to the affordances of the interface and the tools that are provided with it:

- What am I looking at? (Chapter 4: meaningful representation)
- Why would I want to look at it? (Chapter 3: the study of new affordances)
- What can I do with it? (Chapter 2: affordances of prospect)

Research Life Cycle

Our approach to research involves a life cycle that is not necessarily unique, but because it is a product of our interdisciplinary approach and the realities of our funding structures, it might be worth pointing out explicitly. In general terms, we have a design phase, a prototype phase, and a production phase. We try to carry out user studies in all three phases. We try to publish or present results in all three phases. Each phase typically requires a minimum of a year, although with many of the prototypes we have been iteratively progressing for two or three times that long (in some cases there's a renewal of the life cycle with what is partly a continuation of an existing project and partly a new endeavour).

The process often begins with some aspect of what in the business community is called a SWOT analysis: Strengths, Weaknesses, Opportunities, and Threats (Freisner 2010). Given any of these four aspects of a situation, we look at a given area of interest to one of the potential team members. This might be in the form of a domain interest or a research problem. For example, we started looking at visualisations for decision support systems when some of our colleagues in engineering approached us with a series of problems they had been addressing related to making and coordinating decisions in a multi-modal environment. Alternatively, the starting point might be derived from observing an existing trajectory in interface design and thinking of its limitations. An example here is our work on a new kind of timeline that can support multiple conflicting witnesses as well as the concept of subjectivity. It is not unusual for other researchers to be following a similar trajectory, so that for the timeline project, we were able to work with Johanna Drucker and Bethany Nowviskie, whose earlier temporal modeling project produced a wealth of theoretical and practical groundwork.

The real start to the project is a planning meeting where we familiarise ourselves as a team (we often have new collaborators, such as colleagues, clients, or research assistants), we revisit the overall objectives of the project (often described in a grant proposal that led to funding for the project), and we set out tentative timelines and collaborative practices (project governance, modes of communication, and so on).

The next step is often an environmental scan (Albright 2004) and a literature review. An environmental scan proceeds by collecting examples from the internet, combining a series of searches with further investigation of the backlog of visualisation and interface examples sent over time by colleagues. The result is both a subset of selected examples and a report that describes the range. Since not all of the important design innovation is associated with the academic literature, an environmental scan helps us to spot relevant work being done outside the academy. Interestingly, existing environmental scans tend to be easier to find for non-academic projects since academics are not always in the habit of making their preparatory research publicly available. Having realised this more recently, we have become more diligent in making available the full trace of our research work, most often published through a wiki or ticket-tracking system (such as TRAC).

Associated with this activity, we sometimes include the development of personas and scenarios (Cooper 1998). A persona is a written description of a potential user, highlighting specific attributes such as experience and reasons for wanting to use the system. Normally, three or more personas will be necessary, in order to cover a sufficient range of potential users. However, it is important not to multiply personas to the point that they are difficult to remember and use in discussion. It is also a good rule of thumb to avoid giving them comic names, which is often an initial impulse but can tend to become distracting over time.

A scenario, sometimes also referred to as a use case, describes a circumstance of use, typically written as a set of steps that form an outline of the task. The level of detail should be sufficient to include all steps, but not so specific as to constrain the implementation of each step. For example, a typical scenario might begin with "step 1: John opens a file" rather than "step 1: John goes to the File menu and chooses Open." The former version allows any number of mechanisms for opening files, including double-clicking a data file, pushing a button, or choosing a menu option, while the latter version assumes files will be opened only from a file menu within a running application.

The design phase itself usually involves a dozen or more iterations. The politics of design, programming, users, and domain experts become central at this time, as each contributor brings her own background and practices. For example, the domain experts may feel that some particular aspect of the information should be emphasised, while the users express their primary interest in something else. The designers may suggest an approach that the programmers feel will be unnecessarily difficult to implement, while the programmers may have design ideas of their own that seem to the designers to be visually uninspiring. No one agrees on where the bar should be set for ease of use. We negotiate that terrain and end up with a set of sketches. These might be static drawings or sequences of sketches to suggest how the interaction works, or they might be interactive animations with no real data on the back end. We believe that the importance of the design phase cannot be overstated. The involvement of visual communication designers on the research team results in a completely different kind of prototype than would be possible with computer programmers working without designers (we have made it a sine qua non of our projects to integrate a design perspective). No matter how immersed in visual culture the programmers might be, the designers are specialists in visual culture, and the results they are capable of producing through that specialisation show a significant attention to detail that is not otherwise possible (similarly, there are technical aspects that may not be fully understood by the designers). There are innumerable difficulties, however, in finding and training appropriate designers, since they need to learn how to work with computer programmers so that the interaction is positive, fruitful and efficient. Similarly, the programmers need to be open to the idea that design is valuable, time-consuming, and difficult. This awareness can be difficult to establish, since programming education often ignores design entirely, or worse yet, gives it a cursory treatment.

Following (or in delayed lockstep to) the design phase is a programming phase, where a prototype using actual data is created. The goal of the prototype is to allow a more interactive user study, where people can use a working (if preliminary) system. At this point, there are often trade-offs around what components get built, and it is important to keep the dominant project objectives in mind. A prototype is not a production system, so it may actually be missing many of the components that we know are essential in a production system (or even in a planned subsequent prototype), simply because there is nothing to be learned currently from their presence. It is fairly well understood, for instance, that a production system needs a search function and a help system. These two components are not necessary parts of an experimental interface prototype. On the other hand, they are pieces that users will miss if they are not included in a more widely distributed system. If we leave these pieces out, the people responsible for the user study need to be skillful enough to acknowledge their absence and enable the users to move on to the affordances we are interested in examining. However, in some cases, it is simpler just to include a rudimentary version of these kinds of components, so that the user study is easier to conduct. In analysing the results, we put comments about these features into the category "already well understood."

The third research phase is development. In some cases, what we have learned from the designs is sufficient, and we can stop there. At other times, we proceed to a prototype, or better yet, to a set of prototypes. More rarely still, we think that it would be worthwhile to create a working system that is reliable and robust enough for people to use outside the explicit context of a user study. For researchers, development is fraught with peril, first because creating a production system will typically consume five times the resources required for a prototype, and second, because although production software can be seen both as a scholarly activity and as a kind of service to the community, if it comes with a research agenda, that aspect is not primary to the project. We therefore have to remember that we aren't in the software business – we are in the research business. However, it occasionally happens that development environments seem worth the resources they require, and we undertake them. If they are planned properly, they can continue to be the basis for user studies, and can also be a source of information gathered from a large community of users.

The aspects of this research approach that are probably most unusual in the context of tool development in the humanities are the lengthy design phase, combined with the focus on involving visual communication designers as part of the research team. Typically, academic researchers in human–computer interaction (HCI) or human–machine interaction (HMI) will have been educated as computer programmers or engineers rather than as designers, with the result that design often takes the form of hasty scribbles on the back of an envelope. There is also a well-justified fear of vaporware, or software that is described before it exists, resulting in an urgency in the HCI research community to get to a phase that is publishable. The concern is that anyone can imagine a perfect piece of software, but a working prototype demonstrates that it is more than a concept, that the idea has already been reified in a form amenable to testing. We feel on the contrary that imagining a perfect piece of software in detail is much harder than it sounds, that the design phase is worth pursuing on its own merits, and that the sketches produced by a visual communication designer are a form of reification or embodiment of an idea that is worth discussing at that stage, both from the theoretical perspective and as the basis for initial conversations with users. In other words, the design is a deliverable, just like the working tool. In support of this approach, the design community has a tradition of paper prototyping as the basis for user studies (for example, Helmer-Poggenpohl 1999) and there are parallel arguments made for the value of early user feedback on sketches by researchers in information studies (for example, Dillon 2001).

What is the motivation for placing this unusual emphasis on the design phase? We believe that the aesthetic quality of an interface design typically translates into a part of the Gestalt perception of not just the interface, but instead of the project as a whole. An interface is public relations. Our research life-cycle therefore places an emphasis on design as one of the areas of ongoing research, interwoven with prototyping and production, with user studies taking place in all three areas.

Users

In order for an item to be represented in a meaningful way, it is desirable that the designer be familiar with the types of people who will be using the system (if possible), and understand both how they will immediately perceive what they see, and how in the process of working with the interface they will construct an understanding from the materials they have available. It is equally necessary for the designer to understand the nature of the material itself, since the construction of meaningful representations must occur with respect to the contents of the collection.

It is now widely recognised that to design anything is to be involved in an act of communication, and that to communicate effectively requires some common terrain that is recognised by both interlocutors. Language itself is such a terrain, but is only part of the larger environment that also includes the presuppositions of the various parties, their personal experience, the public history of which they are a part, and so on (for example, Frascara 2006). In order to properly "position" a design for a particular audience, the designer needs to be immersed in the visual language of that audience. Immersion in visual culture is not typically a part of the user study process, although there are strategies, such as cultural probes (for example, Gaver et al. 1999), where visual information can be collected from a user community, and help to inform subsequent design work.

It is also important to note that a user is not the same person with the same requirements under all conditions. In fact, even within a single session, using the same collection within the context of the same overall task, a person may adopt different strategies as appropriate for different phases of the task.

Tradition of User Study

In the field of industrial design, the recognition of user input has a relatively long history. The Environmental Design Research Association (EDRA) was founded in 1969 to promote better understanding of product users and to help inform the design process. In visual communication design, on the other hand, recognition of the central role of the user has been slower to emerge, although it has been growing, and various methods for involving the user have either been developed from first principles or imported from the social sciences (Frascara 1997, pp. 33–59). However, in spite of this affirmative stance, in practice the actual interactions between the designer and the end user are often limited in what might be called a product relationship: something is designed and then handed over as a sealed product to the user; no interaction is possible as the communicative process is unilateral.

Difficulties of User Study

Designers may need to know about the intended users of a system, but there are often no such people readily available. For example, in designing a textmining tool for literary scholars, it would be best to find professors or graduate students with research projects that rely on the available collections, and have those people spend the additional time necessary to work with a prototype in carrying out their project. However, professors and graduate students often have more pressing commitments that preclude this kind of engagement. Users who are available for testing may play the part of the end user, but the role is contrived for the purposes of the study and the integrity of the results are likely compromised. Designers may want to know about the intended users, but in some organisations it can happen that the design brief (the document outlining the project) assumes that someone else will be responsible for letting them know what they need to know. It may even be the case that management of the project (especially outside the academic context) requires limiting the contact of the designers from the end users. Typically, this will be done in order to prevent one of the most serious problems a project can face – namely, scope creep, wherein the bounds of the design are modified or expanded as the project proceeds. Serious scope creep can result in a project that can never be completed, or at least never completed within the constraints of available time and budget. Equally problematic can be the relationship between designers and programmers, who need to negotiate, ideally in consultation with the users, not only what needs to be done but also what form it can and should take. In general, the more attention paid to the details of design, the better the outcome, but it is also true that some designs are easier to implement than others, even though they may be of equal quality from the design perspective. Finally, designers may have users available for study, but may simply not have the time or the expertise to find out what is necessary.

From the perspective of identifying users, if the system being designed is a new system in any substantial way, there may not be an existing body of users to draw upon. For example, in creating a tool that allows humanities scholars to visualise a more sophisticated understanding of time than is possible using a conventional timeline, it would be best to recruit participants who have been working with timelines and expressing frustrations at their limitations. If there are users, they may feel that they do not have the expertise necessary to contribute to the design of an interface – that the work is in the domain of the expertise of others, namely the interface designers.

The result is what Mitchell (1993, p. 36) and others have referred to as "the applicability gap," where the usability information that is available is either not appropriate or not used by the designer when the work of creating or refining the design happens.

Given the sometimes overwhelming problems of finding and understanding actual users, many studies make use of study participants who happen to be available, such as students or administrative staff. This approach has the value of at least involving actual people interacting with the designer's ideas. Another strategy, even less connected to actual user-centered design, but very useful as a way of managing client expectations, is the creation of user profiles (or personas), where fictitious people are substituted for actual users (Fleming 1998, pp. 8–9). Discussions of user needs can then be held in the context of the characteristics and needs of the hypothetical person, which serve to reduce the chances for deadlock which sometimes arise between the designer and the client, because there is a third party (albeit a fictitious one) to be referenced in any decision. Since this third party is an invention of the project team, it can be given whatever characteristics seem appropriate to the task at hand. For example, in a project where the team is interested in working within the W3C guidelines for accessibility, it might be useful to introduce a persona named "Ann" who would like to be able to iteratively construct Boolean queries for her project on the history of tobacco. Ann is a 23-year-old graduate student from the Maritimes who suffers from visual impairment and uses screen-reading software. This strategy of raising important criteria through some characteristic of one of the personas is recommended by experts such as Jordan (2003).

Some studies, however, are based on projects where the actual users have been involved in an iterative design that responds to their feedback with revisions to the system. An example of such a project is the Alexandria Digital Library (ADL), which consists of a geographic database containing a variety of information about various points on the surface of Earth. Researchers with the ADL worked extensively with three target user groups: Earth scientists, information specialists, and educators (Hill et al. 2000, p. 250). The partial list of requirements that derived from these users has eight categories, which are extensive enough that they might be used as a general summary of system features: search functions, session management, result display, user workspace, holdings visualisation, user help functions, usability features, and data distribution.

The ADL researchers emphasised that the design of a system for use by a particular community is essentially different from the design of a system that will showcase its own capabilities. These differences include both content and interface (Hill et al. 2000, p. 257). For example, the team might be tempted to provide a range of image manipulation functions, with no real sense of which manipulations might be most important to the user community. As a result, the controls for those manipulations may not find a prominent place in the interface. It is interesting to note, however, that in spite of the nature of the content and the extensive user participation, the ADL is not an example of a project that provides the user with prospect on the contents of the collection.

Interface Aesthetics

The aesthetic knowledge and perspective of artists and designers have either largely been ignored by researchers working with experimental interfaces, or else have contributed in a manner that has not been subject to direct analysis (Bardzell 2009). Whether working with basic web interfaces to text archives, or with projects that combine text and images, or with dynamically interactive experimental prototypes, researchers have the opportunity to extend their understanding through including the study of interface aesthetics alongside more traditional measures of performance and preference.

The significance of the visual is sufficiently evident in all of these cases that aesthetic factors become intrinsically woven with issues of functionality (Dillon 2001, Petersen et al. 2004). For instance, Udsen and Jørgensen (2005) provide a summary of recent studies in interface aesthetics and create a taxonomy of four approaches: the cultural, the functionalistic, the experience-based and the techno-futuristic. Ngo et al. (2002) offer a model of interface aesthetics consisting of 14 distinct characteristics: balance, equilibrium, symmetry, sequence, cohesion, unity, proportion, simplicity, density, regularity, economy, homogeneity, rhythm, and order and complexity. Bertelsen and Pold (2004) suggest adapting the process of art criticism for use in criticising interface aesthetics, using the following categories: stylistic references, standards, materiality and remediation, genre, hybridity, representations, and challenges to expectations and developmental potentials. Hallnäs and Redström (2002) propose the noun "expressional" as a counterbalance to the adjective "functional," with the former term suggesting the components that go into the continuing presence of the designed computational object in everyday life. Fishwick et al. (2005, 2006) discuss the complex effects of art on computing.

We address the issue of graphic design contributions to visualisation research by emphasising what Frascara (1997) calls "the aesthetic function of design." We argue that aesthetic function is a composite that includes attracting viewers, holding their attention, and compelling their trust and respect. Design, in other words, is of utmost importance in expressing both the value and legitimacy of digital cultural heritage materials.

Previous studies have shown a significant relationship between perceived aesthetic quality and perceived usability for a variety of cultures. In Japan, Kurosu and Kashimura (1995) found that apparent usability correlates more strongly to aesthetic aspects of the interface than to actual usability. Tractinsky (1997) replicated their results in Israel. Karvonen (2000) takes this line of reasoning further in her Scandinavian study of the relationship between trust and design, finding that people tended to rate web sites with a clearly professional design quality as being more trustworthy than more vernacular sites. On the other side of the debate, however, it might be argued that there is an anti-aesthetic subtext in certain research areas, since effort spent to engage readers through visual appeal (and its related functionality) might be understood as effort lost to more essential research outcomes.

In any case, the connection between graphic design and academic research has implications for the ongoing need for improved communication between the academic and non-academic worlds; one need only consider the number of technology incubators and commercial research parks at campuses, especially in North America. Several strategies are required at different levels, including public information campaigns, academic contributions to popular media, and a significant presence of the academic in the community. In this context of the academic as a public intellectual, one potential role that design has to play is in visually rewarding the reader of research results. Pujol (2001) points out that the visual qualities of professional design are one of the key signifiers by which we distinguish the individual voice from the institutional. If someone hand-letters a sign to advertise a garage sale, we understand the sale as an amateur activity. If that same person employs graphic design skills and produces a glossy poster, we may interpret the same event, at least until we arrive at the site, as a professional rather than amateur activity.

In brief, the graphic quality of a tool's design, particularly in the areas of visualisation and information design research, can contribute both to the results obtained from user study, and to the reception of those research results. Careful attention to the details of graphic presentation can have a significant impact on the perceived value of a digital collection, the function of a visualisation system, the research results available from analysis of visualisations, and the dissemination of findings both within the academic community and for the larger public audience.

The Aesthetic Experience

Our focus on the aesthetic function of interfaces is in conversation with a considerable body of literature dealing with aesthetic theory, which ranges from the classical interest in discussing aesthetic factors, such as symmetry and balance, to postmodern questions about the cultural role of the aesthetic and the reasons for embracing instead the anti-aesthetic, particularly in fine art (for example, Carroll 2001). From the perspective of perception and response, some theorists focus in particular on the aesthetic experience, which is generally understood to be a form of emotional reaction to a perceived object (Dufrenne 1973).[2] A connection is commonly made between this emotional reaction and its purported function in situating and "civilizing" us:

> The value of beauty, then, is that along with human contact it enables us to break out of the otherwise impregnable spiritual isolation to which every one of us is born and to feel ourselves at home in the world. Beauty and friendship enable us to get outside ourselves and to live as we ought to live, in concord with the world we are part of, and to feel ourselves part of it. (Pye 1978, p. 102)

Whether or not the perceived object needs to be a work of art *per se* is open to debate. Dufrenne (1973) takes it as a given for the purposes of his analysis, while Carroll (2001) challenges the assumption that there is any intrinsic connection, pointing out that many works of art are intended to promote other kinds of responses, and that in any case, the interpretive response is often as central as the aesthetic.

For some researchers, the aesthetic experience is a form of seduction. Khaslavsky and Shedroff (1999) discuss the seductive experience, breaking the process into three phases – enticement, relationship, and fulfillment – which translate into a range of requirements that must be met at different points in the interaction between the user and the object.

Finally, a variety of theorists have attempted to operationalise the study of aesthetic experience, whether in its relation to art or to interfaces. Munro (1956), for instance, suggests an empirical approach using semantic differentials, similar to studies in other branches of sociology and psychology. Attempts have also been made to factor the aesthetic experience into its components. For example,

2 In a related discussion, Höge (1990) connects the aesthetic and affordances, making the observation that one of the features of a painting or image is that it does not provide the affordances that its subject matter would provide.

Jennings (2000) defines the aesthetic experience as occurring when a person is consciously engaged in an activity that is immersive, pleasurable, unique, and personally rewarding.

Related Factors

There are a number of factors that are not strictly aesthetic in nature, yet are associated with the aesthetic, and are influenced by it. These include discernibility, legibility, meaningful and efficient arrangement of visual elements, and logical structure for navigation. The aesthetic, however, is not intrinsically reliant on these factors. That is, each factor can be successfully addressed in either an aesthetic or non-aesthetic way.

The first two factors are those typically discussed in the context of the design of public signage systems. The factors are whether the sign can be seen – whether it is discernible – and once it has been discerned, whether or not it is legible. In both these cases, the choices made by the designer will have an aesthetic dimension. There are instances of signage which are wonderfully discernible against their surroundings, and which are hallmarks for legibility once they have been discerned, for instance, by the anxious traveler. However, it is not essential that in order to meet these criteria, the signage also be beautiful. The aesthetic is possibly a component, but is neither necessary nor sufficient for the signage to perform its function.

A parallel instance occurs in the design of web pages: the suggestion is often made by designers that part of their work consists in establishing a meaningful arrangement of the visual elements, an efficient arrangement of the menu items and other working parts, and a logical structure for navigation. Certainly these aspects of web design are within the purview of the designer. However, as in the case of signage, it is certainly possible to make a web page that features meaningful placement of items, clear navigation, and efficient arrangement of menus that is nonetheless not aesthetically successful. Design can be mechanical and uninteresting, not to mention the potential pitfalls of poorly used features, such as an annoying and encumbering background pattern, a blinking text, or a distracting animated image.

Although the aesthetic can be a component of design decisions that also affect performance, the aesthetic and the functional have also often been disassociated. For instance, in many practical discussions, the two concepts are placed at difference poles, with the somewhat pejorative term "decorative" replacing the more positive connotations of the word "aesthetic." The aesthetic in these cases is almost invariably considered a kind of luxury or indulgence, that can be dismissed until the real work is complete, and added on as a sort of icing or final polish to a project that might just as well do without the extra expense and complication.

Function and aesthetics are also occasionally linked, as in Frank Lloyd Wright's famous modernist formulation "form follows function." The principle here is that a particular kind of aesthetic – one with a minimal or absent amount of ornamentation

– can be seen as deriving from meeting performance requirements. The futuristic, streamlined look of the designs by Raymond Loewy or R. Buckminster Fuller provide good examples.

However, the various factors that involve the aesthetic can be logically identified, and the aesthetic component separately discussed. For example, it is reasonable to think of good typographic practices as involving an aesthetic component. Page layout is often described in terms of balance and harmony, both of which are aesthetic principles, but these attributes also contribute to the usefulness of the page as an object for sustained reading.

However, as in the earlier examples given for electronic media, it is also possible to have a printed page that serves very well as an object for sustained reading, which is not balanced or harmonious. One thinks, for instance, of pages created using a mechanical typewriter, where the conditions of production were not of the kind that could privilege considerations of experimental modification to line length or sophisticated adjustments of leading, and where font choice was minimal or non-existent. Nonetheless, for two centuries people were able to read typewritten pages, which in fact represented an improvement on readability in many cases, as compared with hand-written manuscripts. So although it is possible to associate aesthetic value with page design, it is not reasonable to say that the aesthetic is intrinsic to the success of the page of text. Our expectations and aesthetic preferences evolve along with available technologies. Matters become more complicated, of course, where pages combine both text and image, and various forms of scholarly apparatus increase the complexity still further.

Confidence

Our proposal is that the aesthetic functions are not necessarily those functions that are typically conscious, intentional, or telic. That is, they don't refer to the grosser acts of accomplishing a task. Instead, the aesthetic function is to provide the viewer, or in the case of visualisation research the experimental participant, with implicit associations to the notions of quality and attention to detail. The primary aesthetic function in visualisation research is therefore to inspire confidence, which results in a number of advantages to the researcher, the participant in the research (or eventually the user of the system), and the larger community that receives and assesses the results.

This larger function of inspiring confidence can be divided into three sub-functions, related respectively to trust, willingness, and satisfaction.

Trust

Trust is a factor in associations; it deals with the relationship between the user and the designer. In most cases, however, the designer won't be present when the user is interacting with the interface. It is therefore necessary for the designer to take measures to help instill a sense of trust through the mediation of the interface.

The opposite of trust is mistrust or fear. Trust can become an issue for people using a visualisation tool or computer interface when they fear that their time will be wasted, that they won't get their tasks completed properly or at all, or that the experience will be unpleasant. They may fear potentially nasty surprises, or inaccurate or misleading results. They may fear the lack of control associated with not clearly knowing what is going on. These are all reasonable fears, and they can be mitigated or even forestalled to the point that they never arise, through the provision of various aspects of the design intended to increase cognitive reassurance.

Cognitive reassurance can be provided in a variety of ways, but some of the factors that should be included are the ready availability of help and the provision of an environment that seems appropriate to accomplish the task. Some informed users want to feel that the designers are familiar with current best practices. In some cases, where best practices change rapidly, it may happen that a particular design does not represent current best practice (or perhaps the designer has justifiable reasons for varying from best practice). However, even in these instances, if the design represents a previous best practice that the user can identify, there is a degree of reassurance possible. For example, the metaphor of the typewriter pervades word-processing technology, with keystrokes producing type on a page, even though there is actually no ink or paper.

A similar case can be made for the visual position of the design. Does it accommodate somebody's visual culture? Ideally, it should be positioned for the visual culture of the user; however, if there has clearly been attention paid to positioning it within some visual culture, that may be sufficient to indicate that the designer had some kind of user in mind (Cyr 2010, Lim 2010). In some cases a tool is deliberately designed to be more universally applicable, which is likely to require some compromises with respect to cultural specificities.

Whether the cues are in the form of adoption of best practices or in the choice of visual position, or both, the goal should be to impress the user with every aspect of the tool. If everything about it looks considered, and it is clear that a reasonable allocation of resources has gone into its development, then the effect on the user will be to increase trust in the people responsible, which may include the designer, the researcher, and the developer.

A related set of cues have to do with the provision by the designer of visible indications that the interface or visualisation system has been created in consultation with the relevant domain experts. These visible indications work in both directions: from the content expert to the designer and from the designer to the content expert. In this context, one indication of the professionalism of the researcher or developer who has the ultimate responsibility for the design can be the high level of professionalism apparent in the design. The aesthetic quality of an interface design typically translates into a part of the Gestalt perception of not just the interface, but instead of the project as a whole. An interface is public relations.

Willingness

While trust implies a relationship between the designer and the user, willingness is a factor that reflects the user's internal state during the task. At a basic level, the question is whether or not the user is willing to take on the task at all, given the tools at hand. Subsequently, the question becomes to what extent the user is willing to persevere.

Perseverance is important throughout a task, but is particularly significant when the user perceives that something has gone wrong. The user's willingness to engage in troubleshooting has to be predicated on the belief that the investment will be rewarded with success in overcoming the difficulty. During troubleshooting, the user invests time and effort without necessarily receiving immediate benefit, based on confidence in a later benefit. Good aesthetic function demonstrates that the designer is trying to pack in rewards whenever rewards are possible.

At yet another level, there is the issue of morale, which is related in part to the influence of the environment over time. Morale is in some sense "willingness writ large," and the details that can encourage willingness can also support morale. As Pujol (2001) points out, it is important to consider the change in user experience with repeated exposure to the same design. Novelty and amusement can rapidly turn into repetition and irritation, as fashionable trends indicate in any number of fields, and interface design is no exception. However, it is also possible for the designer to create an environment where the attraction of the interface can persist and even grow through repeated exposure. An example of a repetitive task is the use of Google as a search engine, and though the aesthetic of the main screen is generally minimalistic, the occasional appearance of different logos is a good example of providing some additional engagement (see http://www.google.com/logos/).

Satisfaction

Satisfaction can be derived from several different kinds of pleasurable experience, which may function individually or in harmony. Such pleasure can be understood as occurring at three levels: in the tool as effective and attractive; in the high visual quality of the result of the process of using the tool; and in the fact that the project looks more polished when the findings are presented or published. (Additionally, satisfaction may be indirectly associated with a tool based on the quality of derived work that emerged from use of the tool; however, too many factors enter into play with such secondary levels of satisfaction.)

In its extreme form, this value can result in interfaces that are in some senses autotelic – they can become an end in themselves for some users, who find their characteristics sufficiently compelling to make the system worth further attention, outside the context of any particular research task. For some members of the design community, the development of artifacts that can provide autotelic experiences is understood as one of the inevitable evolutionary consequences of a competitive marketplace (Jordan 2000), where tools that are merely functional are eventually replaced by tools that are functional and also easy to use; these tools in turn are replaced by those that are functional, usable, and also a source of pleasure.

Tools, Experiments, and Theories

In late 2008 and early 2009, the digital humanities community briefly turned its attention, in a discussion thread entitled "Thing Knowledge" on the Humanist Discussion Group listserv, to a question that we consider to be significant for the work we are discussing in this book, namely, what do we believe an experimental interface, a prototype, to be? The possibilities can be loosely categorised as tools, experiments, or theories.

First, recognising that many interfaces serve other ends, we can discuss them as tools. That is, the analysis of an interface can rest on how effective it is in providing an affordance for people carrying out a given task. This metaphor has been particularly useful in the commercial design of interfaces as products. As mentioned briefly above, in the industrial design community (Jordan 2000), there is a spectrum that describes the phases in the design of tools, where the early contenders in the marketplace can survive simply by being functional. They are adequate, because of their historical moment, if they can get the job done. However, once competition arises, the next phase is usability. A tool that is both functional and easy to use will eventually win if placed in competition with a tool that is functional but difficult to use. However, time continues to move on, and eventually, when the merely functional tools have all been replaced by tools that are both functional and usable, a third form of tool will emerge – one that is functional, usable, and pleasurable. In this case, the designer has introduced some aspects of the tool that will reward a more nuanced analysis that includes all three levels of performance. This might be considered a type of Maslow's pyramid of needs for tools.

There are complexities to this somewhat idealised pattern. One is the tendency for people who have learned something with difficulty to persist in its use. Another is the cost-benefit ratio of replacing a working tool with another one just on the basis of the second one being easier to use. A third is with forces of marketing and market-share where design considerations can sometimes be less of a determinant than other forces. A fourth is the added degree of usability or pleasure that the tool can afford, and how that relates to the cost of the tool in comparison to other tools. An example is the Alessi Juicy Salif Citrus juicer, a kind of aluminum spider, designed by Philippe Starke in 1990, that took the domestic kitchen by storm. It was a luxury item, costing two orders of magnitude more than its competition, while performing at the same level of functionality, or arguably even slightly poorer, since it lacked an inner ring to catch seeds and pulp. But it was successful because it introduced pleasure into an area that had stagnated for decades at the stage of usability.

Another way of looking at tools comes from sales and marketing, where they produce what are known as "feature, function, benefit" sheets. A feature is a component of the tool. For example, a laptop might come with a remote control. A function is what the remote control can do – it allows someone to operate some of the laptop's software at a distance. For people who primarily use their laptops for design or spreadsheets or word processing, this function may seem absurd. But the benefit is for people who, for example, use their laptop as a part of their home entertainment system. A remote control allows those people to control audio and video at a distance – they can hook their laptop to their large screen TV and watch digital movies, sitting on the couch with their feet up on the coffee table (potential factors of pleasure facilitated by the tool). In the right context, the feature not only makes sense, it seems essential. The point here is that it is necessary for the design team who created the product, and by extension the salesperson who vaunts its capabilities, to know all three aspects of the tool: what it is, what it does, and why people might want it. As sales guru Kim Hoyer (2000) puts it: "once the pile of benefits is as high as the stack of money, you have the right conditions for a sale."

An alternative way of thinking about prototypes, a different metaphor, is to see them as experiments. This metaphor is most commonly used in interface design within the sciences. The purpose of an experiment is to test a theory, typically by helping to generate evidence around some contestable aspect or implication of the theory, strengthening one competing interpretation over another. This is different from the prototype as a tool in two significant ways. First, an experiment is a process that achieves some result. We use a tool, but we run an experiment, implying that it takes place over time, that it has inputs and outputs. Second, no one expects an experiment to work in production mode for many people over an extended time. It is set up and run for a specific purpose, and once the results are in, the experiment can be set aside.

An experiment is also distinct from an experimental apparatus, which is a tool for doing experiments. A working microscope is not an experiment. However, it is possible that a new kind of microscope can be experimental, in the sense that it will need to be subjected to discussion and analysis for its prospective role as a tool. Many, if not most, of the prototypes that we have worked on, and that are created in human–computer interaction programs, are of this kind.

A third approach is to see a prototype not as an experiment, but instead as the reification or embodiment of a theory or idea. In this case, the prototype is not an object in the service of a theory, whether that might be as an experimental apparatus or as an experiment, but is instead the visual form of an idea (we believe that all prototypes are the embodiment of one or more implicitly or explicitly expressed theories, but it is not always the expression of the theory that is most important). These kinds of prototypes are most commonly seen emerging from new media programs and fine arts departments, although in some cases they are created by more traditional departments of computing science. Taylor et al. (2009), for instance, describe an interactive digital display where images of jellyfish react to various features of a singer's voice.

We have argued (Galey and Ruecker 2010), that it is possible not only to consider a prototype as the embodiment of a theory, but further, to treat that embodied theory as though it were an argument that can be read and evaluated, in much the same way that we read and evaluate scholarly articles. Just as we look for an argument to be contestable, defensible, and substantive (Booth, Colomb, and Williams 2008), so we can look for these aspects in a prototype, in effect reading it as a contribution in the ongoing scholarly activity of thinking through making prototypes. This approach is distinct on the one hand from the descriptive paper that is sometimes pejoratively referred to as "me and my project" and on the other hand from the user study report that treats the prototype as a sort of side effect of the primary research activity, which consists of studying how people work with a given technology.

One advantage of emphasising the interface as reification of a theory is that it can help counteract the tendency to see interfaces – even experimental interfaces – as existing entirely for the purpose of serving some other agenda, such as allowing more people to access an existing affordance or providing a faster means of carrying out an action that is already well accepted. Although interfaces often do serve other agendas, it is also possible to consider them as objects of hermeneutic interpretation in their own right. Experimental interfaces in particular are in the privileged position of serving as a means of focusing attention on the larger intellectual and cultural issues that they and their associated collections of digital cultural heritage intersect.

Interface or Lesson?

In general, we don't subscribe to the belief that an interface is a good means of educating people. For example, if a successful textmining interface for literary scholars has to teach the people who use it what textmining is all about, then either it will be very difficult to use such an interface, or else the years typically necessary to educate a textmining expert have been frivolously wasted by people who could have learned what they needed to know simply by using the right interface. What an interface can do is to make the user interactions with the system as straightforward as possible, by providing, for example, visual forms that represent underlying processes (Ruecker et al. 2009). The aesthetic function also has a role to play here.

The interface designer still needs to decide how much the interface will need to inform the user about the underlying system. The answer is perhaps going to differ based on the nature of the task and the sophistication of the interface. No one expects to know how the Google retrieval algorithms work, since they are proprietary to Google, and it would seem strange and irrelevant for the Google interface to mention that online materials were retrieved using some particular algorithm. The interface to Photoshop, on the other hand, offers the users basic information about how they can expect its algorithmic manipulations of images to perform, comparing them to roughly equivalent darkroom techniques such as burning or dodging. Further along the spectrum is Excel, where users can directly access and manipulate many of the equations via the interface.

As part of the process of deciding how much the interface needs to communicate about its underlying behavior, the designer needs to know what the users can reasonably be expected to know about the system when they first encounter its interface. In the digital humanities community, for example, there is a research stream that uses techniques that were originally developed and popularised by John Burrows. For this community, it is sufficient to indicate, using the domain-specific jargon or shorthand, that Burrows's Delta was the analytical approach taken. Only in modifying Delta or in the choice of certain of the parameters of Delta is it necessary to say more. Such conventions assume that everyone using the interface will be familiar with the kinds of algorithms being used. It is not well advised to attempt to bootstrap less informed users into the same group as expert users by employing the interface as an educational tool. An interface which responds to every user request with a lecture on Burrows's Delta will intimidate naïve users and irritate expert ones.

An ideal interface needs simultaneously to make the underlying processes easy or even pleasurable to use, and to suggest to the user what those processes might be. There are people who feel that command-line interfaces are the high-water mark for human–computer interaction, and every graphical element beyond the command line is superfluous and wasteful. All the interesting work happens on the back end, so why waste computing power on graphics that have nothing to do with the analytics? We believe on the contrary that the command line is too opaque – that it conceals too much behind shorthand function names, cryptic filenames, and single-character switches. Nearly all of our prototypes are graphically intensive, attempting not only to trigger the processes behind the scenes, but also to help the user conceptualise what is going on. The result can be a system that seems to have more graphical analogies for underlying processes than is sometimes the case, even in typical GUIs.

Finally, there is the need to communicate as clearly as possible what the underlying processes are intended to produce. For example, in a supervised classification system, whether using Naïve Bayes or Support Vector Machines, or any one of a dozen other possible approaches, the purpose of the system is to take a set of classes predefined by the user, and find the features those classes have in common, then use the feature sets to add more candidate documents to each class. For a person using such a system, the interface should make clear that the activity of creating "training data" for the supervised classification process consists of defining a number of classes and assigning representative items to them. That is, the minimum that the interface needs to communicate is the appropriate activity or set of activities available to the user, and the outcome to be expected from carrying out each activity. Much less important is that the user have a full understanding of how each of the classification algorithms work.

Design Transferability

One of the consequences of our emphasis on the design phase of software is that we are well positioned to think about the various domains in which a particular type of design might be deployed, producing good conditions for what has been called "design transferability" (Chow and Ruecker 2006). We do not necessarily produce a single design for a particular set of people working on a given task, but instead, we produce a family of prototypes which are related neither by users nor topic area, but instead by a set of design ideas that have been created to work with a specific set of conditions. Our best example is the showcase browsers, where we began with pill identification for seniors (Given et al. 2005, 2007), then moved on to conference delegates (Ruecker et al. 2006), researchers, historic buildings, biodiversity projects, text collections (Giacometti et al. 2008), electron microscope images of wasp-wing features, and engineering textbook diagrams. The felicity conditions that these showcase browsers have in common are:

- hundreds of images
- good metadata for use in grouping items
- a community of people interested in getting an overview of the information and in seeing it grouped in various ways

Similarly, when we were working on the Watching the Script (WtS) project, which was intended to allow people reading plays to think simultaneously about the blocking, we realised that there were many situations where a limited group of people (that is, in WtS, the actors), were moving within a constrained space (that is, a stage), for a prescribed period of time (that is, the duration of the play). We subsequently created designs for a stylised football field and for traffic planning (Sinclair and Ruecker 2006), although these were not fully developed into prototypes. In addition to the benefit for the new context of drawing on previous experiments, another advantage of the transfer is that each new context can help lead to further insights about the tool for the previous contexts.

Design transferability is concerned with leveraging existing assets, in the form of design and prototype software, into new research areas. But it is not about one prototype working in a general way – each of the transferred designs within the family serves a single, situated group of people who have a given task or set of tasks. An alternative approach is to design a system that is general in nature, working with any kind of data but applying the same functions to it. An example of this approach is our Mandala Browser, which allows people to easily create complex queries on an XML file or files by working with a visualisation of the query process. Unlike the showcase family, the design of the Mandala does not necessarily change for every application, although new features may be indicated. For example, in producing a version of Mandala for use with existing collections, it proved useful to modify the system to dynamically query the Application

Programming Interfaces (APIs) rather than reading all the data into the Mandala's own datastore.

Having a single application is a much more common approach, in part because the early phases of the software market have paralleled the early phases of industry, where it was acceptable for reasons of efficiencies of cost to mass produce a single product. However, design of all kinds has become increasingly customisable, and people often expect to see individual variation that is expressive of corporate culture or personal identity. On the web, for instance, we would find it strange to learn that people did not produce individually designed web pages, or personalise their Facebook accounts (in a web context, it is common to develop variant skins or templates to correspond to different contexts). However, because prototypes are more complicated and costly, we typically don't think of them in the same way. With a family of designs, transferred between domains, we are not only able to take advantage of previous assets that we've already developed, but what we are able to learn from each project helps to inform the next one.

Digital Cultural Heritage

Cultural preservation, and management of cultural heritage materials, through the creation and maintenance of digital collections has been, and continues to be, a central occupation of many libraries, museums, galleries, and archival collections. Whether we are dealing with text, photographs, art, audio or video recordings, 3D virtual models, or hybrids, the social, cultural, and political implications of the digital record are evolving rapidly. So too are the affordances we see emerging from the existence and accessibility of the digital cultural archive, with experiments ranging from the crowdsourced transcription of Jeremy Bentham's letters (Terras 2010) to the Library of Congress's folksonomic tagging trials with Flickr Commons (Springer et al. 2008).

What we contribute to the discussion is the specific value of creating rich-prospect browsing interfaces to online collections of digital cultural heritage materials, particularly for the cases described in this book. Rich-prospect browsing interfaces do not reify a theory about a specific kind of users or a particular kind of data. They represent a theory about a set of conditions involving users, data, and metadata, where the collections are of the right size (that is, hundreds or thousands of items, but typically fewer than tens of thousands), have the right conformation (that is, with rich metadata), and are readily represented at the item level. This particular set of conditions comprises the vast majority of digital cultural heritage collections. While the contents of this book may not address the particular complexities of any given project, the principle of design transferability suggests that many of our design approaches can easily be adapted for a wide range of needs.

Research and Development

It might be useful here to add a word of caution about the fundamental nature of experimental interface research, based on experience with a wide range of projects. It can sometimes happen that people mistakenly believe that experimental interface design, especially insofar as it involves visual communication designers and computer programmers, is a form of development or production activity. In software and on the web, there is a spectrum of activity from the conventional to the advanced to the experimental ("experimental" is used here in the sense of innovation rather than in the sense of conducting controlled experiments). Many domain-based projects are not interested in experimental or even advanced issues, but instead require a well-designed database that feeds data to an attractive interface that conforms to contemporary best practices. What we are discussing in this book are systems that are primarily experimental, although in some cases merely advanced, that have taught us a variety of lessons that can hopefully help to inform the next generation of best practices.

Outline of the Book

Following is a brief synopsis of the remaining chapters.

2. I See What I Can Do: Affordances of Prospect

One of the primary ways in which prospect-based interfaces are important is that they provide new affordances that are not found in other kinds of interfaces. An affordance is an opportunity for action in the environment of a given perceiver. The idea was formulated by James Gibson as a way of attempting to find an alternative position in psychology to the schools of behaviorism and mentalism. Gibson felt that, because biological organisms are immersed in an environment, their methods of perception and cognition are directly related to activity in that environment. To distinguish in a somewhat arbitrary way between mental awareness and subsequent action was therefore to miss the point: perception is fundamentally coupled with action. That it is coupled with action in a given environment by a particular creature results in some additional complexity in the theory, which has been one of the grounds for subsequent discussion by researchers in ecological psychology. By placing the significance of the perceptual event in the relationship between the organism and its environment, Gibson emphasised that it is more helpful to examine perception as part of the dynamic process of interaction than it is to see it as a set of discrete steps.

In order to help make the case that prospect-based interfaces provide affordances not found in other kinds of interfaces, one approach is to look at Gibson's concept of affordances as it is currently understood both in the computing science community and among the ecological psychologists who have built on Gibson's work. By examining how affordances have come to be understood, studied, and measured in other areas, it is possible to suggest methods for studying and measuring the affordances of prospect-based interfaces.

Affordances can be complex, taking forms that are nested or sequential, or they can be relatively straightforward. They are distinct from functions, however, in that affordances tend to be multivalent, because human ingenuity can often find more than one opportunity for action when examining an object. Djajadiningrat et al. (2000), in discussing the connection between interaction and aesthetics, describe this multivalence as "richness of actions." Functions, on the other hand, are often defined independent of the perceiver, and are for the most part unitary. This chapter begins by examining the literature from ecological psychology for insights into the nature and purpose of affordances, in an attempt to open the discourse of interface design to include digital artifacts that can be readily used for multiple purposes.

The other theme of this chapter is prospect. Prospect is a view of the world where enough information is available for the perceiver to understand the terrain and have a sense of what it affords, without necessarily seeing all the details. The idea derives from the habitat theories of Appleton (1975), who was generalising from comments made in European studies of landscape painting. There is a variety of new opportunities for action that can be made available to users of digital collections through rich-prospect interfaces. These new affordances are based on the direct visible presence of information about the contents, structure, and other significant features of a collection, such as how it was understood by its developers, how it has been organised, and, in some cases, how it has been encoded with additional interpretive material that is not contained in the actual text.

The discussion includes the composite affordances that are related to prospect, and examines some of the reasons for interpreting prospect, not as implying a relatively literal digital implementation of the landscape metaphor, but rather more broadly as a set of strategies for providing collection insight through meaningful representation of every collection item.

It is in the details of the metadata for actual collections that the principles of rich-prospect interface design come into contact with the kinds of constraints and conditions that need to be addressed as an intrinsic part of the design process. Complicated as they may be, these details serve to test, validate, and refine the concepts in a way that is otherwise impossible.

3. Is This Thing Working? The Study of New Affordances

Having provided some information on how new affordances can be created through rich-prospect interfaces, this chapter introduces the problem of category error, which is a fundamental difficulty in studying new affordances. Category errors occur when two items are compared which simply cannot be compared: apples and oranges; fish and fowl; thermonuclear devices and rubber mice. Since new affordances are not directly comparable to existing affordances, some methods other than comparison under controlled conditions need to be adopted to study them. A strategy is outlined for substituting the comparison of affordance strength for the comparison of affordances, and a vector model of affordance strength is developed and explained. The chapter concludes with a variety of examples of user studies of the new composite affordances of rich-prospect interfaces.

4. I Never Forget a Face: Meaningful and Useful Representation of Items

This chapter deals with some issues that are slightly more technical in nature – namely, the need to find a means of representing every item in a collection in some way that is both meaningful and useful to the end user. Various strategies are available, including manually providing a set of keywords for each document, automatically generating representations from pre-existing indexes or tags defined in SGML or XML, and drawing on library classification processes such as those used in facet analytical theory. The discussion also outlines the characteristics of good candidate collections for rich-prospect interfaces, which should be of a certain size, with documents of an appropriate length, and a fairly high degree of homogeneity. Finally, we conclude with a summary of the kinds of insights that are made possible through the meaningful representation of collection items.

5. Invisible Intelligence: Textual Markup for Digital Collections

Markup systems such as eXtensible Markup Language (XML) can be used to define customised tagsets, so it becomes possible for people to insert invisible intelligence in the text, including interpretive material. The original purpose of text tagging is to facilitate retrieval through applying what is essentially a controlled vocabulary of tags. However, the presence of tagging in a collection provides an opportunity for designers to make the tagged material visible to the users of the collection, in ways that will provide greater prospect and all its related advantages.

This chapter addresses several issues related to collections with markup, including levels of interpretation provided by tagging; the possible new opportunities for action provided by a rich-prospect interface to the tagset (or schema or document type definition); and the possible value of having some form of prospect on the actual tagging of the documents. It also examines several related issues, including the role played by visual culture; the relationship between rich-prospect interfaces and complexity; and how rich prospect relates to the concepts of constraint and natural mapping. This chapter might be summarised as a response to the question: why is prospect on the markup, as opposed to prospect on the contents, potentially useful? The answer relates in part to the kinds of information that the user might obtain by having prospect on the tagset, and how these kinds of information might be applied in understanding and accessing a collection. It also relates to the question of how the user is able to gain confidence with using a collection through having various assurances of what the collection contains, as well as assurances about how it has been understood by the people who created it, and how that understanding might translate into various approaches to accessing the materials.

6. The Design of New Interface Tools

Once the items in the collection are visually available in some form to the person accessing the material, some of the perceptual advantages are immediately present. However, these advantages can be extended through the provision of tools that are associated with the rich-prospect display. These rich-prospect tools allow people to modify the structure of the display through processes such as searching, subsetting, grouping, and otherwise arranging the items. This chapter discusses the design issues involved in creating an appropriate set of rich-prospect interface tools, including the provision of interaction histories, where the user of the interface has the opportunity not only to draw on the previous work of other users, but also to store the results of the current session for possible access by subsequent users.

7. Conclusions

The final chapter draws together the various threads of the discussion, providing a summary of the significant advantages to be gained by applying rich-prospect interface strategies to digital collections. It reiterates the important practical consequences that derive from having designers think in terms of affordances instead of in terms of functions, lists some of the design issues involved, and reinforces the lessons learned from examples based on the prototype interfaces.

Chapter 2
I See What I Can Do: Affordances of Prospect

> The most successful designs are not those that try to fully model the domain in which they operate, but those that are "in alignment" with the fundamental structure of that domain, and that allow for modification and evolution to generate new structural coupling. (Winograd and Flores 1986, p. 53)

The purpose of combining the concepts of affordances and prospect is to create a theoretical basis for rich-prospect browsing. Our contention is that the idea of combining a complete set of item representations (often images) with emergent tools for organising them, while not unique in the literature about interface design, has nonetheless suffered from not being sufficiently grounded in a theoretical framework that can help explain why these kinds of interfaces are desirable and make intuitive sense to people. It is also possible to see how the choices among different approaches to rich-prospect browsing can be informed by referring back to the theoretical framework that we have developed. By examining the concepts of affordances and prospect in the light of our experiments with rich-prospect browsers of various kinds, we can also to help elaborate these concepts or inform our understanding of them in ways that might otherwise not have arisen.

Prospect

The concept of prospect was first introduced by Appleton (1975), who was interested in aesthetic appreciation of landscape painting. He began with the question: "What is it that we like about landscape, and why do we like it?" (p. 1). His approach was to identify, in the context of what he called "habitat theory," two features of landscape that are directly related to survival for people and animals in a natural environment: prospect and refuge: "Where he has an unimpeded opportunity to see we can call it a prospect. Where he has an opportunity to hide, a refuge" (p. 73).

Using these twin concepts as a lens, Appleton examined comments published by art critics in the western world who were looking at European paintings of landscape, and was able to identify and elaborate on the themes of prospect and refuge using their work. His contention is that these features of the landscape, which once had survival value, remain as atavistic tendencies toward certain preferences. These tendencies contribute significantly to the appreciation of those artistic representations that include reference to the appropriate landscape features in some form, either as direct representations or as symbolic elements. In this formulation, various configurations are possible, based on how the symbols of prospect and refuge are deployed in a picture. In some cases, the image will be prospect-dominant, in others refuge-dominant, and in still others there will be a balance. Appleton also introduces a third landscape feature – hazard – which he uses to account for symbols that indicate the sublime. He emphasises that the impact of these symbols is not necessarily related to the rational strength of their connection to what they symbolise:

> In just the same way the symbolic representation of danger may be only vaguely and quite irrationally related to a real danger; a "refuge" may afford no real guarantee of security, and a "prospect" which visually satisfies the observer that his immediate environment is free from danger, may be permeated with radiation hazards or alive with poisonous snakes. Yet the symbolic impact of these environmental phenomena can induce in us a sense either of ease and satisfaction or of unease and disturbance, and it is on these emotional responses rather than on the real potency of the danger, the refuge or the prospect that our aesthetic reactions will depend. (Appleton 1975, p. 81)

Spires, for example, have a strong visual structure indicating elevation over the surrounding territory. It is not usual for people to ascend spires, some of which are actually inaccessible for reasons of physical construction, while others are inaccessible through policy; most often, there is really no purpose in climbing to the top of a spire. The actual use of a spire for obtaining prospect, however, is not important in recognising and acknowledging the spire as a strong symbol of prospect (90). It is this symbolic aspect, Appleton contends, that informs our aesthetic response to spires.

From the perspective of ecological psychology, Appleton implicitly identifies a number of affordances of real and symbolic prospect. If we stretch the definition of affordance somewhat so that perceivable opportunities for action include opportunities for emotional reaction, these include affordances for creating emotional states in the viewer such as ease and satisfaction, or conversely, unease and disturbance. To return to firmer ground, some of the survival-related affordances of prospect that Appleton mentions include advantages in hunting, seeking shelter, identifying positions of concealment, and exploring. He also mentions explicitly interpersonal affordances, such as surveillance activities related to the establishment and maintenance of territory. In cases where the prospect includes elements of the sublime, affordances may also be available for the experience of emotional states such as astonishment, admiration, reverence, or respect. Wayfinding is also a potential affordance of prospect.

Universalism

One of the fundamental objections to Appleton's ideas is that they are predicated on a universalism in human response which is currently unfashionable in academic circles, particularly among post-colonialists. Spawned from the enlightenment, the idea that there exist certain basic truths which apply to all human beings was, in the eighteenth century, a positive force that was wielded politically by members of the anti-slavery movement. Subsequent generations, however, found that universalism was more often than not adopted as an excuse, not for increased humanitarianism, but rather for various forms of cultural imperialism. The underlying argument was that if all human beings are basically the same, then their manifest differences must be the result of ignorance, misunderstanding, or outright wickedness, and should be corrected.

Appleton relies on biology as the basis for his universalism. By basing his theory on the survival value of prospect and refuge, Appleton suggests that natural selection has played a significant role in allowing the continued survival of those members of the species who were able to identify and capitalise on situations where these two factors were crucial. People who were unable to appreciate prospect and refuge were killed, so it is argued, before they were old enough to breed, and their inadequate genes were removed from the gene pool.

It does not seem difficult, however, to posit circumstances in which prospect would not be available, and therefore could not be a significant survival factor, or in which its detection and employment would not be essential for the survival of the individual. Among geese, for instance, it is common for a leader to provide guidance, based on experience (rather than senses), for the rest of the flock in finding water, food, and shelter. It seems reasonable that prehistoric groups of human beings might similarly have relied on previous experience, either individual or collective, rather than on the serendipitous availability of a prominence that afforded prospect to each person in the group. Survival value of group membership would therefore be a predominant factor. Although one of the tools used by one of the leaders might include knowing where to obtain prospect on the area, other successful members might not even be aware of it.

However, the suggestion that prospect and refuge are universally relevant due to human biology is not without merit. Leaving aside natural selection for a moment, it is true that human beings are biological organisms, bipedal, with two highly specialised eyes on the same side of the head and a tremendous amount of brain capacity dedicated to the processes of visual perception. This physical conformation suggests that certain kinds of environments are going to be privileged by this creature, where plenty of visual information is available in the front, and the unobserved back of the head is protected. Appleton's prospect and refuge fit this description nicely.

Subsequent studies of actual landscapes and their perception have looked at potential affordances of prospect that extend beyond the ones originally identified by Appleton. Since the landscapes under investigation are often those involving trees, the researchers are usually interested in some aspect of E.O. Wilson's biophilia hypothesis, which suggests that people benefit in a variety of ways from exposure to other living things and natural environments. As a consequence, prospect has seldom been isolated as a single significant factor, although it is often implicated in the findings, and deserves to be given some attention.

Applying the concept of prospect to human–computer interfaces results in a number of possible avenues for experimentation. We have focused on two approaches, namely increasing the felicity conditions for more affordances by providing various forms of user insight into the collection, and combining these displays with interface tools that allow the user to do something with that insight. Most retrieval and browsing interfaces keep the underlying data in a kind of blackbox; it can be very difficult to assess the scope and the nature of what is inside. In contrast, the insights available to the user of a rich-prospect browser are primarily related to indicating the bounds of discourse that have inevitably been established by the collection – that is, the terms under which the items have been collected, labelled, categorised, and otherwise organised. These areas of direct insight can be grouped into the following categories, which we will consider in more detail below.

- contents
- structure
- context
- features
- limitations
- connections
- trends
- anomalies
- navigation
- reminders
- processes
- reassurance
- reduced helplessness

The ways in which these factors relate to the opportunities for action provided by the system will differ significantly, but one of the primary felicity conditions for each of these affordances is the availability of prospect (an overall view) on the collection.

Insights about Content

By providing a meaningful representation of every item in the collection, a rich-prospect interface allows the user to directly perceive what is available. The user is not dependent on previous experience with the collection, or on having read explanatory material about it, although both of these might of course be useful.

Simply by glancing at the items, the user is able to ascertain with some degree of certainty what the collection is about, how large it is, and whether or not it can contribute to the purpose at hand. In cases where the rich prospect is provided in combination with a search function, direct insight into the contents may also help to establish an appropriate search vocabulary (Pirolli et al. 1996).

It should be emphasised, however, that direct insight is possible only in cases where the system uses terms that the user would consider relevant. As a hypothetical example, in a collection of prescription drugs, if the user is a doctor or other medical professional, it might be useful to organise the display according to the type of drug. An organising scheme in this case might use categories such as "cephalosporins," or "aromatic glycerol ethers." If the same collection were being designed for access by people suffering from some medical condition, however, it might be useful to provide an organising scheme that used categories based on the common name for the disease or other medical problem. In this case, the collection might have categories such as "sinus infection" or "back pain." If the patient attempted to make use of a rich-prospect interface designed for the doctor, it would not necessarily be easy to distinguish which drugs might be suitable for which kinds of medical conditions.

Another approach to providing insight into content might be to draw on facet analytical theory, in the sense that the system might construct representations by combining multiple organising principles into a single composite term. Ranganathan's Idea Plane Canon of Relevance emphasises that the facets used as components for such a term should align with the intention of the collection: its purpose, subject and scope (Spiteri 1998). In the hypothetical case of a collection designed for patients looking for information about medical conditions, for example, a faceted description might include a composite representation that included the part of the body afflicted, the medical condition, and the cost. These three terms represent three facets that are mutually exclusive as categories (though they may share elements), may be of interest to the user of such a collection, and uniquely identify the collection items.

It is also possible for a rich-prospect interface to actually misrepresent the collection (or be overly susceptible to misinterpretation). For instance, if a collection of commentaries on philosophers were organised by the names of the primary authors and their works, some users might interpret the interface as implying that the collection contains the primary materials, when in fact it consists entirely of secondary critical material. Guarding against potential misinterpretations based on alternative presuppositions is arguably one of the most difficult tasks of the designer, because the nature of the problem stems from disparities that are not necessarily explicit either for the designers or the users. Extensive user involvement in the design process, and in testing, can help to forestall these kinds of situations, and iterative approaches to development can help reduce the impact of any which do occur.

Insights about Structure

For interfaces to digital collections, there are two distinct structures involved. First is the structure of the collection itself, in terms of the kinds of objects that it contains and the ways in which the objects are conceptually organised by the collectors or designers of the system. A group of people responsible for designing a digital volume of conference proceedings, for instance, might decide that the digital papers should be collected in groups according to the session of the conference in which they were originally presented. Alternatively, if the papers dealt with topics that were related to national interests, the designers might decide to organise the documents according to the national affiliations of the authors, with papers from the U.K. in one section and papers from Malaysia in another. Yet another possibility might be to organise content by presentation category, with the full papers in one section and the poster sessions in another. Any number of different organisational schemes are possible, and in many cases several schemes can exist concurrently.

The second structure relates to the interface. Independent of how the underlying documents have been organised, the interface designer can provide an organising principle, which might reflect the understanding of the people who created the collection, but which might also reflect alternative understandings, such as those of the users.

If the interface provides an appropriate structure of the first kind, the user can be provided with potential insights into the nature of the collection. For example, a collection of text documents might consist of items that deal with the same subject matter, but that have been written with different audiences in mind. If the interface is designed with the subject matter rather than the audience as a central organising principle, then the user would have an immediate cue to the fact that certain documents that might otherwise appear to be unrelated do in fact have something very central in common with each other – namely, their reference to a common subject. If the interface were to be designed the other way – that is, organised by audience – then the common reference to subject would be occluded, but the different audiences could be made immediately evident as the central theme of each document cluster.

Regardless of whether or not the interface reflects the underlying organisation of the material – depending on the user's current task – some organising principles are going to be more useful than others. The subdivision of the Amazon.com site into different kinds of products is an example of an interface that provides structural information about the elements in the collection. The user can choose to search the entire product line, or can limit the search to books, videos, CDs, and so on. In a rich-prospect form of interface, these categories could serve as an organising principle for the display.

Product format, however, is not necessarily an organising principle that provides the most useful kind of information for the user. One potentially useful organising principle might simply be price. If some consumers are visiting Amazon.com to look for gifts, the ability to organise the products into price ranges, independent of category, might result in a browsing environment that could help generate gift ideas.

An alternative strategy might involve clustering the information by topic areas, with visual cues within the topic cluster used to specify format. A topic cluster for use in Amazon.com might be a subject area such as gardening, with all the available materials, whether books, videos, garden tools, or seeds, shown in proximity to each other. A user looking for a particular plant might therefore find the seeds for it shown in relation to books about how to grow the plant, tools to use in working with the plant, and paintings that feature it as a subject matter.

With the ubiquity of social media, the possibility also arises of allowing the user to suggest organisational strategies. If users are given the facility to create and store structural groupings that can serve as interaction histories for other users, it may be the case that the collection of materials on that particular plant were not created as part of the original system design, but are part of a legacy of structural suggestions made by previous users of the system (recommendation engines may operate either through explicit associations created by users or through statistical analysis of usage patterns such as "people who bought X also bought Y").

In the Searchling project (Figure 2.1)[1], we set out to provide people with the ability to browse a controlled vocabulary for use in query formulation (Stafford et al. 2008; Mehta et al. 2009). Searchling therefore consists primarily of a visual interface for interactively examining a thesaurus. For our initial experiments, we used the Canadian Government CORE subject thesaurus, which has a parallel vocabulary in both English and French. This gave us the opportunity to create a system where the user could enter a search term or phrase in one language and run the query in two languages.

The interface design consists of three related spaces: a table on the left for browsing the thesaurus terms, a query formulation area on the right for working with selected terms in order to create a query, and a results space on the bottom that shows the list of retrieved files. Searchling does not show a representation of all the thesaurus entries at once, making it a restricted kind of rich-prospect interface, which only deals with a selected subset of the entire collection. There is however a hierarchy in use, so that the thesaurus structure informs the interface. In the table on the left, the high-level categories are always visible. Selecting one of those categories brings up a list of the terms it contains. These can be arranged either alphabetically or in their own hierarchy. Above this list is a search box, and next to the terms are a set of columns that indicate how each term in the list relates to the search term.

1 The Searchling interface uses the Canadian Government CORE subject thesaurus to help users assemble queries based on a controlled vocabulary. Since CORE has a parallel vocabulary in English and French, it allows us to formulate queries in one language and run them in both. Design by Ximena Rossello.

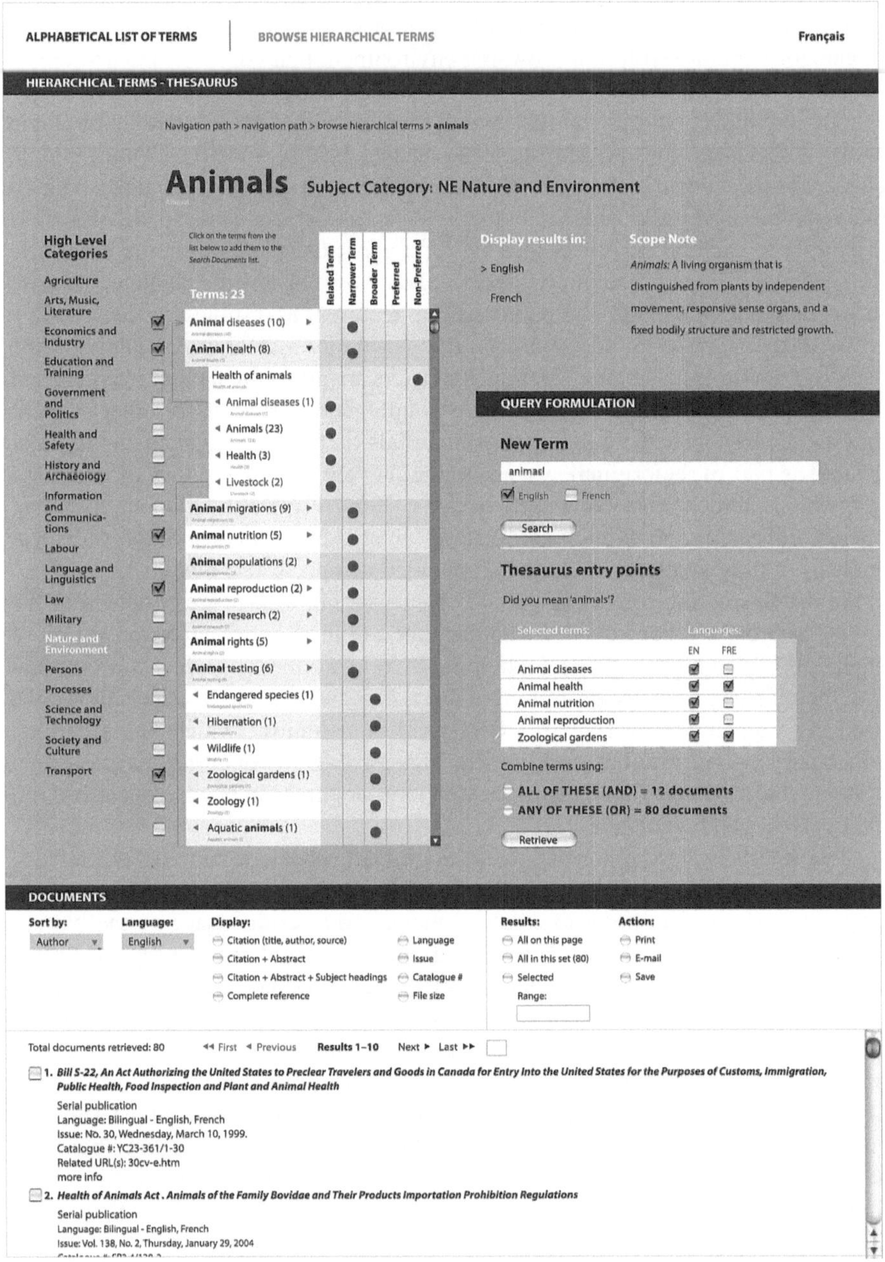

ALPHABETICAL LIST OF TERMS | BROWSE HIERARCHICAL TERMS | Français

HIERARCHICAL TERMS - THESAURUS

Navigation path > navigation path > browse hierarchical terms > **animals**

Animals Subject Category: NE Nature and Environment

High Level Categories

Agriculture
Arts, Music, Literature
Economics and Industry
Education and Training
Government and Politics
Health and Safety
History and Archaeology
Information and Communications
Labour
Language and Linguistics
Law
Military
Nature and Environment
Persons
Processes
Science and Technology
Society and Culture
Transport

Click on the terms from the list below to add them to the Search Documents list.

Terms: 23

Term	Related Term	Narrower Term	Broader Term	Preferred	Non-Preferred
Animal diseases (10)		●			
Animal health (8)		●			
Health of animals					●
Animal diseases (1)	●				
Animals (23)	●				
Health (3)	●				
Livestock (2)	●				
Animal migrations (9)		●			
Animal nutrition (5)		●			
Animal populations (2)		●			
Animal reproduction (2)		●			
Animal research (2)		●			
Animal rights (5)		●			
Animal testing (6)		●			
Endangered species (1)			●		
Hibernation (1)			●		
Wildlife (1)			●		
Zoological gardens (1)			●		
Zoology (1)			●		
Aquatic animals (1)			●		

Display results in:
> English
French

Scope Note
Animals: A living organism that is distinguished from plants by independent movement, responsive sense organs, and a fixed bodily structure and restricted growth.

QUERY FORMULATION

New Term

animasl

English French

Search

Thesaurus entry points

Did you mean 'animals'?

Selected terms:	EN	FRE
Animal diseases	☑	☐
Animal health	☑	☑
Animal nutrition	☑	☐
Animal reproduction	☑	☐
Zoological gardens	☑	☑

Combine terms using:
ALL OF THESE (AND) = 12 documents
ANY OF THESE (OR) = 80 documents

Retrieve

DOCUMENTS

Sort by: Author
Language: English
Display: Citation (title, author, source); Citation + Abstract; Citation + Abstract + Subject headings; Complete reference; Language; Issue; Catalogue #; File size
Results: All on this page; All in this set (80); Selected; Range:
Action: Print; E-mail; Save

Total documents retrieved: 80 ◂◂ First ◂ Previous **Results 1–10** Next ▸ Last ▸▸

1. ***Bill S-22, An Act Authorizing the United States to Preclear Travelers and Goods in Canada for Entry Into the United States for the Purposes of Customs, Immigration, Public Health, Food Inspection and Plant and Animal Health***
Serial publication
Language: Bilingual - English, French
Issue: No. 30, Wednesday, March 10, 1999.
Catalogue #: YC23-361/1-30
Related URL(s): 30cv-e.htm
more info

2. ***Health of Animals Act. Animals of the Family Bovidae and Their Products Importation Prohibition Regulations***
Serial publication
Language: Bilingual - English, French
Issue: Vol. 138, No. 2, Thursday, January 29, 2004

Figure 2.1 The Searchling interface

For the user study, we asked 15 university graduate students and faculty members to carry out a thinkaloud protocol while working with the browser. One thing that we learned is that for the integration to work properly between browsing a thesaurus, constructing queries, and examining the results, it is necessary to put the three spaces in as close a proximity as possible. We know from the Gestalt principles that people will mentally group objects that are in proximity, and in this case the tension is between finding enough screen real estate for the three interface spaces while making it plain that working in one space effects the contents of the others. (Needless to say, there are constraints on interface designs that are dictated by hardware considerations such as screen size and input capabilities (keyboards, mice, touch surfaces, and so on).)

More significantly, in the context of providing structural information about the underlying collection, another finding was that the participants were able to successfully use the interface and understand the results, even though they were not necessarily conversant with the terms of art related to thesauri. They were unclear, for instance, on the definition of a "preferred term" and were not always sure what it meant when the interface indicated that a term was broader or narrower. However, despite these limitations around the vocabulary we had used, the structure was visible in the interface, and the study participants could adequately interpret it.

Insights about Context

There are innumerable collections in the world, whether analog or digital, and some are more clearly defined than others. Depending on the nature of the collection and cultural situation, it may not always be straightforward for users to determine what kind of collection they are currently investigating. Some collections are immediately recognisable for what they are, because they have become culturally recognised as collections. A printed telephone book, for example, is an artifact that has a strong identity. People familiar with phone systems immediately recognise a phone book because of its size, color and poor paper quality, which are consequences of having to annually replace high print runs of large quantities of data for mass distribution.

On the web, there are often very few cues to the context of information, but there are some, such as the taxonomy of URLs. In general, U.S. sites that contain the designation .edu and sites elsewhere marked .ac are associated with academic institutions, while .com sites are commercial or personal enterprises. Sites related to public bodies sometimes, but not always, use a country abbreviation such as .ca, which is usually useful in any case for placing the site geographically (there are exceptions, such as the widely used URL shortening service bit.ly which at first glance seems to be situated in Libya).

In addition to URLs, there are various branding strategies, such as institutional identities, and in some cases there may also be explanatory text that provides the potential user with some idea of the scope and coverage of the site.

There is little that rich-prospect browsing interfaces can contribute to the contextualisation of entire collections within the universe of other collections. Assuming an interface that served as a portal, or a collection of collections, some indications of relative size are possible, and the designers of the portal could also provide some guidance through either the contents or the structural design.

However, if a rich-prospect browsing interface is used for an individual collection, the role of the context for the material can be much clearer. Since individual items in the collection are immediately present to the user within the context of the larger collection, the user has clues, both as to what kind of collection they have found, and to the place of individual items within that collection. For example, someone locating images of historical clothing might have come across a late eighteenth-century dress. Is this the only such dress in a collection that spans the centuries, or is it one dress among hundreds in an elaborate collection that focuses on the eighteenth-century? A rich-prospect browser does not require the user to spend much time in pursuing this question, since the default page provides a view of all the dresses, and perhaps has also organised them into a default configuration that makes the type of collection immediately recognisable (this assumes that each element in a collection can be accessed directly with a unique URL and that the full state of the application can be achieved when parachuted in, such as from a search engine; in practice, this is far from being the case, especially for sites that rely heavily on browser plugins such as Flash).

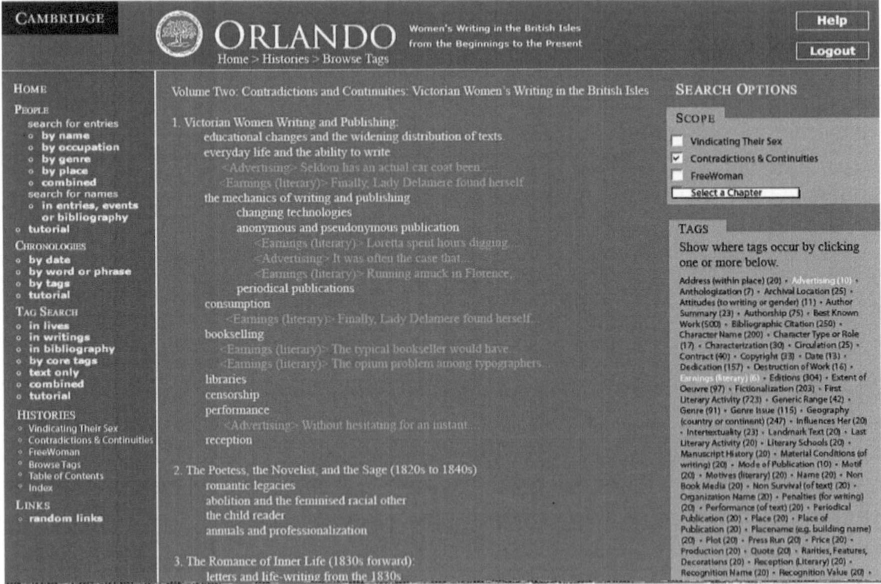

Figure 2.2 The Dynamic Table Of Contexts

Related to the notion of context are questions of reliability, sophistication, and nuance of information. Although there could be various degrees of quality of collections focused on eighteenth-century clothing, in general it would seem likely that an entire dedicated collection would contain more reliable or more sophisticated or more nuanced information than would a collection of dresses spanning the ages.

One of our projects that addressed this issue of providing context as a rich-prospect browsing strategy was the Dynamic Table of Contexts (Figure 2.2).[2]

In a sense, the conventional table of contents is a form of prospect. That is, the items provide a meaningful representation of the chapters. Over the past few centuries, the degree of representation has changed, with a high point occurring in the late Renaissance or early eighteenth century, when chapter titles took the form of paragraphs that summarised the chapter.

The conventional index, on the other hand, is a kind of emergent tool for non-sequential access of the sequential pages. The index does not necessarily provide a whole lot of prospect on a book, although it can provide some in highly fragmented form. However, by combining the table of contents and the index into a single, interactive tool, we have a rich-prospect browser for digital books. In the case of our project, the index is not exactly an index, but is instead based on any available interpretive XML encoding of the document. The person interested in browsing the book can click on the tags (the underlying markup) in the XML, and snippets of the text enclosed by the tags are toggled into the table of contents. Using this approach, the table of contents becomes customisable by the reader to represent areas where his or her interests coincide with the interpretation of whoever was responsible for the encoding and the structure of the document.

In essence, this design provides three kinds of context. Two of them are typically found in books. The first is in the table of contents, where each chapter title is located within the sequence of the other chapter titles. The second is the index, where the terms are located alphabetically next to other terms. The new form of context, however, consists of the dynamic insertion of snippets of tagged text into the table of contents to serve as additional links into the body of the text (this is a type of *transclusion* of content, as described by Ted Nelson (1980) and other early hypertext theorists).

Insights about Features

A collection can have any number of attributes in addition to the content items and the visual language. These attributes can in turn form part of the rich-prospect interface, allowing for their direct perception by the user. An example is the presence or absence of an interpretive tagging system, along with its potential

2 The Dynamic Table of Contexts extends the functionality of the conventional table of contents by allowing the reader to add and subtract brief text snippets, based on the tagging of the document. Design by Stan Ruecker.

complexities in terms of the definitions of the tags, and also in the presence of attributes on the tags and the values of those attributes, all of which are features that can be used for retrieval purposes by the computer, but can also serve as components of a rich-prospect interface. Rich-prospect interfaces for tagged collections will be discussed at greater length in Chapter 5 – Textual Markup for Digital Collections.

Insights about Limitations

Just as prospect can allow the user to identify the strengths of a collection, either in terms of the significant clusters of documents contained or the individual items being sought, so can a prospect-based interface allow the user to identify areas where the collection is not going to be useful or may be useful only with extra effort. For example, if a collection contains a number of documents intended to market electronic products, there may be a combination of promotional items and technical specifications. If a user looking to troubleshoot the product finds a prospect display of the marketing materials, it will be immediately apparent that troubleshooting advice is not part of the collection.

Similarly, a rich-prospect interface can indicate not just that certain kinds of documents are missing, but also that the intentions of the designers of the collection are either going to make the current browsing task easier or more difficult to perform, depending on the level of correspondence between the presuppositions of the designer and those of the user. A typical example might be in the use of keywords as part of the meaningful representation of the items in the collection, where the keywords chosen by the people responsible for creating the index will not necessarily correspond to the definitions used for the same concepts by the people seeking to access the collection. Structuring the display as clusters of documents around each keyword (Figure 2.3) may be one way to suggest to the user the way in which particular keywords have been applied in that system.

In the T-Saurus project (Shiri et al. 2010), our goal was to give people a visual environment for browsing the multilingual thesaurus from UNESCO as a form of controlled vocabulary that could be used for query enhancement. That is, people using this system are visually browsing a thesaurus for keywords that can be automatically added to a query that is run simultaneously in multiple languages. The number of files in the collection is indicated through the size of the box around a selected query term, and the number is also displayed on the box. Related terms of various kinds are clustered around the periphery.

Insights about Connections

If an interface places different meaningful representations together in the display, the Gestalt tendency of proximity will encourage users to consider potential connections among the items. The organisation of the items will naturally tend to strengthen or weaken this tendency. If the display is arranged chronologically, for

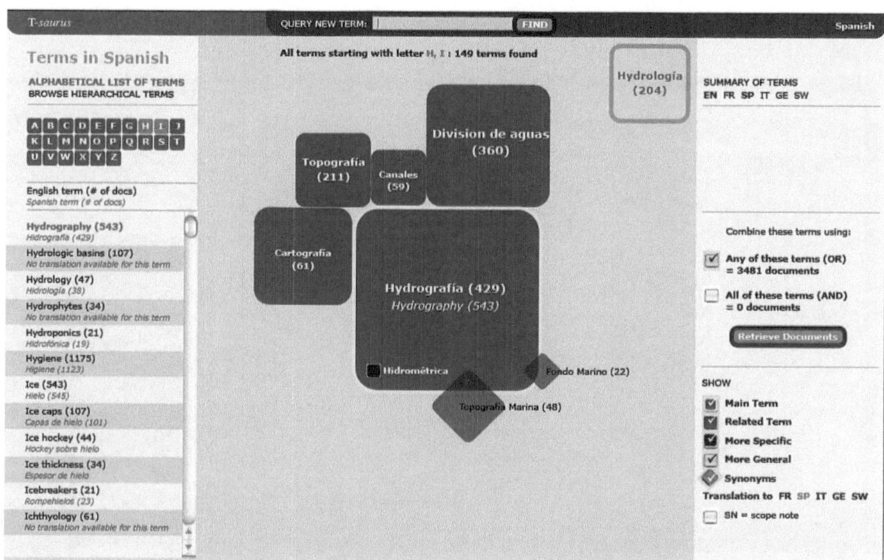

Figure 2.3 The T-Saurus Interface[3]

example, the user may be able to identify items that are part of a thematic interest of a particular era, or people who were contemporaries, or to form some sense of historical narrative such as can be achieved through examining a visual timeline or other sequence.

In the Paper Drill prototype (Figure 2.4), we faced a number of challenges, including the need to be sufficiently clear not only in indicating connections between items, but also in visually expressing some other relatively complex ideas. The Paper Drill prototype was produced under the aegis of the Implementing New Knowledge Environments (INKE) project, led by Ray Siemens at the University of Victoria.

The purpose of the Paper Drill is to automate, insofar as such a thing is possible, the scholarly practice of chaining through articles, which consists of discovering relevant literature by starting with a "seed" article and reading the items from its references section, then reading the articles referenced in those articles, and so on down the line, until a sense of the research area begins to coalesce in the mind of the scholar.

Visually, the Paper Drill prototype includes a home page that shows heatmaps of articles, organised according to how frequently they are cited by other articles in the system. Once the user chooses a seed article or author, the central space changes to one that is filled with the items in the citation chain based on the

3 The T-Saurus Interface is a visual browser for multilingual query enhancement. Design by Carlos Fiorentino.

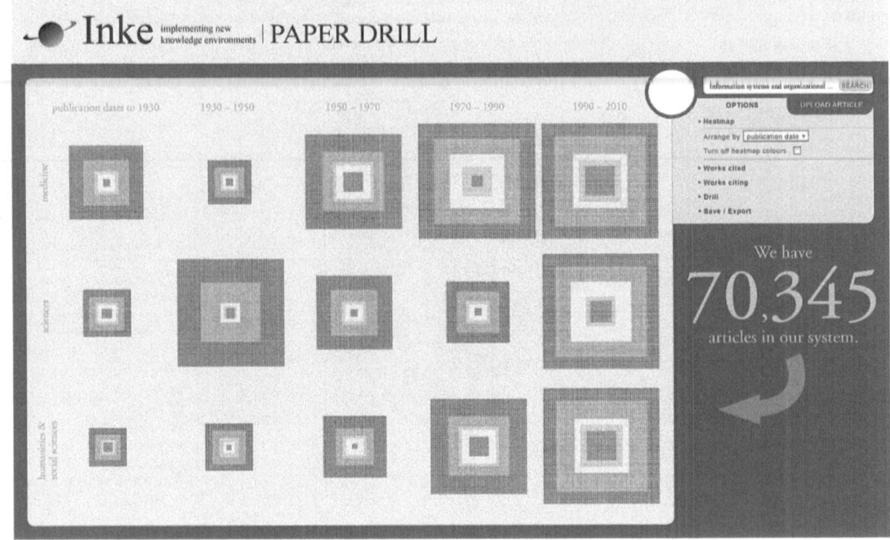

Figure 2.4 The Paper Drill home page[4]

selected starting point. The user is then able to further refine this field of items by dragging and dropping a small object, a droplet, onto the collection. The droplet triggers an oil and water effect that pushes most of the items to the side and draws into the cleared area some more details about the top five or ten authors or articles within the chain. The visual complexity of the droplet increases with the number of changes the user makes to the default settings. The user is also able to select among a variety of pre-defined droplet types, with the goal of making the configuration easier to identify for subsequent reuse.

The droplet idea was originally designed for use in textmining (Ruecker et al. 2009), where we were using supervised classification to allow literary scholars to provide clusters of examples of some phenomenon of interest. These examples provide a training set for a system to use in proposing other candidate items to add to the clusters. The original manual clustering task can be difficult and time-consuming.[5] We felt it was therefore important not only to provide a means to

---

4 The Paper Drill attempts to provide prospect on the citation chain (what texts cite this text and what texts are cited by this text) for a given author or article, while at the same time visually representing the depth of the search. This home page shows heatmaps of citation activity, plotted against the domain of the journal and the period of publication. Design by Milena Radzikowska.

5 Sara Steger, who experimented with this approach for her PhD dissertation on sentimental fiction, clustered roughly 400 episodes in her training set, before running the process against nearly 4,000 novels, which returned an additional 1,348 chapters (Clement et al. 2008).

save the training as it proceeded, but also to provide some visual clues as to how much training had been done, and how many parameters had been set up, so that someone returning to the task could quickly get back up to speed.

There are a number of challenges in designing and building this kind of prototype. First, under the hood we needed to include several methods for dealing with inconsistent formatting of metadata about the materials being cited. Just reconciling the many different citation standards is a challenge, as is locating, retrieving, and parsing documents that aren't part of a system that has regularised metadata for citations. Fortunately, there are several systems that do provide this kind of standardised information – our partners for the project include the Synergies umbrella for open source digital journals, as well as one of their partners – the Open Journal Systems. For the rest, we have been working on a combination web scraper and file parser.

However, in order to test a prototype, it is possible to work with pre-packaged data, rather than relying on application programming interfaces from other projects to provide the data "live." For the Paper Drill, our questions have to do with how well people are able to understand and use the various affordances such as selecting depth of chaining, and how they feel about some of the more experimental animations such as the oil and water effect.

Insights about Trends

Independent of the structure of the interface or the structure of the underlying collection, there may also be trends in the collection that are potentially significant to the user but would not be obvious to someone just looking at the individual documents. For example, a collection arranged chronologically may prove to have strong holdings in one particular period but very few holdings in another. A chronological rich-prospect display would make that difference immediately apparent to the user, since the number of items showing in the historical period with a lot of holdings would form a comparatively larger group on the screen.

A generalised approach to identifying trends is to create a structured surface as the basis for the rich-prospect browser, then look for gaps in the placement of the items (Ruecker and Liepert 2006). An example is the sketch we produced for a tabular interface to the Victorian Women Writers Project (Ruecker and Liepert 2004), which shows that the collection actually contains material published after the Victorian period. The rationale is clear once the information is visible – these documents are included because their authors are considered Victorian writers, independent of when the material was actually published.

Insights about Anomalies

With a rich-prospect interface, the user may have the opportunity to identify individual items or groups of items which seem to be out of place in the collection or are in some other way anomalous.

As Shneiderman et al. (1992) point out, one of the common activities of information foraging in western culture involves looking for bargains. For a user interested in identifying an item that can be purchased at a discount, a collection interface that uses price as a structuring principle would quickly allow identification of possible bargains. An even more useful organisation of the interface, however, would be one that emphasised the comparison of items that were similar across every dimension except price. For example, a list of houses organised by street or neighborhood could potentially show anomalous pricing more clearly than it could be shown by an interface organised by price range.

Insights about Navigation

If the design of the rich-prospect interface is such that it contains information about the structure of the underlying collection, then the interface also has the potential to serve as a navigational aid. As Winograd and Flores (1986) point out, an even more optimal situation is one in which the user has the opportunity to either modify existing strategies for communicating with the collection, or else has some means of establishing new ones.

Some interesting possibilities have been investigated by previous researchers. Wexelblat and Maes (1999), for instance, developed a suite of "footprint" tools to provide interaction histories, both for the current user and for subsequent users who might want to take advantage of previous work: "One of the primary benefits of interaction history is to give newcomers the benefits of work done in the past" (Wexelblat and Maes 1999, p. 217). The record of past work in a footprint can include paths through the collection, as suggested in Bush's (1945) famous description of the memex with its trails, although in order to increase their usefulness for others, it is helpful to find ways of conveying not just where they went, but also who did it, why they did what they did, and how the history was created (that is, automatically by the system, or subject to selection or editing by the user). It is worth noting that very little of the shared histories functionality described by Bush and others is apparent on the web or in our browsers.

Reminders

If some meaningful representation of items is available to the user, there is the possibility that the person will look at the representation and be reminded of collection items that are of potential interest, either because the user knew about them at some point and has forgotten, or else because they are something new that would not have occurred to the user if the system had not offered them up for observation. This affordance is a digital analog to the opportunity available to the library patron who scans the stacks looking for items that might be related to the title already found, or are otherwise of interest, sometimes serendipitously. In the case of the library, the affordance is made available through the organisation of the shelves by subject. In a computer interface, the opportunity exists to look at the same information arranged under different organisational schemes.

An example of the reminder value of rich-prospect browsing is our Delegate Browser (Figure 2.5) project. The Delegate Browser is an experimental interface to help conference delegates manage their social capital both during a conference and afterward (Ruecker et al. 2006). The system provides the user with a photo of every person attending the conference. The images can be grouped by visual characteristics such as hair color, as well as by professional information such as the keywords that apply to this year's conference presentation.

One of the fundamental purposes for conferences is to allow delegates to see what work their colleagues are doing. However, that kind of information transfer does not necessitate a face-to-face meeting: it is possible to publish and even to pre-publish research results, and to keep track of colleagues in the same field by these

Figure 2.5 The Delegate Browser[6]

6 The Delegate Browser shows photos of everyone at a conference, combining information about appearance with information about professional activity. This screenshot shows a preliminary mockup using photos scraped from the web. Design by Michael Lewcio.

means. However, a conference also affords opportunities for networking, whether that be in the form of establishing, maintaining, or building on existing social capital.

Our goal was therefore essentially to provide an interactive memory aid. The system needed to contain information about colleagues that was worth knowing, but not so much information that it would be overwhelming. It needed to contain the kinds of information that provide a quick snapshot of what can be learned through social interactions that have occurred at intervals that may be as long as a year or several years. It needed to include a mechanism for quickly identifying a colleague of interest, someone who might be standing at the front of the room and presenting, standing across the room at the bar, or walking across the room to say hello.

We included a dozen kinds of grouping information, all of which were divided into two categories. The first category consisted of a set of items about the visual appearance of the person: hair color, eye color, gender, wearing or not wearing eyeglasses. The second category contained information about the person's professional activities: city, university affiliation, keywords associated with presentations where this person was an author.

Other features of the system included a crumbtrail that allowed users to retrace their sequence of steps in using the system, an advanced query line where the syntax for a particular grouping could be modified without using the navigation buttons, and a magnification tool so that users could zoom in on individual photos without having to subgroup until they were as large as desired.

In addition to the interface home page, where photos of delegates could be dynamically grouped by the users, each photo also served as a link to a page of detailed information about the delegate, including an annotation field, so that the users could take notes about their colleagues. Navigation between the detailed pages and the home page was simplified by having the system spawn tabs for each new detailed page, so that they could be quickly traversed while the home page retained its current state.

We were interested in finding out how people would use these groups of information (personal attributes and professional details). Would they combine them or use them one at a time? Would there be some that would be used by everyone and others that would be used by only a select few, and if so, which items fell into which groups? Our study in this case used a logging method. We had 84 people attending the 2006 TEI conference in Victoria who agreed to try out the system, and we logged their activities for the three days of the conference, then for three months afterwards.

As has happened repeatedly in this research, we were surprised by the result. Conventional wisdom for web site design suggests that it is the job of the designer to figure out the navigation model that will make intuitive sense to the majority of users. Working with questionnaires, interviews, focus groups, and using specialised techniques like card sorts (where users organise cards to represent the hierarchy as they understand it), the designer tries to determine how people conceive of a particular body of information, so that the site can be structured in a way that will make sense to the majority of people who use it.

However, when we provided our participants with 14 buttons that could be used in any order at any time, and logged their use over three months, we found that they used each of the buttons roughly equally. What this suggests to us is that there is some benefit to exposing metadata to the users, although we aren't sure yet what the upper limits on the amount of metadata might be, and to what extent the benefits are offset by having some forms of metadata that are either not useful for the end user, or else are too obscure to be readily understood. It may also be that during some of the initial usage, participants were exploring the system and trying everything – perhaps a balanced usage pattern would not be sustained by people who used the system at more than one conference.

Processes

Processes, or possible sequences of actions, are a type of information that has been traditionally available but can be difficult to study. If one thinks, for instance, of instructions for assembling prefabricated furniture, it becomes clear that there are better and worse ways of providing this kind of information, and the ability to browse through an entire process from the vantage point of a prospect view can help forestall difficulties of the kind where an early ambiguity or misinterpretation can result in the subsequent need to retrace one's steps and undo actions already completed. There is also a combinatorics of complexity as the number of potential processes – and variants within those processes – become available (assembling furniture usually leads to a single outcome, but most tools in the humanities are far more open-ended).

One of the purposes for providing prospect on processes is to allow the user to gain additional information at critical decision points. Another of the purposes is to enable to the user to identify critical decision points. A third purpose is to facilitate troubleshooting in the case where the first two purposes have not been adequately met.

In the case of document collections, the need for prospect into process is particularly indicated when the system provides not only a means of accessing the material, but also includes a number of tools for manipulating either the display or the document contents. An analogy might be in the development of macros, where an identical series of actions involving documents can be predefined and run against a set of documents that share common features that are amenable to having an identical series of actions run against them. Not all document collections, of course, contain items where the processes necessary can be automated to such a high degree. However, by providing the user with an overview, both of the processes possible and of their usual sequence, a system might be designed that could support document manipulations through allowing the user to step in and out of the actions, providing manual interventions where necessary but otherwise working through a well-defined sequence that may also contain automated components.

In No One Remembers Acronyms (NORA) and Metadata Open New Knowledge (MONK), we worked on the design of two "workbenches" that were intended to provide literary scholars with an opportunity to use textmining algorithms. For each project, we produced a variety of interface designs, some quite conservative and others more experimental, with the goal of making the process of working with textmining analytics as straightforward and understandable as possible for people who are not in the habit of using such tools.

We believe, for example, that while it is important that the user have access to detailed explanations of the underlying principles, and that numeric data should be available when requested, the default interfaces should not *necessitate* an awareness of the underlying principles or the numeric data that the system produces.

For almost as long as computer-assisted literary analysis has existed – since the middle of the last century – there has been debate about the utility for textual scholars of sophisticated analytical routines (for an overview of early text analysis and stylometrics work, see these two retrospectives: Milic (1967) and Potter (1991)). More recently, researchers like Ramsay (2003), Moretti (2005), and Unsworth (2005) have all provided thoughts on the subject, especially with respect to large-scale textmining, largely to the effect that such systems should provide the basis for studying patterns that would otherwise be difficult to observe, without degenerating to overly positivistic perspectives of textual phenomena. The consensus appears to be that sophisticated textmining analytics will not be an end in themselves for literary scholars, but will instead provide a lens onto material that can serve as one of the stages of the hermeneutic or interpretive activities that form the core interest of the discipline.

Bringing textmining into the research lives of literary scholars remains, however, an interesting and challenging task. On the one hand, the opportunity exists to create working environments that will allow the scholarly community to apply sophisticated analytical techniques to large bodies of digital text. On the other, there is not yet a large group of literary scholars who have found a strong motivation to use such techniques. We believe the decisive moment in this chicken or egg scenario will come when a reputed literary scholar adopts digital methods to provide a compelling exemplar to other literary scholars. Certainly it is true that there is a small, dedicated coterie of digital humanists who are willing to endure any kind of interface for the opportunity to carry out analytical processes on their text collections. But we had hopes of producing interfaces that would be simple and attractive enough to extend to colleagues outside this specialised group.

Funded by the Mellon Foundation, the NORA project was led by John Unsworth and was an attempt to produce a working prototype of a supervised classification system for humanities scholars. We created four conceptually distinct designs and developed a fifth. These consisted of designs for a 3-step system, an interactive tree, an oil and water browser, and a scanner, followed by a working prototype based on a space divided by moveable shutters.

3-step sequence

In our 3-step interface design for NORA (Figure 2.6), we had the mental model of a recommender system, except that algorithmic processes (so-called intelligent agents that could demonstrate contextual awareness) would replace the behavior of previous users as the basis for recommendations. In this design, a simple sequence exists from the beginning to the end of the process. In step one, the researcher chooses a large body of material to work with. In step two, good and bad examples of some phenomenon are selected. The system automatically identifies the features the examples have in common with each other (unsupervised classification in the jargon of datamining), then uses those features to find other similar documents, which are presented to the user in step three.

This is not an unreasonable design, and has the virtue of simplicity for first-time users. However, it has the disadvantage that for literary scholars, the underlying

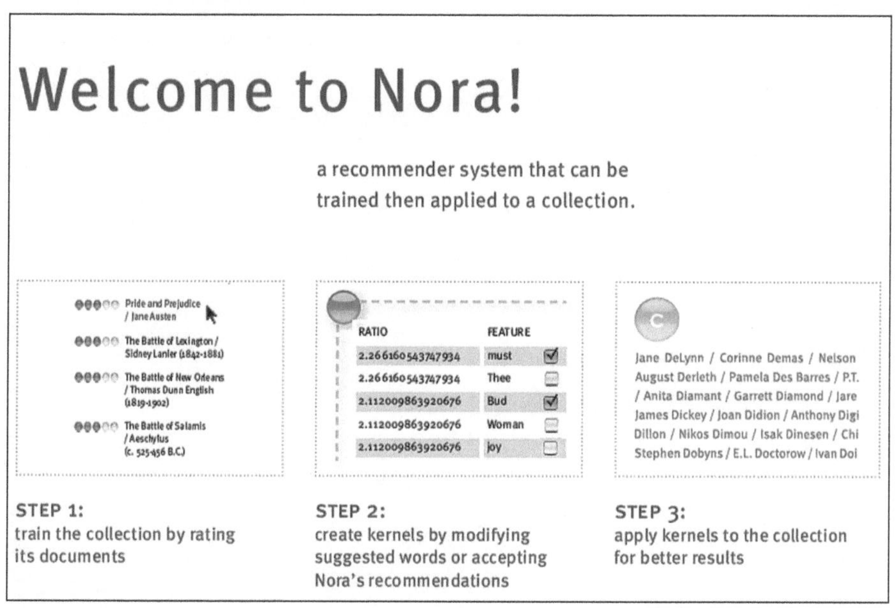

Figure 2.6 The home page sketch for the NORA three-step sequential process[7]

7 The home page sketch for the NORA three-step sequential process, which is simple to understand but highly constrained. The implied sequence is also not particularly useful for literary scholars, who may prefer a more iterative approach. Design by Milena Radzikowska.

details are often the most important aspect of the scholarly activity, and the ability to manipulate them in an iterative way is an affordance that makes the process more useful. Questions about the underlying details arise naturally, since the literary scholar has some rationale for providing the examples (we might be skeptical of scholars willing to accept computer-generated results without any understanding of the underlying mechanisms). This might be a set of passages, for example, that are rich in a particular figure of speech. Alternatively, it might be a set where some literary motif is present. It might represent a set rich in emotion, or devoid of emotion, or very stilted, or particularly purple, or full of lies, or speculative thinking, or anaphoric references to time. Whatever the case might be, it is natural to wonder what the algorithm sees as the features that the passages in the set have in common with each other, in addition to seeing the set of new documents that the system recognises as belonging to the same set. Further, once the features are displayed, it is a reasonable assumption that many users will want to have the ability to adjust the set, adding new items and removing items that seem clearly irrelevant or mistaken in light of the intention behind assembling the original training set.

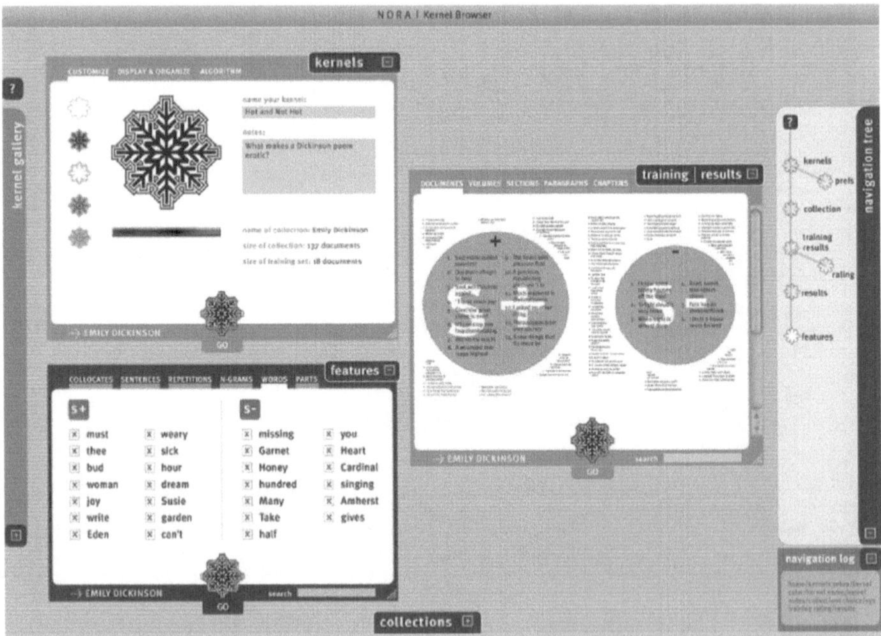

Figure 2.7 The Oil and Water Browser

The 3-step design also included a rudimentary use of the "kernel" or "droplet" concept, where a small visual object was used to store the previous steps in the process for subsequent re-use, either in the context of the existing study or else in connection with a different set of data.

Oil and water

The oil and water browser (Figure 2.7)[8] was based on the idea that users would encapsulate previous steps of the process in little droplets that could be applied to a collection by dragging and dropping them onto it. Each droplet might contain textmining training data, as well as choices about what information to display about each item and how to organise the items on display.

Interactive tree

Like the 3-Step design, the interactive tree browser (Figure 2.8)[9] provided the user with a stepwise process, but was intended to leverage the fact that literary scholars could be expected to be more comfortable with text than with visual objects such as droplets. The sequence proceeded through having the user make choices at the nodes of horizontal branches, which would then expand to provide the next step. The primary disadvantage of this design is that the nodes at the ends of branches do not necessarily lend themselves to providing sufficiently complex information for the user to be able to easily make the decision as to which node it would be best to choose. The design also quickly extended to the right of the screen and off the page, requiring some form of truncation on the left or automated scrolling to the right.

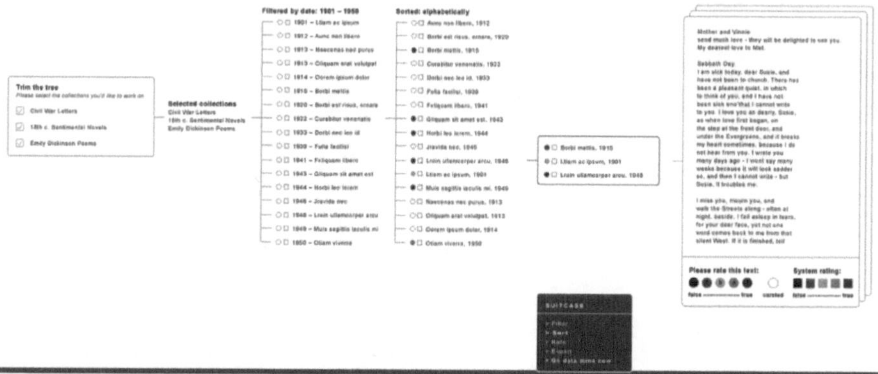

Figure 2.8 An interactive textmining tree

8 Droplets in the Oil and Water Browser would interact with a screenful of collection items by separating out the items of interest. This sketch shows various palettes where the user has trained and used a droplet shaped like a blue snowflake. Design by Milena Radzikowska.

9 The interactive textmining tree suggested a series of steps by having the user make selections on the rightmost nodes of the emerging branches. Design by Milena Radzikowska.

In order to provide more information to the user about the current state of the system, and also to allow users to move back and forth through the process, a slider bar with a popup menu system was provided at the bottom of the screen.

Scanner design

As another alternative to working with textmining droplets, we also produced a design that was loosely based on the mechanism of a flatbed scanner or photocopier (Figure 2.9). That is, the user would assign selected functions to a vertical bar that would then traverse a screenful of items, first highlighting the ones of interest, then collecting them in a second pass that dropped them into a bin off to one side. The scanner bar would in many respects serve like the droplets in the oil and water design, acting like a repository for the choices made by the user. The scanner bars would be somewhat simpler for the programmers to implement, but would not lend themselves to mixing and matching in the same way that the droplets would. There is also some question about the underlying metaphor, which might be unattractive to potential users who either find the visual connection to scanning spurious or else associate photocopying with a level of intellectual activity that is not congruent with textmining.

This concept sketch leaves many of the important details for further development, including all of the iterative processes where the user trains the system for a

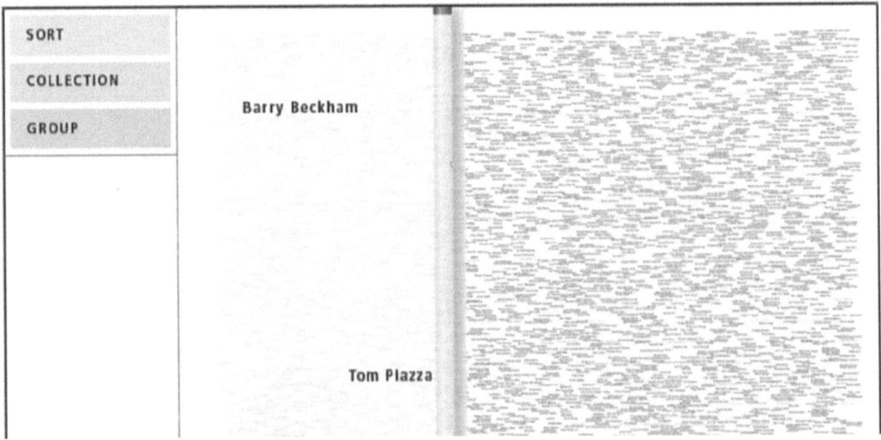

Figure 2.9 The Scanner Design for Textmining[10]

particular classification and examines the features. What the sketch does show is how the system is applied to a given collection once the training is complete. In

10 The Scanner Design for Textmining shows a vertical yellow bar passing from left to right over a collection and highlighting the items that match the criteria assigned by the user. Design by Bernie Roessler.

fact, it is probably a better design for a system that performs "search by example," where the goal is to find documents that match a single training set rather than a set that has been trained by grouping examples in to multiple clusters.

Moveable Shutters

In the end, the NORA interface we developed (Figure 2.10) used parts that were somewhat more off-the-shelf, in the form of moveable shutters (panels of tools that could open, close and resize as needed). We applied the shutters to the problem of creating a design that would prompt novice users through a sequential process while allowing more advanced users to go back and revisit any of the steps. One of the difficulties with this design is that the preferences panel is not a main shutter, but instead sits in a sub-palette of the first panel. For NORA that wasn't a big sacrifice, since there were very few options available to the user, but in a more advanced system, where many choices could be possible, the ability to set parameters should probably be more central to the process.

Subsequent to NORA, we worked on the Metadata Offer New Knowledge (MONK) project, which was funded by the Mellon Foundation and led by PIs

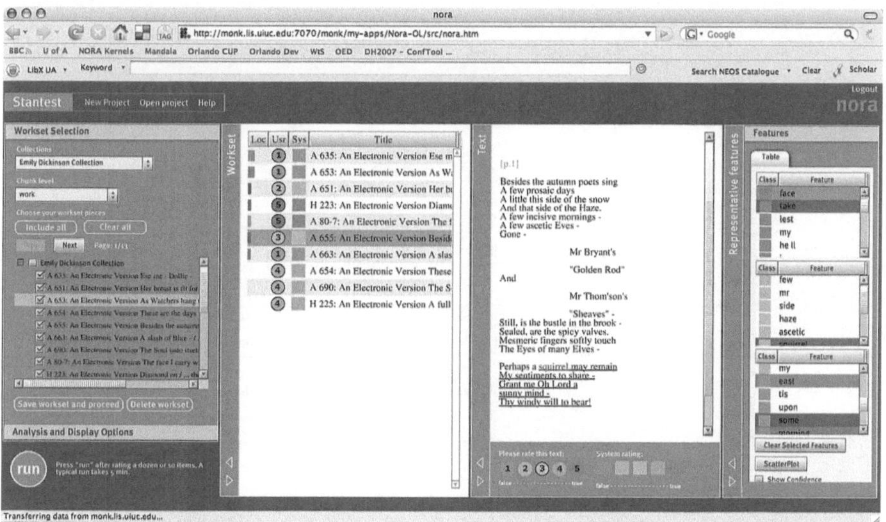

Figure 2.10 The NORA shutters design[11]

John Unsworth at UIUC and Martin Mueller at Northwestern. The goal of MONK was to build on previous work done separately in NORA and Wordhoard (a stand-

11 The NORA shutters design was the one we eventually implemented. It guides the user through the process by opening and closing vertical panes. Design by Piotr Michura and Milena Radzikowska.

alone application built primarily to do analytics on the plays of Shakespeare), by combining into one system collection level-analytics and lexical-level details about words and lemmas in context. The resulting design was the MONK workbench (Figure 2.11), where a variety of tools are available and the user has the opportunity to work either with a pre-defined toolset (a sequence of steps where each step is composed of one or more composition of interacting tools) or else create a custom toolset that can also be saved for later re-use. Common tools include workset selection, where the user chooses a subset of all available documents to work on, workset rating, where training data is created by the user and associated with a workset (training data help refine the datamining operations that will be performed by the system on new, unclassified documents), a document reader, where the user can see the text of a given work, and a results display, which can take various forms. There are also tools specifically designed for searching and sorting documents.

We attempted in MONK several innovations that promised to make the management of this project, distributed as it was across seven universities in two

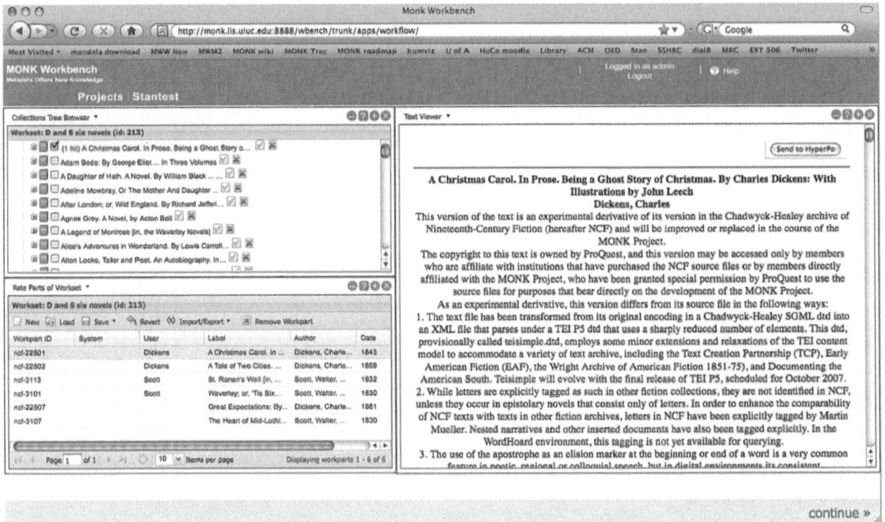

Figure 2.11 The MONK interface[12]

countries, as successful as possible. For one thing, we agreed that access to the data and analytics be mediated through a proxy layer or API, which would allow the interface group the opportunity to produce the workbench and its tools with

12 The MONK interface is based on the concept of a workbench with a set of tools that can be configured into toolsets. The system comes with some predefined toolsets, but the user is also able to define new custom toolsets. Design by Milena Radzikowska.

some degree of isolation from the developments of the other groups (a strategy that emerged at the end of the NORA project where front-end and back-end development were more closely coupled and vulnerable to delays). In practice, this turned out to be both difficult to accomplish and invaluable. It was difficult because it meant that every analytical routine had to have what was essentially a second means of calling it, and although it could in principle happen that we could receive analytical calls in the proxy layer that were not yet really available, in practice there was some reluctance to produce these speculative routines and use them. It was invaluable because it did effectively isolate the workbench development from the details of the data and analytics that were proceeding in parallel.

Although we have had the opportunity to create a number of designs for textmining systems for literary scholars, we are still at an early stage in the analysis of these designs in the context of actual use. Of the various alternatives we have discussed, only two prototypes have been built: one had a limited dataset available, while the other is ongoing. Clearly the next steps in this process should involve user studies of the designs as well as the prototypes, involving literary scholars making use of the tools in the context of literary research. Plans are currently underway to carry out these studies.

Reassurance

If the prospect display is attached to the results of a search process, it has the possibility of providing the user with a means of understanding the search results within their context. For instance, a dictionary search might result in the display not only of the word found (or not found), but also of the dozen or more words that occur alphabetically before and after the target word. This strategy can help to reduce the consequences of some minor spelling difficulties by providing the user with a picklist of alternative words that begin with a similar character string. It can also suggest related words that might vary slightly from the target, provided that the spelling begins with a similar string, as it frequently does in English. Other strategies for producing potential matches include finding variations of characters anywhere in a string (the Levenshtein distance is a common algorithm for this) or a calculation of phonetically similar strings.

Reduced Helplessness

When everything else fails, a user working with a retrieval interface can face the troubling situation of facing an empty box or a null search result. With a rich-prospect browsing interface, the worst case is that the user is faced with the entire contents of the collection. When we ran one of our first studies, looking at pill identification for seniors interested in online health information, we had one participant who did not notice any of the tools for manipulating the display, but who confidently undertook the task by the simple expedient of moving her finger along the screen, comparing each of the pills in the rich-prospect display with the one she held in her hand.

Affordances

> An important fact about the affordances of the environment is that they are in a sense objective, real, and physical, unlike values and meanings, which are often supposed to be subjective, phenomenal, and mental. But, actually, an affordance is neither an objective property nor a subjective property; or it is both if you like. An affordance cuts across the dichotomy of subjective-objective and helps us to understand its inadequacy. It is equally a fact of the environment and a fact of behavior. It is both physical and psychical, yet neither. An affordance points both ways, to the environment and to the observer. (Gibson 1979, p. 129)

The concept of affordances has undergone some significant developments since it was first developed by Gibson in the first half of the twentieth century. In originally choosing to use the term "affordance," Gibson was relating his ideas to a concept suggested in 1926 by the German phenomenologist Kurt Lewin ("Aufforderungscharakter"). Gibson was also influenced by the ideas of Kurt Koffka, a Gestalt psychologist who had been Gibson's colleague at Smith College during the 1930s, and who used the term "demand-character" to describe the relationship between the perceiver and the environment (Gibson 1979, pp. 138–9). Gibson objected to Lewin and Koffka on the grounds that they described affordances primarily as phenomenological or psychological in nature, while he felt it was important to stress that affordances were relational. Gibson expanded on the idea in his now-classic book *The Ecological Approach to Visual Perception* (1979).

Theories based on perception of an affordance are distinct from other theories of perception in that the affordance represents an acknowledgment of an interface between the perceiver and the environment which consists of the possibilities for action in that environment on the part of the perceiver. In fact, it might be said that the concept of affordances confounds the distinction between perceiver and environment. Affordances involve both an environmental property and some capacity of the perceiver to use that property for an action. Gibson also argued that affordances could be directly perceived, rather than being constructed by the perceiver using smaller individual pieces of visual or other perceptual information.

The concept of affordances is one of the most controversial aspects of Gibson's work. By emphasising the process of direct perception, he was choosing to ignore the possibility that significant levels of mental activity were required by the perceiver. As Ullman (1980) points out, Gibson can be understood as adopting a two-level model of perception, where the highest level directly represents information about the opportunities for action in the environment, and the lowest level consists of the physiological mechanisms that provide the information. These physiological mechanisms do not rely exclusively on mental activity, but are rather a result of the actions of the organism as a whole. There is some evidence to suggest, for instance, that the dynamic movements of the eye during foveal saccades (discreet jumps in the field of perception that are nonetheless perceived as being a smooth continuum by the human mind) are essential to the perception of contrast. The retina also contains specialised receptors which respond only to particular kinds of light. The eye would therefore appear to be not so much a static receptor – a kind of camera connected to the brain – as it is an active part of the processing system for visual information.

Inasmuch as it proposes a human perceptual system composed of a paired mechanical and higher order mental process, Gibson's two-level model is similar to previous psychological models of the Graz and Würzburg schools (Koffka 1935, pp. 559–60). Faced with the question of how sensations become construed as shapes, the Graz school introduced the concept of a higher mental function they called "production," which served as a label for the end result of a process that was not elaborated further. Similarly, the Würzburg school, in looking at how memory develops from associations, suggested a higher mental function called the "determining tendency."

These schools were explicitly criticised by Koffka as being vitalistic – which is to say they implied that something like the soul was required to explain human mental capacities. Gibson's model of direct perception of affordances might be similarly accused of implying vitalism, although the counter-argument can also be made that purposeful perception and subsequent action might be developed as species characteristics through natural selection. In any case, Gibsonian affordances are certainly not specific to humans.

It has also been suggested that the two-level model fails to account for all the facts. Research involving perceptual misperceptions and ambiguities or illusions suggests that there should be an intermediate level of study, dealing with algorithmic processes and possible internal representations that can form the basis for mental transformations of perceived objects (Ullman 1980, pp. 379–81). Although followers of Gibson have tended to ignore this algorithmic arena of research for programmatic reasons, there seems to be no reason to reject research from other groups that might inform this area, such as the neurophysiologists.

Perception of Affordances

In terms of human visual perception, the current mainstream neurophysiological stance is that the system is based on the development and exploitation of information, as opposed to being based on the capture and storage of data. That is to say, the process and mechanism of vision consists not of image transmission, where an accurate image of the outside world has somehow been sent through the machinery to be recorded in the brain as a faithful image of the outside world, but rather of the extraction of optical information from the environment in a form that is useful to the organism (Livingstone 2002, p. 24). This optical information is manipulated at each step in a complex path from the moment that light impinges on the photoreceptors on the retina, on through to the thalamus in the center of the brain, and from there to the primary visual cortex at the back.

After the primary visual cortex, there is some fairly convincing further evidence for the existence of two structurally distinct but related mechanisms in the higher processing areas of the brain (Milner and Goodale 1995). The first stream, which is associated with vision for conceptualisation, follows a ventral path forward from the primary visual cortex to the inferior temporal lobes. The second stream, which, since Milner and Goodale, has become associated with vision for action, follows a dorsal path from the primary visual cortex to the posterior parietal lobes. The evidence for the existence of these two streams and their associated functions comes from studies involving two different types of participants: those who have suffered damage to their brains and those who have not.

In the former class is the woman D.F., who suffered damage to the ventral stream and experienced visual agnosia after a case of carbon monoxide poisoning. She could use everyday objects but had problems identifying them and their characteristics. The opposite condition is called optical ataxia, where patients with damage to the dorsal stream can verbally describe common objects, but have trouble using them (Michaels 2000, p. 243).

In the latter class (experiments on people without brain damage) are results that show: disparities between description and action for visual illusions; effects on perception but not action from visual masks which appear after the original stimulus; effects on action but not perception of visual precues; and effects on action but not perception of target repositioning during saccadic eye movement.

Van der Kamp et al. (2001, p. 168) similarly report that the interceptive timing of hand closure in one-handed catching experiments does not appear to rely on the optical variables that distinguish time to contact (that is, on perceptual information), but rather on a combination of the relevant rates of change (that is, on a more complex form of information appropriate for action).

If this distinction between visual streams for different purposes exists, there are several implications for the study of affordances. Firstly, since different information is available from the two different visual streams, it will be necessary to set up experiments that collect information based both on action, or at least on reports of imagined action, as well as on user reports involving conceptualisation.

Secondly, the kinds of experiments called for may vary according to the stream being studied. Michaels suggests, for example, that one of the differences between the two streams is that dorsal stream (action-related) visual information may be tacit, while ventral stream (conceptualisation-related) visual information may be explicit. She also suggests that there is possibly some distinction between the two streams in terms of their time scale. D.F. experienced increasing difficulty when she had to delay her actions. In Michaels's phrase, "the dorsal stream seems to be very much a use-it-or-lose-it system" (Michaels 2000, p. 252).

Here is Michaels's complete list of ways in which the two streams may vary:

- the information is likely to be different
- the phenomenological experiences may be different
- the principles of learning may be different
- the mechanisms of information detection might be different
- they may operate on different time scales
- they may differ as to the importance of spatial viewpoint
- vision for action may be tacit while vision for perception is explicit

The distinction between the dorsal and ventral streams may not, however, be as clear-cut as Milner and Goodale suggest. Kotchoubey (2000), for instance, points out that neurophysiological evidence has traditionally been found to support whatever the current psychological theories required it to support, since basically everything in the brain can be shown to be connected to everything else one way or another. He also makes the suggestion that, since the studies of D.F. relied on verbal reporting of her conceptualisation activity, it is not possible to distinguish in her case between perception and speech, which confounds the clear distinction between vision for conceptualisation and vision for action by turning the reporting of conceptualisation into a second kind of action.

Some of the supporting experimental evidence has, however, been revisited by subsequent research projects, which in general have confirmed that there seems to be some reproducible difference between vision for reporting and vision for action, but that the details still need to be further investigated. Ellis et al. (1999), for instance, carried out experiments using, respectively, a modified form of the Müller-Lyer illusion and the Ponzo illusion. The Müller-Lyer illusion uses arrowheads pointing either inward or outward at the ends of parallel lines to create an illusion of extended or reduced length. In the Ellis experiments, both arrowheads pointed in the same direction, which can cause perceivers to misjudge the center of mass. The Ponzo illusion similarly causes mistaken impressions of center of mass by laying a rectangle onto a background of converging lines so that the rectangle appears to be wedge-shaped. In both cases, participants significantly misjudged the center of mass, both in the situation where the judgment was indicated by verbally directing someone else to place a mark and in the situation where the judgment was indicated by picking up the bar. However, the latter judgment – the one indicated by the action of the participant – was found to be significantly closer to the reality of the situation than the former.

One interesting avenue of future research might involve attempts to identify and study situations in which the ventral stream perception is more accurate than the dorsal stream perception. If the ventral stream is, under certain conditions, superior, then there should be cases where action is significantly influenced by an illusion that is less effective on perception. That is, participants should not necessarily verbally identify an illusion that nonetheless interferes with their actions.

The theory of affordances may therefore have flaws or inherent limitations, but it has nonetheless played a significant role in a wide range of fruitful research and debate. Researchers have looked at a variety of the issues relating to affordances, including the following areas, which will be elaborated below:

- ontology
- intention
- learning
- nesting
- sequencing
- using
- static, kinematic, and dynamic
- modality
- properties of the environment
- reflexivity
- relationship to Gestalt
- social affordances
- constraints and natural mappings
- pleasure

Affordances: Ontology of Affordances and Effectivities

According to Gibson, an affordance is a perceptual primitive. Although it is possible to subdivide an affordance into details of perception related to the optics of surfaces, to undertake that subdivision is misleading because the perceiver does not construct an awareness out of smaller visual components, but rather experiences it as a complete whole.

It is well established that the human visual system perceives surfaces. This aspect had been widely studied by perceptual psychologists prior to Gibson. Gibson proposed extending the significance of surfaces by equating them with direct awareness of what actions their perception suggests, or in his terms, what they afford the perceiver (Gibson 1979, p. 127).

Prior to Gibson's ecological theory, the field of psychology could largely be understood as divided into two camps, which had their roots in Descartes and the duality of mind and body. In their psychological guise, these themes were expressed as behaviorism and mentalism, depending on the research emphasis placed, on the one hand, on physical responses and activities, and, on the other hand, on mental constructs and processes. Yet Gibson emphasised that affordances are not based on a subject-object duality, but are to be understood as forming a middle ground between the organism and its environment. It seems clear that he was attempting to establish an alternative basis for research that ascribed to neither of the two existing camps.

Despite this orientation, one modification of Gibson's ideas that has been suggested relates to an expansion of the mechanisms involved in the role of the perceiver. The implication is that the original formulations were not completely spelled out in all their details (Turvey and Shaw 1979), and that, in fact, the meaning of the word "affordances" needed to be shifted slightly, so that an affordance is not the interface between perceiver and environment, but rather exists as a property of an object or of the environment, independent of the perceiver. New factors are therefore introduced to account for the role of the perceiver. These new factors are effectivities (or sometimes abilities) and intentions, which represent, respectively, the capacity of the organism to perceive and make use of the affordance available, and the motivation or goal of the organism that may bring it to the point of taking advantage of a perceived affordance.

> The term *effectivity* is offered to complement the term *affordance*, and it is defined subject to revision as follows: The effectivity of any living thing is a specific combination of the functions of its tissues and organs taken with reference to an environment. (Turvey and Shaw 1979, pp. 9–10)

Factoring an affordance into the aspects that pertain to the object and the aspects that pertain to the perceiver seems like a promising approach to take in attempting to operationalise the concept of affordance for the purposes of research. One problem, however, with Turvey and Shaw's approach is that it would still be useful to retain some term for the designation of the relational aspect. It might be useful to adopt a second set of terms to deal with the environmental properties, which could be substituted for Turvey and Shaw's "affordance," leaving that term as the over-arching specification of the larger interrelation. It seems likely that at least two terms would be required. The first term would deal with the actual value of the object as it offers a particular potential function. A hammer, for instance, offers a very good potential for pounding. A screwdriver, on the other hand, has only a limited use in this area, primarily through inversion from its normal position in the hand and repurposing of the handle as a form of hammer. The potential of the hammer for pounding would therefore be said to exceed the potential of the screwdriver for pounding.

The second term would deal with the situated potential of the object and its property. It is not very useful to say that a hammer offers better opportunities for pounding than a screwdriver does, if all that is available at the moment is the screwdriver.

There is a sense, however, in which the act of factoring the affordance, on the one hand, and the effectivity, on the other, simply reintroduces the subject-object duality that Gibson was seeking to reject in the first place (Sanders 1997, p. 104). Gibson's point was that a rationalism that depends on the existence of subject and that object misconstrues the nature of visual perception by not accounting for the central role of the perceiver as an active participant in the environment. In place of this duality, he therefore placed a form of visual perception which provides the perceiver with information related to successfully continued existence in the environment, rather than with alternative conceptions of visual perception (such as the one that suggests that the function of visual perception is to provide faithful images that internally reproduce the external world).

Given that the visual spectrum comprises such a tiny segment of the electromagnetic spectrum, and that the human mechanisms for perception of even that tiny segment have their intrinsic limitations, it would be difficult to make the case that human visual perception provides anything but a small sample of the available environmental information. Whether it is better to understand this sample as being primarily representative of some external reality, or simply as one of the perceptual components that form the basis for human action, is the question that Gibson addressed with the concept of affordances.

Affordances: Intention

Another potential factor in the perception of affordances relates to the current intentions of the perceiver. When people look at objects with the intent to accomplish some predetermined tasks with them, they are obviously more likely than otherwise to perceive whether or not the task can be undertaken using affordances of the object. A different scenario is where someone is looking for one affordance but spots another. For example, it is one thing to look for a coffee cup when the goal is to have a cup of coffee. It is somewhat different to see a coffee cup during the course of the day when coffee isn't at issue, and different again when the goal is to get ready for bed. In the first case, the intention to get coffee makes the multiple situated potentials of the coffee cup consciously significant to the perceiver. The cup affords containing hot liquid, grasping, lifting with either one hand or two, and drinking. In the second case, the irrelevance of these affordances to the task at hand means that they are given only cursory, if any, attention. In the third case, the alternative goal may serve as a barrier to even considering the coffee cup.

In the design of human–computer interfaces, one of the very difficult challenges lies in attempting to distinguish between the three kinds of situations described above (clear application corresponding with intent, irrelevance to intent, contradiction of intent). One of the reasons for the tendency to design for functions instead of affordances is that the specificity of a function can help to reduce instances where the user is looking for one function but is confused, irritated, or even obstructed by other functions. One of the risks, however, is that a function can be an action that is too narrowly defined and is less useful than a system with a multivalence of functionality.

The argument can also be made that addressing this challenge is one of the principal reasons for the variety of approaches to user study. Determining the likelihood of various user intentions – actual intentions, in a situated environment, as opposed to speculations of theoretically likely intentions – seems to necessitate examining the interactions between users and prototypes from as many perspectives and in as many contexts as possible. Since there are limits to what is possible, different research groups have tended to privilege one set of methods over another, depending on the extent to which the approach seems to yield useful results.

Complicating the issue of intentionality is the fact that Gibson made clear that one of the distinctions between his theory of affordances and previous ideas by Gestaltists such as Koffka was that affordances were to be understood as invariants that did not rely on user intention:

> The affordance of something does not change as the need of the observer changes. The observer may or may not perceive or attend to the affordance, according to his needs, but the affordance, being invariant, is always there to be perceived. An affordance is not bestowed upon an object by a need of an observer and his act of perceiving it. The object offers what it does because it is what it is. (Gibson 1979, pp. 138–9)

Gibson's stance on this issue of user need suggests, among other things, that attraction (the appeal of an object for a given task) should not be equated with perception. It also might be understood to suggest that there is an objective quality to the affordance – that it is a quality of the environment, rather than a fact about the interface between the perceiver and the environment. The case can be made, however, that Gibson's purpose was not to reopen the question of subject-object duality, but rather to prevent the extreme of "mentalism," in which the emphasis in the relation shifts entirely to the side of the perceiver. The term he uses for the object's role in the interaction is the active verb "offer," which implies that there is a perceiver receiving the offer. Since English syntax is predicated on an inherent dualism of subject-object distinctions, confusions of this kind are inevitable when discussions of relations are the focus.

The question still remains whether or not, in perceiving the cup at all, people also immediately and commensurately perceive all of its potential affordances (Hecht 2000, p. 59). One test case in this situation is the infant. As Sanders (1997) points out, a baby in proximity to an electron microscope will perceive a wide range of affordances. There will be knobs for turning and shiny surfaces that reflect, there will be some removable parts that may or may not afford swallowing, and, depending on the strength of the infant and leverage conditions of the microscope, there is always the possibility that the device will afford tipping over. The infant will not, however, be consciously aware of the primary affordance of the electron microscope, which is to visually magnify down to a molecular scale, nor of the related affordances, such as the possibility of winning a Nobel prize (Sanders 1997, pp. 107–8).

The infant's limitations, on the other hand, are not necessarily a deciding factor in the question of whether perception of affordances is holistic or not, because those limitations mean that the device does not afford those actions for that child at that time. It does seem clear that perception of affordances cannot be said to be holistic in the sense that a perceiver is immediately aware of all possible affordances for all possible perceivers, although certainly it is the case that some affordances can be perceived on behalf of other organisms on some occasions. A dog owner, for example, can perceive the affordance of a dog dish for holding dog food for the consumption of the dog, even though the owner has no personal intention of eating the dog food out of the dish.

There is also some evidence to suggest that intention does influence perception. For example, Hommel (1993) reports two experiments designed to investigate the Simon effect (where stimulus-response times are influenced by spatial information that is irrelevant to the task). In a typical experiment on the Simon effect, participants might be asked to respond to a binary stimulus, consisting of a high or low auditory tone, by pushing an appropriate left or right key on a panel in front of them. If each key is associated with a light that comes on when the key is pushed, then there are a total of three spatial objects in the experiment: the source of the tone; the keys; and the lights. By varying the placement of these objects, it is possible to show that response times are faster when the objects are physically associated, even when physical placement is irrelevant to the task.

In light of these and other related results, Hommel was interested in finding out whether the mental model of the perceiver concerning the task could influence the Simon effect. He found that the effect could be inverted by explaining to different groups of participants that their task was either to press a key in response to the stimulus, or else to turn on a light as the response. Depending on the nature of the instruction, the location of either the key or the light became the relevant factor, even though the actual action was identical to an external observer.

The implication of these studies for research design for user interface performance seems straightforward. In order to understand the details of user interactions, it is necessary to establish that the mental models held at the time of the experiments concerning the task are also well-understood and documented as part of the study. It also seems probable that pre-existing mental models based on relevant domain expertise will be a significant factor, whether that expertise relates to content, procedures, or previous experience with interfaces used for research in the given field. It is therefore likely that results will vary based on whether the participants in the study are currently active in the domain for which the interface has been developed.

Affordances: Learning

Gibson acknowledged explicitly that people have to learn to recognise and use affordances, beginning, as E. Gibson points out, with an exploratory toolbox that is limited to a few basic functions, such as sucking and looking (E. Gibson 2000, p. 55). How people proceed from there has been the subject of educational theorists for centuries. Within that larger terrain, however, there have been some research projects looking specifically at the learning of affordances. In their study of expert, novice, and inexpert wall climbers, for example, Boschker et al. (2002) identified a number of the factors that differentiate those groups. Expert climbers were able to recall more information that was specifically relevant to the task by clustering it according to the climbing affordances of the wall, whereas inexpert climbers focused on less-significant features and spoke in structural terms rather than in terms of climbing opportunities. Climbing walls use two kinds of holds: footholds, which are too small and smooth to afford grasping, and hand holds which are larger and more contoured for grasping, and can also afford standing. In reconstructing a climbing wall with an easy lower section, critically important middle section, and difficult top section, experts focused on learning first the position and orientation of the hand holds (which are more crucial to success). They also concentrated first on the middle section and difficult upper section, which were the sections that presented the greatest climbing challenges. Inexperts, on the other hand, did not differentiate among the sections of the wall, and treated all holds as equally important. Finally, expert climbers tended to perform climbing gestures or movements during their explanations of the climbing choreography, while inexperts did not use their bodies during their explanations (Boschker et al. 2002, p. 34).

Body theorists insist that learning as a field of activity is not confined to cognitive processes, but that the body itself is something that is learned within the context of a particular culture and environment. In a seminal article in that field, Mauss (1935) compiles an impressive list of body techniques that vary by culture, including walking, running, dancing, marching, swimming, jumping, climbing, descending, holding, throwing, washing, spitting, eating, drinking, massaging, and reproducing. His own education in France in the late Victorian period included learning to swallow water and spit it out again while swimming: "In my day swimmers thought of themselves as a kind of steam-boat" (Mauss 1935, p. 71). It seems likely that a swimming technique of this kind, as opposed to a technique where the water is not swallowed, would tend to limit the detection of affordances for swimming to bodies of water that were clear enough to be safely ingested. He also tells the story of British troops in the First World War who were working in alternating shifts with French troops in digging trenches. The army was obliged to provide different spades to each group, because the English could not (or perhaps would not) dig with French spades and vice versa. The learned techniques of the body can therefore have profound effects on both the perception of affordances and choice of whether or not to use them. A corollary of this observation is that it is possible to introduce new affordances to people, but that the process may require training. Without appropriate learning at some level, it is not reasonable to expect people to be able to climb the wall, use a new kind of spade, or otherwise behave in an expert manner with respect to a given affordance.

On his list of the learned techniques of the body, Mauss also lists education in vision, which is not one of the topics he elaborates. Some degree of visual perception is inherent from birth, but the differentiation of the visual field is part of the natural development of the child. The relationship between development and education, however, is a subject of debate among educators. As Vygotsky (1978, p. 80) points out, various theorists interested in education have adopted each of the possible positions, including the idea that development necessarily precedes learning (Piaget and Binet), that the two are actual synonymous (William James), and that they interdigitate, with one feeding the other, then the reverse

(Koffka). Whatever the case may be (and perhaps it depends on a given set of circumstances), the learning or development of visual perception should be classed among the learned techniques of the body which are implicated in the perception of affordances.

Mauss also includes education in composure, or the deliberate suspension of activity. The relationship between inactivity and affordances has received some attention by ecological psychologists, who appear uncertain what status should be given to inaction as a form of action. Since the behavior of someone who is choosing not to act on an available affordance may be indistinguishable from the behavior of someone who is unaware of the affordance, or of someone who is aware but lacks the ability to use it, the problem is a complex one to analyse (for that matter, the reverse is true as well: the correspondance between behaviors and affordances may be a matter of chance, not always of awareness). Proponents of certain forms of inaction, however, would stress that the force of intention and volition are significant, and that the resulting effects on the environment are also important. An example might be an ecological awareness resulting in unwillingness to purchase or consume products with a negative environmental impact. Another more concrete example would be Mahatma Gandhi's principle of satyagraha or nonviolent resistance and how it contributed to dramatic cultural changes in India and Britain in the twentieth century. Finally, inaction in a context of strong environmental support for action is a clear indication of volition, as in the cases of people acting collectively to protect worker interests by holding a strike.

Affordances: Nesting

Although Gibson suggests that affordances should be treated as perceptual primitives, it is possible to distinguish among different kinds of affordance, based on the manner in which they interact with other affordances. One such interaction is the nesting of affordances, where several different affordances are intrinsically related to each other by being grouped together spatially. Within this larger category of nested affordances, there are sub-categories, including: invisible nesting; metonymic nesting; and nesting across different planes of experience.

The first kind of nesting involves a combination of visible and invisible affordances, where some of the affordances in a nested group are initially invisible but become apparent upon investigation. An example of this kind of nested affordances is a doorknob. It is not always possible to determine by visual examination whether a particular doorknob is locked or unlocked, or whether it should be turned clockwise, counterclockwise, or if either direction will work the same. But for people with the appropriate physiology and experience, the doorknob does afford grasping – that much information is available to visual examination – and the hand that grasps it can be used to determine whether it also affords turning and, if so, in which directions.

A second kind of nested affordance is one where the presence of the entire collection can be signaled by the visual presence of an object or object property that stands in a metonymic relation to the whole. An example of this kind of object is a printed book. Whereas a doorknob might be locked or unlocked, and those two conditions represent a state that is one of the affordances of the doorknob, there is usually no corresponding mystery about a book. If a person is literate in the language and has the appropriate visual acuity and lighting conditions, then a book affords grasping, opening, and reading. In most cases, the cues for language are available in a printed form on the cover or spine, so it is not necessary for the perceiver to open the book in order to decide whether or not it is printed in a language he or she reads. The language used for printing the spine or cover of the book is therefore an example where an object property, as opposed to the entire object, serves in this iconic or metonymic fashion.

A related but distinct kind of nesting occurs in cases where several affordances occur simultaneously at different cognitive or experiential planes. For example, a cat may afford petting by its owner; the petting affords pleasure for the cat; the petting affords pleasure for the owner; the petting and the cat's pleasure afford a sense of companionship for the cat owner (and arguably for the cat, too). The pet-ability of the cat is a mechanical affordance. The pleasure of the two creatures involved is an affective affordance. The companionship is a social affordance. It is possible to have any of these affordances without the others. The cat may still afford companionship even if it is not currently in the mood for being petted. The cat may also afford petting but fail to experience pleasure, and so on. The cat is also unlike the book in that its willingness to afford petting in the first place is volitional – the book cannot actively resist reading, by, for instance, jumping up on top of the refrigerator.

Given that affordances can be nested in these various ways, it is not necessary to perceive all the details of an affordance in order to be able to identify and begin using it. In the case of invisible affordances, such as the locked or unlocked doorknob, it is only necessary to perceive that the doorknob affords grasping and either to know or guess that it may afford turning. In the case of the book, it is not necessary to know ahead of time the various mental states that reading the book will afford – it is sufficient to realise that it affords reading. With respect to petting the cat, the person does not have to anticipate that the petting may result in a sense of companionship – it is enough for either the owner or the cat to initiate the negotiation and see where it leads.

Affordances: Sequencing

The complex nesting of affordances involved in petting the cat introduces a related concept that deals not so much with the nesting of one affordance inside another as with either the changing nature of a given affordance or else the sequential relationship of different affordances across time. To continue the example of the doorknob, the turning of the doorknob may introduce another affordance, namely the affordance that the door has for opening. The movement of the door will reach a point where the doorway it has previously blocked is now cleared, and the doorway will begin to afford entrance. This sequential unfolding of affordances allows the perceiver to interact in a continuous manner with the environment (Bingham 2000, p. 31).

There are similar examples in the natural world directly related to the affordances of prospect. The perceiver of a landscape from a perspective of prominence does not necessarily see the details of the landscape, but the details are not essential to the value of the prospect. It is sufficient to be able to identify areas of potential shelter, danger, food, water, and so on. Upon entering the environment, the prior experience of prospect may contribute to wayfinding, helping to guide the perceiver into the desired situations, as for example in approaching a stream in order to get a drink of water. Although the general path might have been observable from a position of prospect, the details of approach to the stream will not necessarily have formed part of the information available, and may have to be worked out once the perceiver has sufficiently advanced toward the water. As in the case of nested affordances, sequential affordances therefore do not require complete perception, but are amenable to exploration once any component affordance has been recognised.

Affordances: Using

Once a perceiver begins to make use of an affordance, the situation can quickly become complex, and we shift from the study of affordances, or perceivable opportunities for action, into the study of activities, events, or behaviors. The complexity arises to a certain extent because it is in the nature of affordances that, for the most part, they allow for multiple behaviors. Bingham points out, for example, that a floor which affords support for locomotion for a human adult does not necessarily predetermine the form of locomotion that a given perceiver will adopt. A person may crawl, skip, walk, or dance, and may do any of these actions efficiently or inefficiently, gracefully or gracelessly, and at different possible speeds (Bingham 2000, p. 31).

The distinction between affordance and behavior is therefore significant in several ways. First, it is the case that the behavior is ontologically dependent on the affordance: every behavior is predicated on the existence of an affordance that makes it possible. Second, learning to identify affordances is one form of knowledge, but learning how to perform behaviors is another; a person can perceive that a wall has an affordance for climbing, but initially be unable to climb the wall. After training, the affordance remains the same, but the behavior changes.

Behavior is also distinct from ability (or Turvey and Shaw's effectivity), which is the potential for action on the part of the perceiver. When we set out to factor affordances as an approach to operationalising them for the purposes of research, we identified that ability or effectivities are one of the perceiver-side factors. Effectivities differ from behavior in that behavior is action, whereas effectivity is potential.

Another factor in behavior is, therefore, that even though it may be based on a general effectivity and intention that are characteristic of the agent, the actual behavior is not necessarily predictable or consistent. A professional ice skater can slip in the middle of an international competition; a person who has learned to strike a falling ball can have inconsistent results in actually accomplishing the movement and striking the ball. The ball nonetheless affords striking and the person has the necessary effectivity and intention; only the behavior is unsuccessful.

Affordances: Static, Kinematic, and Dynamic

Human beings can perceive affordances that derive from complex information about objects or the environment. For example, the human visual system is capable of detecting affordances of objects that are either in uniform motion or under accelerated motion.

Static affordances are those which do not involve objects in motion, although the case has been made that, notwithstanding the perceived immobility of an object, no perception is truly static from the perspective of the perceiver, because the nature of the human eye dictates that vision involves frequent foveal saccades, making movement an intrinsic part of perception over time (for example, Livingstone 2002). There is also a tendency for people to move during information-seeking behaviors. Given these caveats, however, there is still a valid taxonomic distinction based on the role played by the motion of the object. For example, to perceive that a ball sitting motionless on the floor is of a size that affords one-handed grasping is to perceive a static affordance of the ball.

The next level of complexity is in the case of objects in uniform motion (that is, not subject to accelerations indicated by changes of motion or velocity). To perceive that a ball rolled along the floor by another person affords trapping between the knees – ignoring the somewhat more complex effects of gravity and friction, which are actually accelerations rather than kinematic effects – is to perceive a kinematic affordance of the ball. Another way of describing this second kind of affordance is to say that it is the first derivative of the position of the ball as it changes over time.

Finally, human beings can perceive affordances that are derived from objects under acceleration. To perceive that a flyball falling from the sky affords catching in a baseball glove is to perceive a dynamic affordance of the ball, since the position is not constant, as in the static affordance of grasping, nor is the position changing at a uniform rate, as in the kinematic affordance of the rolling ball. Instead, the ball is subject to acceleration due to gravity. Another way of describing this kind of affordance is to say that it is the second derivative of the position of the ball (as it changes over the square of time, or accelerates). People are able to perceive all of these different kinds of affordances, and more. With respect to the design or implementation of new affordances in computer–human interfaces, it is therefore counterproductive in most cases to restrict the discussion to static features.

Affordances: Modality

Although much of the research on perception of affordances deals with visual perception, Gibson and others have not altogether neglected the role of the other perceptual systems. Perception of affordances can therefore be understood to occur across various sensory modes.

For example, a person in the autumn who is deciding whether or not to wear a winter coat might begin by looking out the window to see what the weather is like, then extend the process of information exploration by putting a hand against a window, and complete the process by going to the front door, stepping outside to feel the air, and concurrently listening to the wind. In this case, the variety of sensory modes used (vision, haptics in several forms, sound) is helpful in determining whether the weather will permit prolonged exposure of the body without additional protection.

In fact, one of the tenets of ecological psychology is that intermodal information is often fundamental to action. Not only does someone, while carrying out an action, perceive visually, but the action itself will often involve senses such as touch, smell, and sound, as well as bodily awareness (proprioception) and the awareness of the physical surround (exteroception), all of which contribute to the recognition and use of the larger affordance.

Affordances: Properties of the Environment

One of the intriguing characteristics of affordances is that, while they have been primarily defined and discussed by researchers subsequent to Gibson in terms of the relationship between perceivers and object properties, an entire class of affordances exists independent of discrete objects. These affordances exists as properties of the environment, or perhaps, to use Gibson's taxonomy, as properties associated with the medium (air), other substances (water and various solids), or places. As Chemero (2001, p. 114) points out, many affordances of this class are signaled in speech or writing by feature-placing sentences such as "It's hot in here," or "It looks like rain," where the intention of the communication is to identify a feature of the environment that has implications for human activity but is not directly associated with any particular object (Strawson 1959, pp. 202ff, 214ff).

In the domain of landscape perception, or more precisely in the field of prospect on landscapes, the perception of properties of the environment is primary to the experience. There are any number of potential properties that are observable within the composite of prospect affordances, from the condition of the weather to the current state of development of this year's crop. Some of the more common affordances that are provided to the perceiver by properties of the environment relate to wayfinding. Wayfinding has implications for everything from map design to traffic safety to web navigation, and has therefore been widely studied in a variety of contexts. In one project intended to outline the potential implications of analog methods of wayfinding for digital environments, Vinson (1999) drew on Kevin Lynch's classic *The Image of the City* (1960) in identifying five types of features that are typically used by people in the process of navigating in the real world. These navigational features, which may be useful in the design of computer–human interfaces with some form of prospect, are: paths, edges, districts, nodes, and landmarks (some of these terms are recognisable from network and graph theory).

Affordances: Reflexivity

Affordances are not restricted to aspects of interactions between a perceiver and natural objects or properties of the natural environment. Human artifacts also provide affordances for human beings (and other animals), and in this way a mutuality relation is established between the artifacts and the people by virtue of the affordances.

Human artifacts are to be found at a variety of ontological levels. By applying the concept of human factors to the ontology of artifacts, it is possible to formulate a taxonomy that includes the physical, cognitive, interpersonal, and cultural. Each of these levels of artifact has the potential to serve within a reflexive cycle that enables people to define themselves, or provides a context for definition which is continuously available to processes of modification (Pickering 2000, p. 74). These categories are not necessarily mutually exclusive, since affordances can be nested across experiential levels (as in the case of the petted cat).

The simplest form of artifact to understand in this context is the physical. Physical artifacts can range from those that are microscopic (perfumes, for example), to many at the scale appropriate for grasping (for example, hand tools), through to those that create an entirely constructed environment. By building cities, for example, people have significantly modified their surroundings, and living within that new urban landscape has consequences for how people understand themselves and their behaviors, and includes a whole range of new opportunities for action.

Cognitive artifacts are those which have no physical form, but represent the consequences of human activity in the mental sphere. Cognitive artifacts are to a large extent the consequences of learning, and include language, philosophy, intellectual skills, and so on. Language has a reflexive effect on the person who uses the language. Related classes of artifacts are those which are imaginative, metaphoric, or symbolic. An example of a symbolic affordance provided by an artifact would be the affordance of a sense of domestic security provided for a child by that child's favorite blanket.

Interpersonal artifacts that are neither physical nor cognitive include emotional or affective states that develop through involvement with other perceivers. An example of an interpersonal artifact is the spontaneous arising of compassion felt in observing a suffering animal. Compassion is an interpersonal artifact in the sense that it requires an object in order for it to arise in the perceiver; once compassion has been experienced, it can have further consequences for the actions of the person, such as the affordance of compassion to increase the inclination for the person to act in an altruistic manner.[13]

Cultural artifacts are those which are created and maintained at the larger level of society. Examples of cultural artifacts include institutions or collective forms of activity and their mechanisms, such as businesses or governmental bodies, legislation, news, marketing and other broadcast phenomena, and so on. An example of a cultural artifact is the internet community, where the individuals together form a collective that can take on an active role in providing new affordances to the members. An example of such an affordance is the idea of spam-blocking by vote, where email users in a given group agree to pool their opinions about the messages they receive to determine which will be filtered at the server level on behalf of the collective (Spamnet 2010).

Affordances: Relationship to Gestalt

The concept of affordances had its genesis in Gibson's interest in the ideas of the Gestalt psychologists, and the intellectual descendants of the Gestalt school continue to take an interest in Gibson's idea of affordances. One provocative suggestion is that a new Gestalt tendency should be identified to account for the human ability to perceive complex nested or sequenced affordances. The argument is that, in the same way that the human systems of visual perception have a tendency to fill in the missing pieces under a variety of conditions (for example, in visual association of items in proximity, closure of incomplete outlines, association of objects that are in alignment, and implied relations among similar objects – these phenomena are often exploited in visual illusions), so the human perceptual systems that allow for perception of affordances have a tendency to create a Gestalt or holistic impression of those affordances that are related either by proximity or sequence over time (Van Leeuwen and Stins 1994).

For Van Leeuwan and Stins, the mechanism of this holistic perception is related to the compounding of affordances across multiple orders of complexity. Construction tools provide a good example. A pair of pliers affords grasping, which in Van Leeuwan's system is a simple, first-order affordance. The primary purpose of a pair of pliers, however, involves considerably more than its ability to afford grasping. There are several other first-order affordances, such as opening, closing, applying pressure, and gripping. In a particular situation, there may be other affordances that are also first-order, such as reachability from the perceiver's current position, or visibility among the other tools in the toolbox or workshop. The second-order affordance of the pair of pliers, however, is that it affords the tight holding and squeezing of objects that fit within the jaws (usually to turn or

13 The generation and subsequent cultivation of compassion is the distinct basis of the mental exercises employed by Tibetan Mahayana Buddhists; in this context, the affordance would have to be said to be cultural as well as interpersonal.

to compress objects). For a person with the requisite knowledge of the tool, to perceive a pair of pliers is therefore to perceive an entire array of both first-order and second-order affordances.

A relationship between the affordances of prospect and refuge and the Gestalt tendencies has also been outlined by Nelson et al. (2001, p. 323). Having established that participants correlated completeness of the canopy of a tree with both its fecundity and visual attractiveness, Nelson et al. suggest that the Gestalt figural tendencies, and in particular the principle of closure, may be vestigial mechanisms related to perception of a sub-class of affordances related to survival.

Affordances: Social Affordances

Somewhat distinct from the affordances of interpersonal or even cultural artifacts, the internet and other digital technologies like mobile phones are now widely used as means of creating and maintaining various forms of social capital. Researchers such as the designer Bill Gaver (1996) have examined social interaction as a form of affordance, resulting in a wide range of interesting experimental installations, including the history tablecloth, which retains for an indefinite length of time some visible traces of objects placed upon it (Gaver et al. 2006), or the two-storey office desk, which was actively resisted by the office workers where it was placed.

Affordances: Constraints and Natural Mappings

Norman (1990) creates a clear association for designers between the three related concepts of affordances, constraints, and natural mappings. For Norman, the perception and use of an affordance is inevitably linked to the perception of the constraints that surround the affordance, and a good designer will make intelligent use of both. Constraints can be understood as a negative space around an affordance, helping to both define it and to reduce the risk of it being misinterpreted or ineffectively applied. On a somewhat similar trajectory, the sociologist Hutchby (2001, 2003) has proposed the use of affordances, and more particularly the constraints on affordances, as a means of reconciling the sociological position of constructivism with the less nuanced belief in realism.

Affordances: Pleasure

In an unpublished manuscript dating from approximately the same period as the first edition of *The Ecological Approach to Visual Perception*, Gibson briefly discusses the question of how affordances are related to pleasure (Gibson 1979u). He distinguishes three kinds of pleasure related to the viewing of surfaces, depending on whether the surface has an affordance, stands for other things, or invites inspection for its own sake. This taxonomy relates in part to a taxonomy he proposes of modifications to artifacts, whether to modify their affordances, display additional information, or enhance appearance.

The idea that perception of affordances might relate to pleasure or satisfaction seems like a natural outcome of the role of action in human and other life. One of the areas in which the relationship has arguably been further developed is in the work of Appleton's habitat theory, and in particular in the context of his discussion of the affordances of prospect.

We shift now from a general consideration of affordances to an examination of affordances in the context of digital tools and their interfaces, and in particular to the affordance strength model, which we propose as a means of facilitating the study of new affordances.

Chapter 3
Is This Thing Working? The Study of New Affordances

The improvement of the world must be highly contextualized. – Hans Rosling

For computer interface designers attempting to create experimental software prototypes that provide new affordances, a perennial problem exists concerning how best to study an affordance that was not previously available. Comparisons against previous interfaces with different affordances tend toward category error (comparing apples to oranges), and comparisons against interfaces with similar affordances but different designs tend to be studies of design rather than of opportunities for action. We therefore propose a strategy of evaluating not the affordance per se, but rather the strength of the affordance in a given context of use by a particular group of people.[1] Using this approach, researchers can begin to compare the affordance strength of different kinds of software tools, providing essential information to interface designers at different stages in the process. In the early stages, user feedback on affordance strength can allow the researchers to concentrate their efforts on the stronger candidates, and in later stages, this feedback can help them to think in terms of maximising the affordance strength through attention to details that might not otherwise be foregrounded as areas of concern.

Relational Factors of Affordances

Ideally, an operational definition of the strength of affordances should allow only for analysis of various aspects of the relationship, rather than analysis of the perceiver and some quality of the object or feature of the environment being perceived. This analysis of relational factors should be specific enough to capture the various kinds of information that are relevant to both the perception and use

1 It might be worthwhile to note explicitly that this approach is distinct from the Ecological Interface Design (EID) framework developed by Vicente and others at the University of Toronto in the late 1980s. EID is primarily intended to produce interfaces that will support industrial workers in adaptive problem solving. (Vicente 2002, p. 62). On the other hand, we do consider ourselves to be responding to the challenge articulated by Lintern (2000, p. 68) and others to leverage affordance theory into a research program that can give coherence to the practice of interface design.

of the affordance by a given perceiver at a given time, and yet general enough that it will apply to all the different kinds of affordances, whether static, kinematic, dynamic, physical, cognitive, interpersonal, cultural, or any other.

In order to discuss the strength of affordances appropriately, it is therefore necessary first to establish which are the necessary components that constitute the relation between the perceiver and the perceived object property or environmental feature. It is also necessary to establish to a satisfactory degree that the list of components is sufficient to serve as a pragmatically useful indication of a situated potential for action for a given perceiver, at a given time.

A factor is relational if it does not make sense to discuss it outside the context of a particular affordance. For example, the primary affordance of a pen is that it can be used to write on a piece of paper. Within the context of using a pen for writing, it is reasonable to talk about whether or not it has ink in it, and if so how much ink, and whether or not the pen allows the ink to flow out in a smooth stream onto the paper. It is also reasonable to ask whether the pen affords grasping by a particular person who wishes to write with it. However, if the person is looking for a pen in order to use the side of it as a straight edge in order to draw a straight line, then the amount of ink in the pen and how it flows are irrelevant factors. If the affordance of the pen is that it can serve as a straight edge, then graspability is still a relevant factor, but the new relevant factors become the length of the straight section and the smoothness of the pen shaft.

Given the need to specify the significant relational factors that characterise the strength of an affordance, it is possible to distinguish five factors that together represent the relational aspects of the object, the perceiver, and the dynamics of the context: tacit capacity, availability, tendency, ability, agential support (we will explore each of these in more detail below). These factors together can be used as the basis for user study questions that help the designer to understand the relational aspects of affordance strength in an operational way. An interesting and useful property shared by all these factors is that if any one of them is negated, the entire affordance disappears.

As an extended example of how the affordance strength analysis works, we will take the case of someone who wishes to use an object to facilitate walking in the rain while keeping as dry as possible. In this case, the necessary affordances of the object are the twin capacities of being of the right size and configuration to be carried while walking and, simultaneously, to keep someone dry. The object in question might be anything that is large enough to cover at least the top surface of the head, light enough to be held up there, and impervious to rain. A range of objects are possible, from specialised devices like umbrellas or rain hats, to makeshift ones such as newspapers or briefcases, to the objects of last resort, such as the back of the coat pulled up over the back of the head or a covering made of the two hands. Although it is possible to measure objective features of the various candidate objects, such as their size, weight, slope, imperviousness to water, tendency to sustain water damage, monetary value, and so on, each of these features is only important in this situation because the person wants to stay dry while walking in the rain. For practical purposes, it may therefore be sufficient to aggregate these features into one larger relational factor, a sub-component of the affordance as whole, that represents how well the object can perform the task at hand.

We call this first factor the tacit capacity of the object to provide the affordance in a given situation. In this case, the tacit capacity of the umbrella in situations where a person needs to walk in the rain while staying dry would be very high, while the tacit capacity of, for example, a wrench, would be negligible. The wrench has an excellent tacit capacity for other types of actions. In fact, because it is a specialised tool (like the umbrella), it has a primary affordance. But for the work at hand it is useless.

It is possible but not necessarily helpful to subdivide the tacit capacity into sub-features such as the weight of the umbrella or the slope of the dome or the nature of its fabric, since the perception of the tacit capacity is in a sense given. Every adult in our society knows that umbrellas have this affordance – that it is, in fact, their primary affordance. The direct perception of the affordance is also a central point of Gibson's approach. It would therefore only be helpful to address further sub-features in cases where the tacit capacity is open to contention. An example of this kind of situation might be at the occasion of the original purchase of the umbrella, where factors such as expense vs. utility may need to be considered.

The second necessary relational factor is the availability of the object, which is subdivided into situated potential, awareness, and environmental support. Understanding the availability of the object requires that it be studied within a situated context, not in the hypothetical circumstances of our example, but in one particular situation at one particular time. It is all very well for the person about to walk in the rain to realise that an umbrella has an excellent tacit capacity for keeping a person dry, when at the point of setting out there is no umbrella available, or the umbrella that is available is torn. The same can be said for awareness. For the person about to walk in the rain, a perfectly good umbrella might be sitting ready to hand, but if the person is distracted or confused or in a rush, the umbrella might not be perceived, and for all of its high tacit capacity and situated potential, the umbrella still stays dry while the person gets wet.

The final sub-factor of availability is contextual support, where aspects of the environment that are not directly part of the affordance have an influence one way or the other on the perceiver's interaction with the affordance. There are a wide range of possible contextual supports, including aspects of the situation that are physical, cognitive, and environmental, and the precise nature of the contextual supports in a given situation should be outlined during the process of analysing the affordance as a whole.

In the example of someone who wishes to stay dry in the rain, the contextual factors would include environmental facts such as how hard it is raining, whether it is warm or cold outside, how hard the wind is blowing and in what fashion, and so on. If it were raining hard and was cold enough that the rain was almost turning into sleet, and the wind was blowing hard in a fairly horizontal direction, then this context renders the umbrella's affordances virtually useless. On the other hand, if the sun is shining through the rain and it seems likely to clear within a couple of minutes, the perceiver's motivation to find an umbrella or some other object with appropriate affordances may be dramatically reduced in favor of the strategy of waiting for the rain to stop.

The definition of the context factor as a positive one providing support is important in order to keep the list of affordance strength factors homogeneous. An alternative definition might use the idea that contextual factors should be characterised in terms of their interference with a particular affordance. However, since the other factors are all framed as positive elements in the affordance, it makes sense to approach the context in the same way.

The two factors discussed so far – tacit capacity and availability – are relational attributes where the attention of the researcher is directed toward the object or environment and its relevant affordances for action. There are other factors that treat the relational aspects of the agent, where the researcher's attention is directed at Turvcy and Shaw's effectivities (1979).

The first of the effectivity factors is tendency, which includes the sub-factors motivation, preference, and habit. If the person in question wants to walk in the rain and would prefer not to get wet but does not really mind it all that much, that person's tendency to seek and adopt an available affordance is significantly reduced in comparison with the person who hates getting wet, has just had a cold, and is wearing clothes that will be damaged by the rain. The former person may casually take up an available umbrella if one were available, since the tacit capacity and availability are high enough that the action has an appropriately low resource load. If only a newspaper is available, the lower tacit capacity might be such that the person would prefer to simply get rained on. For the latter person, it is likely that the high motivation and absence of an umbrella would lead to extremes of behavior such as deciding not to walk but take a taxi instead, or perhaps going back into the building to see if an umbrella could be found somewhere.

Like many of the other factors, motivation is a composite of a wide range of sub-factors, including the whole complex terrain of personality traits and their expression under various circumstances; previous experience or behavioral conditioning; and perception of risk and the tendency to either accept or avoid it when perceived. In spite of the complexity of the terrain, however, it is not unreasonable to ask someone with respect to a given scenario: "How motivated would you say you would be to carry out such and such an action, in the course of performing this particular task?"

The next sub-factor related to the perceiver's tendency toward making use of an available affordance is the role played by individual preference. All other factors being equal or even roughly equal, it is often the case that individual adoption of affordances depends at least to some extent on personal preferences. In the case of the person who wants to stay dry in the rain, if there are two umbrellas available and one is a color that the person finds attractive, that will probably be the one that gets employed. Preference can be based on any one of a dozen sub-factors, ranging from aesthetic considerations to interpersonal influence to previous personal experience. Preference is distinct, however, from ability, and although preference is related to motivation, the two are not equivalent. A person might be highly motivated, for example, to perform an action that should probably not be correctly characterised as a preference, as when soldiers fling themselves on live grenades in order to save the lives of their comrades.

Finally, tendency is also related to habit. Given a history of use of a particular affordance, the person establishes and strengthens a likelihood of continued use. For the person who wants to stay dry in the rain, the habit of carrying and using an umbrella whenever it rains is possibly one of the strongest indicators that in a given situation that person will have that umbrella available and will use it. In the context of experimental software design, it is often apparent that habits of users will become a significant factor in how they perceive and adopt new affordances, so it is useful to obtain some information about their habits. Perhaps surprisingly, however, there is evidence that habits in some circumstances are not particularly difficult to overcome (Luis and Dyson 2008), which makes the role of conventions perhaps less significant than is often believed.

The second relational factor that is associated with the perceiver is ability. For a person with a physical disability that makes grasping difficult or lifting the arm problematic, the option of carrying anything above the head may simply not be available. In this case, all the other factors may be present, including an available umbrella with high tacit capacity and a strong tendency to use it. But inability to grasp the handle renders the affordance zero for this particular person at this particular time. Ability is related to a variety of issues discussed earlier, including the socio-cultural aspect of the perceiver being able to recognise and use new affordances through education or training. Another factor in ability is the current condition of the perceiver: a person suffering from extremes of fatigue, hunger, or thirst, for example, is less able than the same person when not afflicted. Talent, natural proclivity, and intelligence of various kinds are also involved.

The other feature that has not been accounted for yet in an explicit form is the role of other agents in the scenario. Agential support includes those features relating to the roles of the other people, animals, insects, and so on who are also potentially part of the situation. Agents are distinct from other factors of the environment in that they have agency, which is to say volition, goals, and actions of their own, which may have some bearing either directly or indirectly on the particular affordance.

For instance, for the person who wishes to stay dry in the rain, it may turn out that there are other people present who also wish to walk outside. One of them might be elderly or frail and lacking an umbrella, in which case our perceiver could be motivated to behave altruistically and turn over the superior affordance of the umbrella to the other perceiver, choosing instead an inferior solution such as a folded newspaper.

To summarise, our affordance strength model has the following components: tacit capacity, availability (including situated potential, awareness and environmental support), tendency (including motivation, preference, and habit), ability, and agential support.

Interaction of the Affordance Strength Factors

Although the factors involved in the affordance strength model are relatively independent of one another, it is possible to identify mechanisms whereby the various factors interact. For example, there is a potential inverse correspondence between tacit capacity and ability, in cases where improvement to the capacity of the object to provide a given affordance increases the complexity or novelty of the object in such a way that the ability of the user is adversely affected.

A classic example is provided by the cockpits of jet aircraft, some of which are sufficiently complex that they have been described as having reached the thresholds of human capacity to monitor all the relevant instruments (Norman 1993). Although the tacit capacity of the cockpit instrumentation to afford information to the pilots is very high, the ability of a non-pilot to receive the information and carry out the appropriate actions is reduced in proportion to that capacity. Only through extensive training and experience have qualified pilots been able to develop a level of ability that corresponds to the tacit capacity of the instrumentation.

Another pair of factors that can influence each other is tendency and agential support. A given person can be either encouraged to act or discouraged from acting by other people. Agential support can also have a paradoxical inverse effect, as in the case when a person acts out of a sense of rebellion against social expectations. Although a particular behavior might have strong agential support in the form of interpersonal or cultural approval, for the person motivated by a spirit of rebellion, the very strength of the agential support can serve to reinforce the negative preference.

The Affordance Strength Model in Interviews

Our primary use of the affordance strength model in user studies to date has involved introducing questions into our interviews or semi-structured interviews that involve the different factors in the model.

1. Tacit capacity:
    - "How well would you say the feature works?"
2. Availability (including situated potential, awareness, and environmental support):
    - "How easy would you say the feature is to access?"
    - "How well is this feature supported by the context in which you would normally be using it?"
3. Tendency (including motivation, preference, and habit):

- "How aware were you of the feature and its use?"
- "If you had a choice of this among other features that provided the same function, how would you rate your personal preference of this feature?"
- "How strongly would you be motivated to use such a feature?"

4. Ability:
   - "How would you rate yourself as a user of this kind of feature?"
5. Agential support:
   - "If you used this prototype in your work, would you know people you could go to in order to get any help you might need?"

The Affordance Strength Model as a Quantitative Tool

In addition to using the model in qualitative questions for user study participants, it is possible to obtain some estimates in numbers. There are several options available for assigning values to the different factors in the affordance strength model, but perhaps the simplest method is to choose a common Likert scale that can be used for all the factors. Each of the items might be rated, for example, on a scale of 0 to 5, where 0 means the affordance factor is such that the entire affordance is rendered null, and 5 means that the affordance factor is as strong as it needs to be for all practical purposes.

Likert scales are a form of ordinal (or ordered) scale, which means they are useful in discerning difference. However, because it is difficult to establish that various respondents agree as to the precise meaning of the anchor values, Likert scales are not usually treated as interval scales. That is, the distance between a zero and a one is not necessarily the same as the distance between a two and three.[2]

The primary advantage of a Likert scale is that it is easy to apply. The primary disadvantage is that it reduces what may be fairly complex qualitative information into a simple number, rather than preserving the complexity. It also requires that the evaluation be carried out in terms of a choice between one whole number and another, rather than as a point on a full continuum.

In short, the simplicity of Likert scales is simultaneously their strength and their weakness. One means of reducing the weakness is to capture additional information that is more qualitative by allowing participants using the scale to provide comments, either as written addenda to each question or else in the form of an interview.

In terms of the design of the Likert scale, there are several decisions that need to be made concerning the relative values of each item. If the same numeric scale

---

2 If the intervals between the individual items were equal to each other, then it would be meaningful to calculate a mean score for all respondents. An example of a scale of this kind would be one developed using the Thurstone method of equal-appearing intervals. The Thurstone method assembles statements from participants on a common topic, then collects ratings that place the statements at equal intervals on a scale.

is used for the different factors, then they each count as equivalent elements in the whole ranking. An alternative strategy would be to weight some of the factors so they contribute either more or less than the others. One means of adjusting the weights only slightly would be to adopt different Likert scales for various factors. Another stronger weighting strategy would be to use the same scale but add a multiplier.

It would also be possible, of course, to establish more complex research criteria related to each of the factors, so that values might be assigned through decomposition of each factor into sub-factors that were subjected to rigorous study, then aggregated to create a total. The introduction of this additional level of complexity should be reserved, however, until such time as the simpler method proves insufficient.

Using the vector space based on a six-point Likert scale, it is possible to have an individual evaluate a particular affordance in a given situation. The assessment will be more convincing, however, if it is performed by a larger number of people who have equivalent characteristics in the relevant aspects of their profiles (samples of, say, a dozen, can provide useful preliminary results, but do not constitute statistically significant numbers). It may also be useful to have ratings both from the actual participants and from observers, who can provide a form of cross-check by guessing from the behavior of participants what their ratings might be.

Vector Anchors

In defining Likert scales for the various factors, one approach is to label each of the numbers on the scale with its own anchor text. This strategy provides the user with a maximum amount of specific information concerning the intended meaning of each value. In some cases, however, it is preferable to label only the extreme ends of the scale. Providing evaluators with only the extreme anchors can result in some minor variation in interpretation of the intermediate values, but has the advantage of making the task less demanding. If they are not required to read the text on each value, study participants are able to react more naturally to the implicit ranking suggested by the numbers. In an ideal situation, the task would be even further simplified by having the same anchors apply throughout the vector space. The normal strategy for this approach is to rephrase each question as a statement, which allows participants to choose among points on a spectrum from "strongly disagree" to "strongly agree." However, because the factors in the affordance strength vector differ from each other quite dramatically, the following discussion provides the finest level of granularity, with anchors spelled out explicitly for each point on the scales for the various factors.

Tacit Capacity

In many cases, tacit capacity may be one of the most difficult of the affordances to evaluate. Where the object in question is a dedicated tool with a single primary function, the situation is relatively straightforward, but even in cases of this kind the individual variation among different evaluators may prove to be significant. Part of the reason for predicting disparity among perceivers is that there is arguably a mainstream cultural bias toward emphasising product feature variation in western capitalism (to help promote sales of version upgrades, for instance). Minor differences among dedicated devices form part of the niche approach to marketing that drives the economy of the western world, and as such they tend to receive a high degree of attention. It may prove difficult, in fact, to separate evaluation of tacit capacity and individual preference. Given these reservations, a Likert scale for tacit capacity might use the following anchors:

0 – useless
1 – very poor
2 – poor
3 – acceptable
4 – good
5 – great

Availability (including situated potential, awareness, and environmental support)

Inter-evaluator perceptions of availability, on the other hand, seem likely to vary less significantly, since there is no comparable cultural mechanism in place to emphasise different values for what is ready to hand. The evaluation of the availability of an affordance primarily consists of its proximity to the perceiver, although there are possible confounding circumstances in special cases, as when a tool can be seen but not grasped because a fence is in the way, or where it is visible but out of immediate reach on a high shelf. The degree of imagination of the perceiver may also be a consideration; what might be called the MacGuyver factor for resourcefulness. A Likert scale for availability might use the following anchors:

0 – not available
1 – available with extreme effort
2 – available with considerable effort
3 – available with some effort
4 – easily available
5 – effortlessly available

Tendency (including motivation, preference, and habit)

A Likert scale for tendency would need to allow for conditions ranging from a degree of inclination that is effectively non-existent through to a strong, immediate desire to accomplish the action in question. The suggested anchors are:

0 – will not act
1 – will act under coercion
2 – grudgingly willing
3 – willing
4 – highly motivated
5 – absolutely determined

Ability

Ability is a complex factor that may involve: prior learning; experience; physical or mental qualities such as dexterity, strength, or determination; age; health; and even confidence, predilection and talent. A Likert scale for ability might use the following anchors:

0 – incapable
1 – beginner
2 – novice
3 – intermediate
4 – advanced
5 – expert

Agential Support

As with contextual support, agential support is composed of any number of possible sub-components relating to the activities of other people or sentient creatures. A Likert scale similar to the one used for contextual support may prove useful, consisting of the following anchors:

0 – aggressive interference
1 – partial interference
2 – minor interference
3 – neutral
4 – partial encouragement
5 – active encouragement

Conclusion

Although it is impossible to compare different affordances per se, it is possible to compare the strength of affordances within a given context of use by an individual carrying out a specified task. By isolating the key factors that help establish the strength of an affordance, both a set of discussion questions and a vector model of affordance strength can be adopted by interface designers who require some means of exploring, not only the opportunities for action that are currently available in an interface, but also the opportunities that could potentially be provided.

User studies

As described in more detail earlier, over the course of our various experiments with rich-prospect browsers, we have developed a process that admits for testing, including addressing affordance strength questions, at three different points. First, we have a conceptual discussion and identify what exactly we are interested in studying. The project designers begin to iteratively develop sketches that reify these concepts (we have found it essential to develop multiple sketches to help explore the possibilities, some ranging from very practical to much more creative, artistic or experimental). At some point, we feel that there has been enough design thinking for us to be able to hold some conversations with potential users. This is the first opportunity for user study. We show them the sketches in one or more of the following formats:

- on paper
- as still images on screen
- as sequenced images on screen, usually in a PDF
- as kinetic or animated sketches, usually in Flash

Based on what we learn from the user observations of the sketches, and from our own ideas about what we think might be interesting, we proceed to the next step, which is to choose the designs that we will expand into working prototypes. Originally, we would follow the conventional wisdom of developing either a vertical or horizontal prototype, where the former doesn't include all functionality but does include a single important feature fully implemented, and the latter doesn't include any single feature fully implemented but does include a nod to at least most things that a full system would require. The problem with these approaches is that they make user study surrounding the concept of the design more difficult, since users will inevitably tend to focus on the parts of the system that would typically be required but haven't been implemented to the point where they can be ignored in the discussion of what is unique.

A search box is a typical example. We are interested in browsing interfaces, and we know that every browsing interface also needs a search box. We also know that it takes time and money to include one, and those resources could be better spent in elaborating the experimental aspect of the interface. However, it is difficult to get users to ignore the absence of a search box if one hasn't been included, but quite easy to get them to ignore its presence. So in the interest of having more effective discussions with users, we will sacrifice some development resources to include standard interface features that we aren't interested in, but which can then be checked off in the user's mental checklist of what they will need.

It is also possible, once we have a working prototype, to try it out with people. However, since we are typically working with experimental designs, rather than variations on functions that already exist, it is often most useful to embed any performance measures within a larger discussion with the users about their experience in trying out the interface, in which the affordance strength questions can play a significant role.

Finally, there is a third step in the process, where in some cases we have been able to create a production system (or advanced prototype) rather than simply an initial prototype. With these systems, it is possible to carry out user studies like the ones that can be done with earlier prototypes, but it is also possible to log the activities of actual users working in their normal patterns with the system, and to question them about behavior over a longer period of time than is typical with prototypes. It also requires less cognitive work for the participants to ignore unfinished or unimplemented features.

Results

The first question that we believed needed to be addressed in thinking about rich-prospect interfaces is whether or not they would simply represent a case of information overload. That is, if people are used to running their query first and seeing results afterward, would seeing an entire collection filling their screens feel overwhelming, independent of whatever else we were able to do?

We approached this question in a couple of ways, first by developing the pill identification system (Figure 3.1), which included a thousand photos of pills and some basic information about each of them (Given et al. 2007).

Taking our lead in this instance from the research methods of David Sless and his team at the Communication Research Institute (Sless and Wiseman 1997), we invited a group of users who had an interest in accessing this kind of information but were most likely also at risk to fail in using the interface. Sless argues that design studies with these kinds of users are a very good way of identifying the major design problems. In this case, we put posters up in public libraries, apartment buildings for seniors only, and community centers, in order to recruit a dozen people aged 65 and older to come in and try to find three pills using the existing online retrieval system at drugs.com and three pills using our experimental visual showcase browser. We found that they had difficulties with both systems, but we had expected they would. What we were also able to observe is that they didn't appear to be overwhelmed by the thousand photos of pills in our prototype.

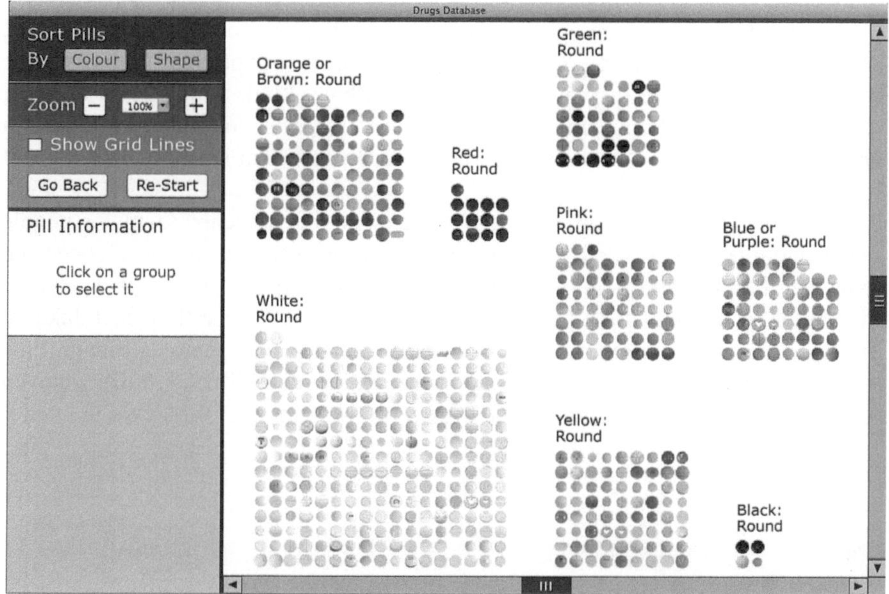

Figure 3.1 The Pill Identification System[3]

On the contrary, what seemed to be a common response is what we refer to as "cognitive reassurance," where they were pleased to be able to see everything available, so that they wouldn't have doubts about the contents of the collection, and in particular, whether or not they had missed anything in their search (which was a common difficulty with the retrieval system). We had predicted that people wouldn't feel overwhelmed because they would have control of the system through the tools that could be used to group the images. However, in this group, there were people who never spotted the tools, and who nonetheless undertook the pill identification task using the full display of all 1,000 items – without grouping them, and without magnifying the images to make them easier to see.

This was a surprising result. It implied that we should modify the browser to increase the sense of cognitive reassurance, which we did in subsequent prototypes in the showcase family by always keeping all the images on the screen. Whereas in the pill identification system the user could focus on a group of pills by clicking on the group (with the other groups disappearing from view), in later showcase browsers, we still included an affordance for the user to focus on a group of images, but the other groups were minimised into an "unselected" strip across the bottom of the screen. That is, images were resized, but no image ever left the screen.

3 The Pill Identification System allows people to carry out a visual search for pills. Metadata and pill images courtesy of www.drugs.com. Design by Andrea Ruskin.

In summary, even those people at risk of failing to use a technology didn't seem to be overwhelmed by photos of a thousand pills. But perhaps they would be overwhelmed by other displays that showed different kinds of images. However, we haven't observed this "information overload" response to any major degree in any subsequent studies, so we are becoming fairly confident in saying that it is not really a factor.

We have, however, come across one design that appears to make people uncomfortable or even overwhelmed – random placement of the images. It occurred to us that the pill identification browser set the items on a Cartesian grid. That is, the photos of the pills are all roughly the same size, or at least they each take up the same amount of room on the screen, and we've placed them as though they were in a spreadsheet. In fact, against the strong advice of Tufte (1990), we even included a checkbox to allow people to turn on the gridlines. When we pointed it

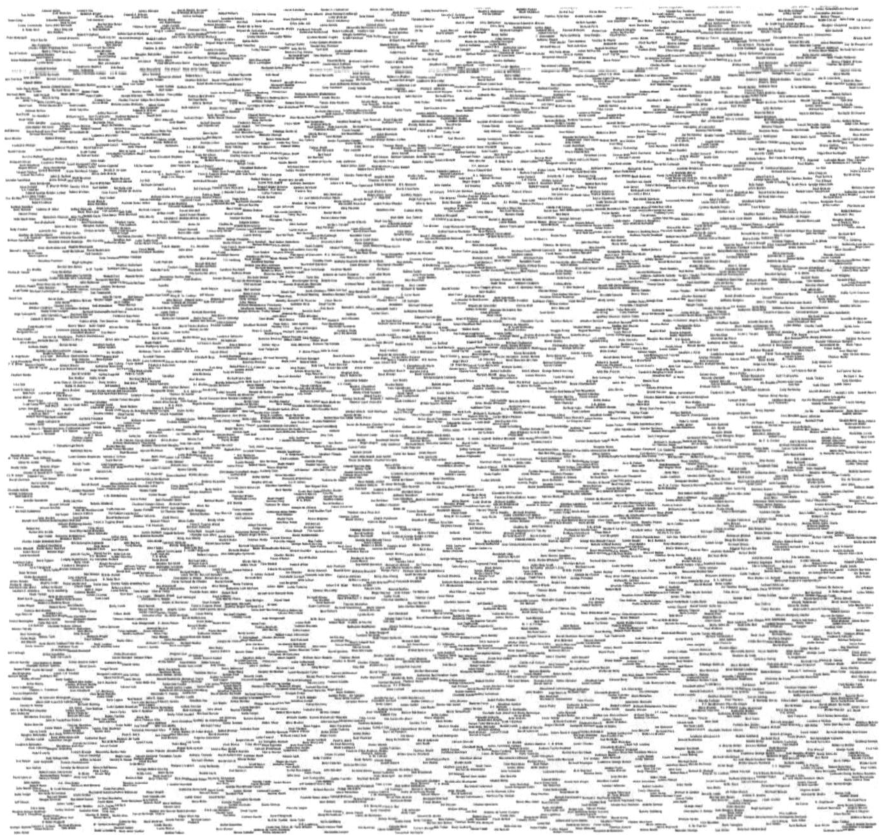

Figure 3.2 Randomly placed text

out to people, they didn't seem to feel one way or another about it, and they left it turned off.

However, placement on a grid implies some kind of order to the images. In fact, they weren't in any particular order, but they seemed to be, in part because they were located in an orderly manner and in part because the colors seemed to occur more or less in rows. We were worried that this was misleading, and perhaps worse, suggested that we wanted people to start with some default organisation of the system, when in fact we wanted it to start with a random placement of images that the people using the system could subsequently choose to organise in ways that were supported by our metadata and yet made sense to them.

So we created some designs for the pill identification system, and for a subsequent system for text mining for literary scholars (No One Remembers Acronyms, or NORA), where the images were placed randomly on the screen (Figure 3.2).[4] In the case of the pill identification system, the idea was to have the pills resemble a scattering of pills in a tray, and in NORA, where we were using the names of authors, the words were just not on a grid.

People did not seem to respond well to these random initial displays. We aren't sure why. Perhaps it is a matter of unfamiliarity – people aren't used to seeing randomness, especially random placement of words. Perhaps the random placement emphasises the number of images, whereas an organised placement helps to reassure people that even though there are a lot of items on display, they are under control. We ran into a similar issue when we were testing the Texttiles browser (Giacometti et al. 2008) and some of the organising principles weren't immediately obvious to people. So we have added to our list of rich-prospect browsing principles the idea that the organisation of the images should always be meaningful to the users (even if the choice of the initial organisational principle seems a bit arbitrary).

We learned two other things in our study of the Texttiles browser (Figure 3.3).[5] The first was a surprising answer to one of our research questions, and the second was gravy. Our research question had to do with placing the meaningful representation under the control of the user. In Texttiles, we were primarily interested in seeing if the concept of the showcase browser could be transferred from collections where photos were available to collections where the meaningful representation consisted of text. So words would appear on the "tiles." Now, if the users were able to add or subtract information from each tile, what would they add and subtract, and how would those changes correspond to the task they were working on with the browser? We set a default text, then provided checkboxes that could be used for each of the pieces of metadata available about the documents.

4 A design for the NORA system where the initial screen shows the author names randomly located, rather than placed on a grid. It seems to make people uncomfortable.

5 The Texttiles Browser allows users to add and subtract metadata from each tile by clicking the checkboxes on the left. Tiles can also be grouped using the same criteria. Design by Ian Craig.

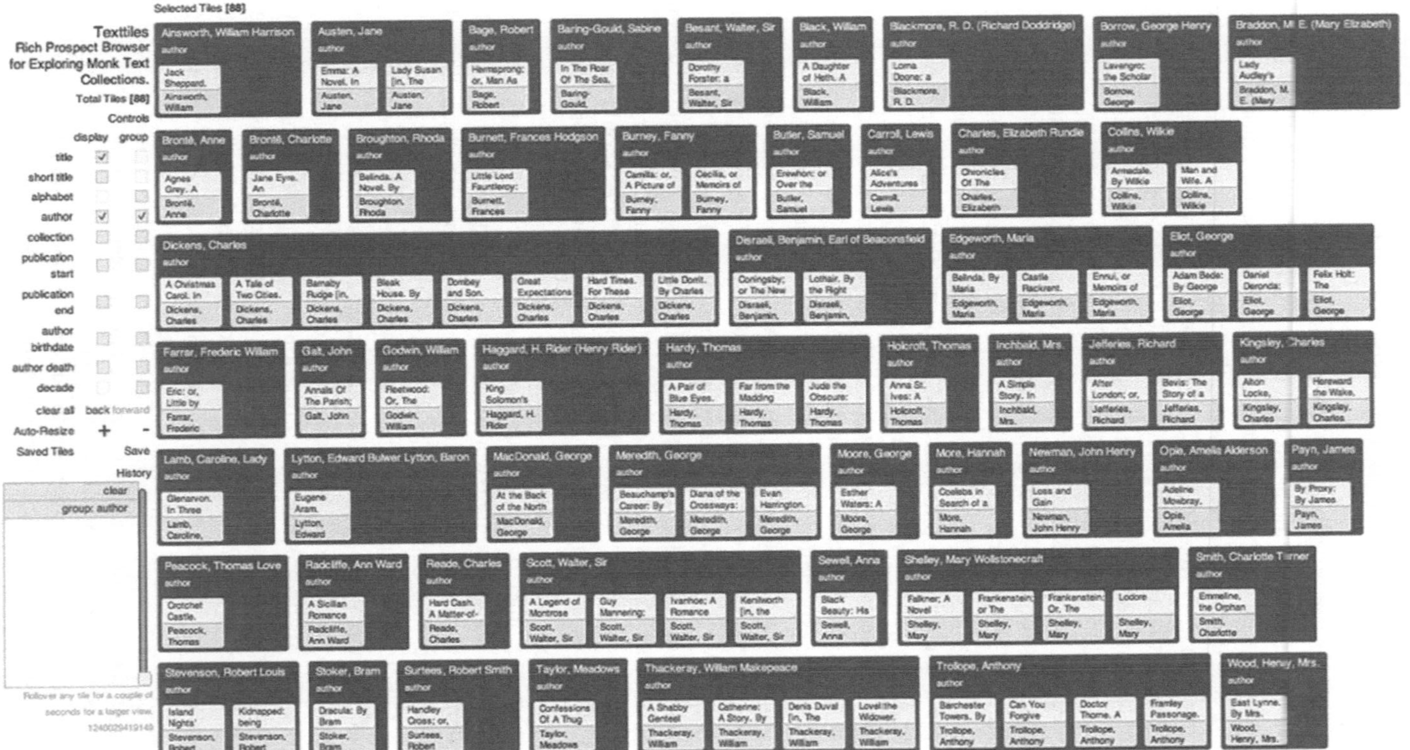

Figure 3.3 The Texttiles Browser

A parallel column of checkboxes also allowed the user to group the images by the same criteria. We had a dozen items of metadata on the list.

Our study participants consisted of 14 graduate students at the University of Alberta. What we observed while they were using Texttiles is that they did take the opportunity to turn information on and off in the tiles. But what was surprising is that they didn't tend to keep any particular piece of information turned on for any length of time. Instead, they would turn on a piece of metadata, look at the results, then turn it off again and use it instead as a grouping criterion. It didn't seem to be necessary to have extra information persistent on each tile when the same information could be captured by the meaningful arrangement of items into groups, and the information could be accessed at the push of a button whenever it was needed.

The second thing we learned in the Texttiles study should have far-reaching consequences, not only for the design of rich-prospect interfaces, but for interfaces of many kinds. What we saw was that the study participants would group the items one way, look in detail at a few of them, then group them another way, at which point their interactions with the few that they'd looked at in detail would be lost. There was no way to keep track of what they had looked at, other than by remembering the location of those tiles on the screen, and reordering the tiles removed that piece of information. We therefore added another new principle, namely that it is not enough to be able to interact with the arrangement of images, but it should also be possible to mark them (or have them retain an easily recognisable characteristic, like placement).

There is quite an extensive literature developing on the subject of digital annotation (for example, Marshall and Brush 2004), but in this case, we aren't thinking of anything as extensive as writing marginal text or drawing marginal images, or creating links between images, but instead simply being able to stick a colored dot or some other slightly customisable mark or tag on an image. We say "customisable" because it is only a short step from being able to mark a tile or image to creating a taxonomy of marks, even something as straightforward as "yes, this is one I want to remember later," to "no, not helpful" or "maybe." To make these marks persistent across sessions would require a username and password or data importing and exporting functionality, but even within the current session, they can prove very useful, and the current prototype of the Texttiles browser provides a means for the user to color selected tiles with a small set of colors. We have also provided for a toggle on dots in the Mandala browser, so that clicking on a dot to view the text also changes the shape and color of the dot to indicate it has been examined. In both Texttiles and the Mandala, these changes persist throughout the current session, or until the user toggles them off.

In our research program, there were a variety of browsers that came between the pill identification system and Texttiles. Like the pill identification system, these other showcase browsers also used images, but they included more elaborate metadata, which allowed us to investigate questions about how people would make use of the emergent tools. One of the most significant observations we made had to do with the use of metadata for grouping images. In the pill identification system, our metadata only included color and shape, so there were two buttons that could be used in any order. In subsequent members of the showcase browser family, we provided increasingly more ways of grouping items, until with Texttiles we included not only grouping affordances, but also the ability to turn the display of specific pieces of content off and on.

An example of the difficulty in representing complex interactions visually arose in our study of a decision support visualisation (Paredes-Olea et al. 2008). We had produced a series of interactive sketches that showed how a person might manipulate a central object to try to find optimal configurations of variables. Our

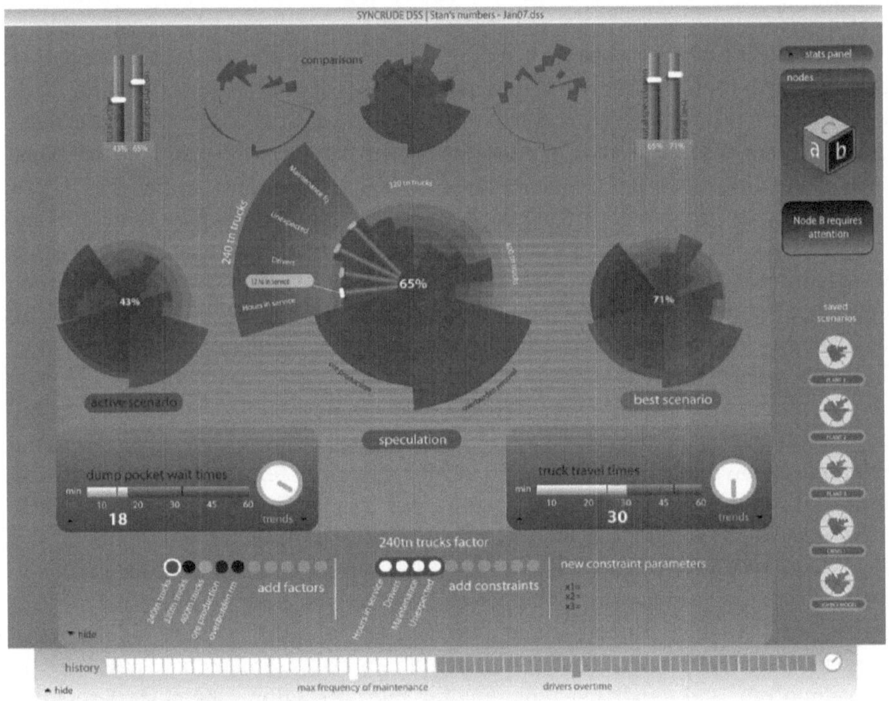

Figure 3.4 Decision support with Florence Nightingale's rose diagrams[6]

goal was to provide sufficient context for the user to understand how different factors influenced each other in making decisions (Figure 3.4).

6 The first iteration of our visualisation for decision support used a set of sliders superimposed on one of Florence Nightingale's rose diagrams, with a timeline along the bottom as a useful but not central element. Design by Carlos Fiorentino.

In particular, we were interested in encouraging users to experiment with the "shadow prices" (also known as marginal costs or Lagrange multipliers), which represent the areas where the system can be adjusted to take advantage of opportunities for additional benefit. To that end, we provided a central image, a kind of radar plot where each of the wedges was intended to represent a cluster of related factors, while all the wedges taken together provided an overview of all the factors relevant to the current decision. In this case, we decided it was too difficult to attempt to include unrelated factors in the visualisation, since these factors could easily number in the tens if not hundreds of thousands. However, for any given decision, a couple of dozen factors would typically represent all the active decision variables.

The user interacts with the system by clicking on any of the wedges, which calls up a set of sliders – one per active decision variable. By moving the sliders, the user is able to see their effect on the other sliders within the same wedge or in other wedges.

Since the design was for a multimodal system, we included a node in the top right corner that could change color in order to alert the operator to potential difficulties within other modes of the operation. To study this prototype, we created a kinetic sketch in Flash, then interviewed decision-makers in four different industries: mining, shipping, construction, and hospitals. The system included, almost as an afterthought, a timeline across the bottom that would allow the user to revisit earlier configurations. We created the system for one industry, then showed it to study participants in a total of four industries, to try to determine the extent to which the design might be portable.

One of the surprising results for us was that participants across all four industries, in remarking on the situations in which they typically made or examined decisions, depending on their role in the hierarchy as tactical or strategic decision-makers, explained that the bulk of their decisions were definitely associated with time. There were days of the week or month, and hours in the day, when certain decisions typically needed to be made. The timeline along the bottom of the design was just too peripheral in the context of typical decision-making. In addition, people at a higher management level would prefer to have a simple means of reviewing decisions in order to understand what kinds of changes they resulted in subsequently. We began to rethink some of the basic premises of the design, and are currently working on a new iteration (Figure 3.5) where the calendar and clock have become central metaphors as well as components in the system.

What haven't we looked into yet?

We have had the opportunity to study a number of features of rich-prospect browsing interfaces, but there are some further areas to investigate. For instance, our showcase browsers to this point have always included a single set of images. Some of the pill photos had front and back, but we only used the front image for the browser, and relegated the back images, where we had them, to the information

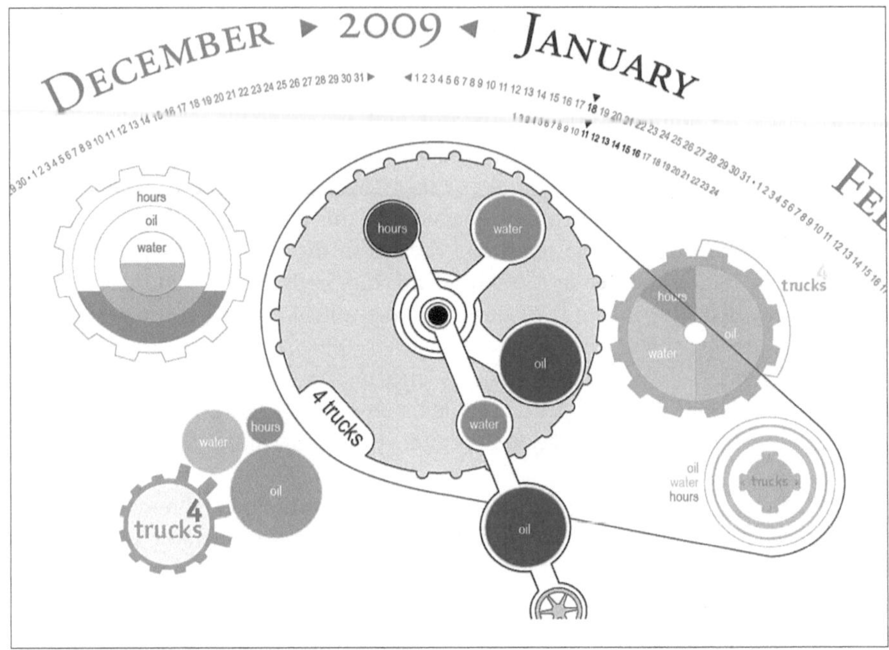

Figure 3.5 Decision support cogs[7]

panel that appeared when a photo was clicked by the user. Ideally, it would be useful to know more about the provision of alternative images. Would people really be interested in swapping one set for another, flipping, for instance, all the front images of pills for back images? Our Texttiles results suggests not, but in that case we were adding and subtracting text rather than replacing the entire image with a new one. We also need to further explore optimal representations of items that are not conducive to being shown as small thumbnail images; for instance, how to meaningfully distinguish the paragraphs of a novel at an iconic level? We will discuss this further in the next chapter.

Another aspect we haven't yet looked into is the threshold in the quantity of metadata associated with each item; at what point, if any, does the quantity become unmanageable? In our showcase browsers, we typically have at least half a dozen items that can be used for grouping, and we have sometimes included three times that number, which required a two-level hierarchy in a collapsible menu.

7 A later iteration of our decision support interface places the entire system within a calendar and clock. Design by Milena Radzikowska.

Chapter 4
I Never Forget a Face: Meaningful and Useful Representation of Items[1]

One of the principles of rich-prospect browsing is that the default interface should show a meaningful representation, not of some kind of hierarchical system, but of every single item in the collection (or in the search results). A meaningful representation will be different things for different types of collections. In the Delegate Browser, for instance, which is intended to help conference participants manage their social capital, the meaningful representation is a photo of the face. In the Historical Building showcase, the representation is a photo of the front of the building. Clearly, it would also be possible to show other perspectives on the buildings, including interior views. Under some conditions, the interior may be more meaningful than the exterior. For instance, when we were searching for models of stages and sets to use in the SET project, we found that there were a great many 3D models of exteriors of theatres, which we could recognise adequately (that is, they were meaningful), but they weren't useful to us.

Relying on images is one approach to providing a meaningful representation of collection items, but it is not the only approach. In our Mandala Browser (Figure 4.1), which allows for nuanced visual searching of XML-encoded documents, we have used colored dots as the fundamental unit of representation.

In using the Mandala, the user begins the process by opening a file, and while loading the contents, defines what unit of text a dot will represent. For someone studying one or more of Shakespeare's plays, a useful unit for subdividing the play is the speech (possibly identified in an XML document with the XPath expression //speech). For someone studying prose, an equally useful unit might be the paragraph (identifiable as an XPath expression //p. Choosing an appropriate granularity for the dots is one of the skills that Mandala users develop over time. Once the dots are defined, they appear around the periphery of the Mandala. The user constructs queries of the dots by creating magnets which sit within the circle of the Mandala, and simultaneously pull the dots in from the periphery and attach color to them. When the dots are attracted to more than one magnet at the same time, a new pie-colored magnet is created in order to represent the intersection, and the dots take on the same pie colors. Although there is a default sequence of magnet colors based on a palette designed to provide for a maximum of color variation, it is also possible for the user to specify what colors should be used for each magnet. This affordance allows someone interested, for instance, in studying

1 Thanks to Maryanne Wynne for this title.

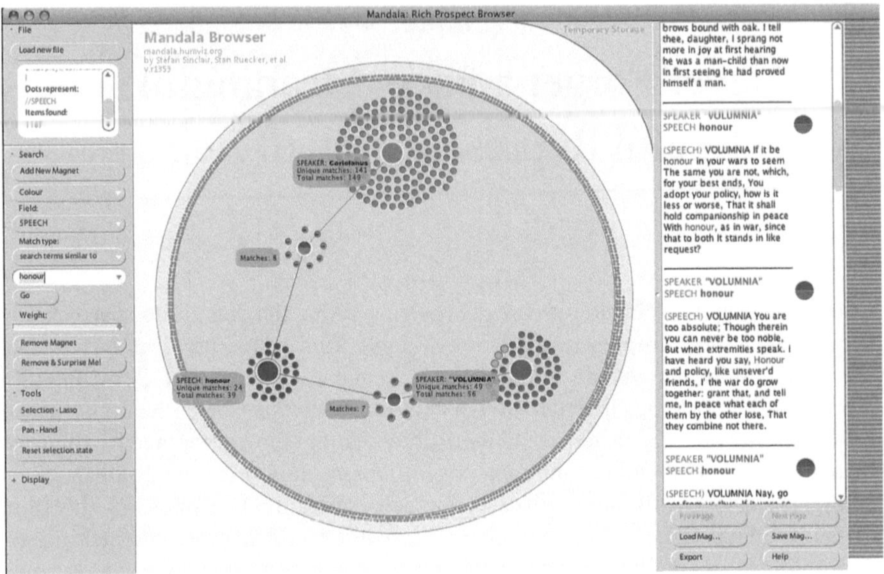

Figure 4.1 The Mandala Browser[2]

texts related to politics, to assign the colors to magnets that are conventionally associated with the colors of different political parties.

Although it might be argued that a dot is not intrinsically very meaningful, the combination of visual elements that goes into working with the Mandala results in the dots being more or less as meaningful as they need to be within the context of the system. In this case we have made a deliberate compromise between the meaningfulness of the representation and the applicability of the tool to a very broad range of contexts (any valid XML file from any domain can be used, and we have other specialised adapters for reading formats such as plain text and comma-separated values). The meaning of the dots is nonetheless enhanced by the fact that the user chooses what the dots will represent from an automatically generated list of suggested XML tags, which includes all the tags that enclose more than 80 percent of the text in a given file. For those who want to work with a smaller proportion of the text, it is also possible to type in a custom XPath. The meaning

2 The Mandala Browser uses dots to represent text units within an XML file, or across multiple files. The interface is shown here in grayscale, but the working system is in color, and the dots change color to match the magnet that attracts them. Dots shared by more than one magnet are divided into pie-shaped slices of different colors. This screenshot shows the 1,107 speeches in Shakespeare's *Coriolanus*, with magnets attracting all the speeches by Coriolanus and his mother, and a third magnet for any speech where someone says the word "honour." Initial concept by Oksana Cheypesh; design team led by Sandra Gabriele.

is also supported by the colored magnets, which represent search terms, again as entered by the user, and by the fact that the color of the dots directly reflects the search term or terms that have attracted it from the periphery. Finally, each dot supports the rich prospect browsing principle of connecting directly to more data – in this case, the text behind the dot, which appears in a reading panel on the right whenever a dot is clicked or lassoed.

Our next example takes us on a different trajectory, partly in an analogue mode. Designed by Piotr Michura, Repetition Loops (Figure 4.2) use a meaningful representation of a text that consists of every word in the text (Ruecker et al. 2008).

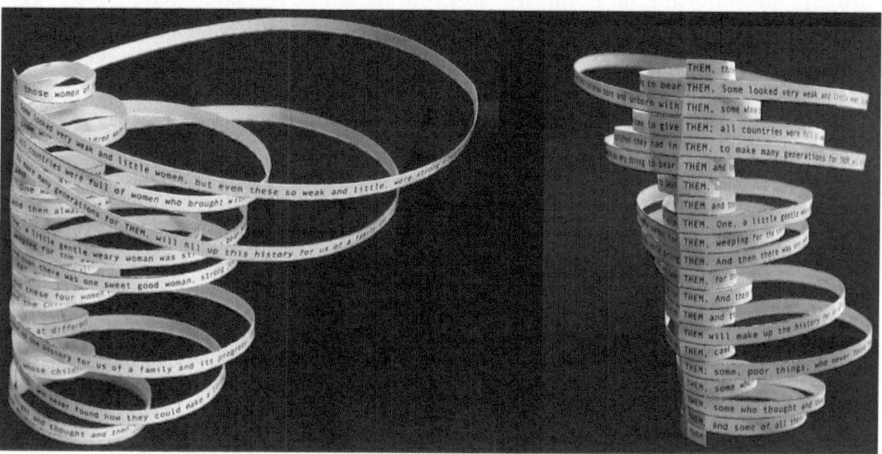

Figure 4.2 Repetition Loops[3]

What is different about this approach is that it begins by abandoning all of the other codex conventions. There are no text blocks, no paragraphs, no page margins, no pages. Instead, there is a string of words that begins with the first word in the document and continues sequentially to the last word. Then, starting from this string of words, the design adds information in the form of the physical configuration of the object. Beginning with the first instance of the search term or phrase, the string of words is looped back on itself so that the repetitions form a spine. The size of the loops represents the distance between repetitions. In order to make the objects as meaningful as possible, a mono-spaced font is used, so that each character takes up the same amount of space (unlike properly kerned fonts, which adjust the spaces between letters to accommodate their different shapes).

In rich-prospect browsing terms, the words are the representations, and the choice of repeated words or phrases chosen by the user are the means of

3 Repetition Loops are intended for studying patterns of repetition in a document. The repeated word or phrase appears along the spine; the length of the loops indicates the number of words occurring between repetitions. Design by Piotr Michura.

manipulating the display. Rather than the affordance of grouping items, as shown in the Biodiversity Browser or the Mandala Browser, the visual organisation of the Repetition Loops is the combination of loops and spine.

Taking their inspiration from the Repetition Loops, two designs by Carlos Fiorentino employ still different approaches to meaningful representation. In this case, the interfaces visualise where search terms appear in multiple documents. In Bubblelines (Figure 4.3), the complete document is represented by a horizontal line – albeit a line that is significantly shorter than the lines used in Repetition Loops. Setting the horizontal lines in Bubblelines one above another does not provide any information about the absolute length of the documents, but it does show us their relative lengths in comparison with each other.

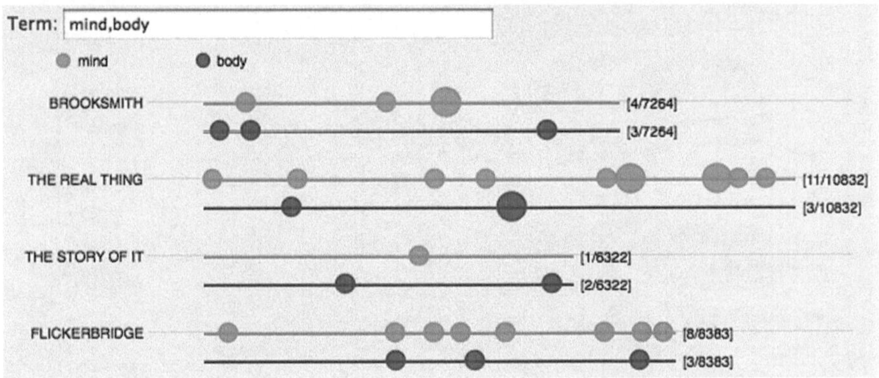

Figure 4.3 Bubblelines[4]

Once the relative length of each document in the set is visible, it is possible to use this overview as a means of locating search terms. The circles on each line in Figure 4.3 represent these locations. The numbers at the end of the line give the total number of search hits for the current term, and the total number of words in each document. We also plan to provide a vertical scrubber line that will allow the user to look at points of congruence across books, examining places where a given vocabulary item is used most frequently at the beginning, middle, and end of a book.

Bubblelines is an excellent visual means of comparing search terms as they are found within multiple documents. It employs two kinds of representation, using lines for novels and bubbles for the occurrence of search terms. Putting the two together in a single line provides information about search term location within a single document. Putting several documents together at once begins to show

4 Bubblelines is intended to show where search hits occur in multiple documents. Design by Carlos Fiorentino.

patterns across an entire collection. Clicking on any bubble or set of bubbles opens a reading panel with the associated text.

Fiorentino's other design for visualising search terms similarly begins with a single line representing an entire text. Referred to as Knots (Figure 4.4), this tool allows the user to visually compare a series of search terms by overlapping one line for each term. The lines are color-coded to match the search terms, and bend at 30 degrees whenever a term is encountered.

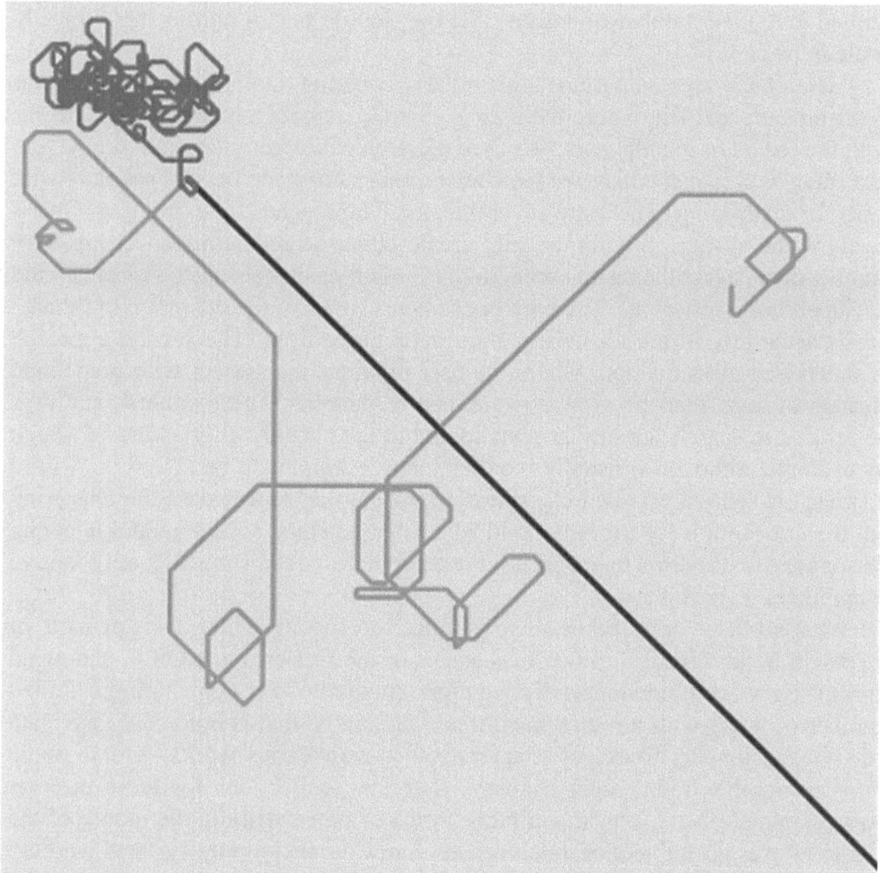

Figure 4.4 Knots[5]

5 The Knots visualization represents each document with a colored line. The lines bend at 30 degrees whenever a search term is encountered. Here we see the words "painting," "that" and "boy" in Charles Dickens's novel *A Christmas Carol.* Design by Carlos Fiorentino.

In Knots, the representation combines a line, the effects of a search term on the shape of the line, and a color.

In order to make clear the distinction between meaningful representation of every item in a collection and other forms of overview, we can contrast the examples so far with designs that use either a selective representation or else a hierarchical one. Both of these approaches are attempts to give people access to a large amount of information without trying to put it all on one screen.

Another conventional form of selective representation consists of lists that are limited to a fixed number of entries, like the Google search returns that typically come in batches of 10.

Hierarchical representations are similarly common. One of the most familiar is the alphabetical list, where the user is able to navigate a hierarchy that begins with the letters of the alphabet. We used hierarchical representation in the NORA and MONK projects, where we were attempting to provide literary scholars with tools for textmining. There are several general approaches to textmining. One is to allow the system to automatically create either a predetermined or arbitrary number of clusters of texts that seem to share common characteristics of some kind (unsupervised clustering). The kind of characteristics and the definition of "share" varies according to the clustering algorithms being used. The second approach is supervised classification, where the user provides the system with predefined clusters of texts that the system examines for patterns. These patterns can then be re-used to search for similar texts to add to the clusters. It is a kind of search by example, although it usually requires many examples to be effective. A third approach is semi-supervised classification, where the system does the clustering but the user iteratively examines and adjusts parameters, accepting and rejecting clusters and texts within them, until some acceptable outcome is achieved (adaptive spam filters work this way).

What all these approaches share is a need to specify which texts or parts of texts will be involved in the various stages of the process. In NORA, and again in MONK, we combined the selective representation of a list containing a limited number of items with a hierarchical tree structure so that people could navigate into the documents to select chapters rather than entire works, and in some cases paragraphs rather than chapters. Since the collections for these projects also contained poetry, plays, and other forms of prose writing, the nature of the hierarchy was the subject of much debate. Since the textmining systems work by comparing chunks of text, we also had to consider what it might mean to cross genres, so that a training set that had been prepared, for instance, with a set of plays, might then be used for mining novels.

The main problem, however, is that selective representation in practical terms limits the browsing that most people are willing to do. Google researchers have reported that the vast majority of people never leave the first page of search returns – the top 10 hits – and that the vanishingly few numbers of people who do go further rarely extend beyond the first 20 or 30. With a hierarchical display that can collapse and expand, like the ones we used for NORA and MONK, even the first

10 items on the list can quickly become overwhelming, if the user needs to open the hierarchy down to the paragraph level. A typical novel might contain anywhere from 500 to 2,000 paragraphs, making the expansion of even a single item in a collection into a very difficult list to work with. In contrast with this approach, if an entire screen is dedicated to collection browsing, it is not that difficult to put 2,000 items on a computer screen.

Some collections are also better candidates than others for rich-prospect browsing interfaces. The relevant characteristics that need to be considered are:

- the possible uses of the collection
- the number of items in the collection
- the characteristics of the individual items
- the degree of homogeneity among items
- the possibility of providing some logical, consistent and meaningful representation of each item
- the extent of the markup of the collection

The Possible Uses of the Collection

Some collections may have been created for a specific purpose that precludes the necessity of any user ever wanting prospect over them. For example, an archive of historical technical specifications from a turn-of-the-century manufacturer might be labelled with part numbers that are found in an index somewhere and used to retrieve the specific documents that were once required by the technical staff. Within the constraints of that archive, the need for a rich-prospect interface showing a representation of all the technical materials seems minimal, especially if it were to consist of the relatively meaningless part numbers.

However, even in such an extreme case it is possible to suggest scenarios involving users and tasks that might find prospect useful on such a collection. For someone carrying out historical research on the economics of manufacturing, for instance, it might be helpful to have an overview of the technical documentation, especially if the representation of the items in that case included additional information such as cost or maintenance cycles or sales totals.

For an archivist in charge not only of the technical documentation system, but also of the parts it documents, a rich-prospect interface might also help to provide reassurance that all the parts are where they should be, and that no documents have been mislaid or overwritten, especially if the display were to contain additional information on items such as a date and time for most recent update, current file size in some meaningful units, or current status.

Similarly, the potential usefulness of prospect on something like a dictionary is relatively limited, since the primary function of the dictionary is to facilitate retrieval of information about a single word at a time. However, even in the case of a dictionary, some degree of prospect can be beneficial in certain scenarios. For instance, when the user is uncertain about the spelling of a word, a list of the words surrounding the word being sought can provide some cognitive reassurance, either that the correct word has been located, or that variants may be available that differ in relatively minor ways, such as in their inflectional morphology. The online Oxford English Dictionary is a good example of this kind of limited prospect.

The Number of Items in the Collection

There are undoubtedly limits to what a human perceiver can integrate from a rich-prospect interface in a useful way, but those limits will likely vary according to a number of factors such as learning, experience, visual acuity, and motivation. Monitor size is also an issue, of course. A 21-inch monitor at a resolution of 1,024 × 768, full of text, without vertical scrolling, can hold in excess of 2,000 words of 12 point single-spaced Verdana, which is a reasonable size and font for screen display for most users. An iPhone screen, on the other hand, can display roughly an order of magnitude fewer words: perhaps 200–300, if the font is fairly small to accommodate a closer reading distance. If one of the criteria of the design is that the prospect should not involve vertical scrolling, a good candidate collection for the iPhone might therefore be one that contains only 200 items or fewer. There does not seem to be, however, any a priori reason to disallow scrolling or page flipping from a prospect-based interface (all items are represented and readily accessible, although an overall single impression of all items is not available).

The naive limits on text display mentioned above are not necessarily realistic either. The designer of a rich-prospect interface is able to employ any number of techniques to structure the information in ways that make it more accessible – some of these techniques may allow increased prospect on larger collections without compromising the advantages that accrue to the strategy of showing a meaningful representation of each item. It seems likely, however, that an upper limit on the number of items that can be reasonably displayed using current desktop monitors might be a few tens of thousands (for example, Figure 2.4, the Paper Drill).

The Characteristics of the Individual Items

The principle of return on investment for both the designer and the user can be applied in considering the kinds of collections that are good candidates. One way of applying this principle is to examine the individual items in the collection in terms of how useful they might potentially be. If, for example, the collection is fairly small and consists of very small items, such as single images or single sentences or paragraphs, or small structured records, it may be possible to create a display that shows the entire contents of the collection. On the other hand, if the collection has short items in the hundreds of thousands or millions, a search system may be the optimum solution, and browsing solutions may not be possible (though a hybrid may be useful, where a large number of search items are selected for rich-prospect browsing from an even larger aggregate collection). Finally, if the collection consists of fairly large items that are individually rich sources of information, then the overhead involved in designing a rich-prospect interface may be easier to justify.

Some kinds of data may also lend themselves more readily than others to the creation of meaningful representations, although in general all kinds of information are routinely catalogued, indexed, and displayed in one form or another. An extreme case might be a collection of artifacts obtained in an archeological site, which might contain everything from pot shards to bones and inscriptions (for example, Meredith-Lobay 2009). If an archivist is tasked with recording diverse collections of artifacts, ranging from physical objects of unknown purpose to texts in undeciphered languages, it is necessary to create some form of useful labels, if nothing else than as indexes to a set of images or objects. These labels can also be used in a rich-prospect interface, although they will only be as meaningful there as they are elsewhere.

The Degree of Homogeneity among Items

Within any given digital collection there can be a wide range of items that are not necessarily of the same class or in the same form. There might be, for example, sound files, video clips, text documents of various kinds, and digital images in any number of formats. Even collections of text documents can contain diverse kinds of items. General Electric Energy Services, for example, has in its research and development area the mandate of creating electrical substation automation hardware and software. Each component of the system has a set of associated text documents, including in-house testing reports, technical documentation intended for client use, and marketing materials. In order to provide a meaningful representation of every item in this collection, it may be necessary to indicate in some way not only the content, but also the system components and the intended audience.

One means of providing some homogeneity is through a meta-tagging system that provides a similar structure for the information about each document, which is stored along with the documents. The Dublin Core, for example, consists of a set of 15 meta-tags that can be used as part of a document header to provide the information needed to characterise a digital document for cataloguing purposes. These tags are: title, creator, subject, description, publisher, contributor, date, type, format, identifier, source, language, relation, coverage, and rights (Dublin Core 2010).

The contents of any or all of these tags could be used as the basis for a rich-prospect display, depending on the information needs and intentions of the user.

There are also more complex encoding standards, such as the Metadata Encoding and Transmission Standard (METS), which is an XML schema developed by the

Library of Congress (METS 2010). A METS document may include tags in the following five areas:

- descriptive metadata
- administrative metadata
- file groups
- structural map
- behavior (METS 2010)

Material from any one of these sections may be useful in developing ways of representing heterogeneous documents.

Other meta-tagging systems for document definition include the MARC encoding standard, which, like METS, was defined for use by library scientists, the Text Encoding Initiative (TEI) header (Renear 2004) and COCOA, which was used by the Oxford Concordance Program and was later extended for use in TACT (Hockey 2000, p. 27). Tagging schemes such as Standard Generalised Markup Language (SGML) and eXtensible Markup Languages (XML) also allow developers to define tagging systems which can contain meta-tags for document definition.

The Possibility of Providing Meaningful Representation of Each Item

If metadata has been used and contains information that is meaningful to the user, the rich-prospect interface can be based on it. Whether metadata is available or not, it is necessary to consider what the user brings to a given task in terms of prior knowledge about the field and expectations of what is appropriate or useful. For someone unfamiliar with law, for instance, it might seem reasonable to access a collection of case documents by the judge involved. Each case requires a judge; the judge's name is included in every document; and the decisions that set different kinds of precedent might reasonably be expected to cluster around particular judges. However, in the legal field, precedent cases are not conventionally accessed by judge, but rather by the names of the plaintiff and defendant. A collection of cases that used an interface based on the names of judges might therefore be of interest to the public, or to academic researchers, but would be largely useless to lawyers.

Different searches require different kinds of information: this fact is widely acknowledged in the design of search interfaces to library collections, where it is not uncommon to have different interfaces to allow access by author, title, publisher information, or keywords – that is, based on the various metadata that have been used to define the document records. Similarly, it may be useful to have different kinds of rich-prospect display for different kinds of browsing activity.

Another solution is to provide the user with a variety of information about each item. This strategy has been widely implemented by web browsers, which respond to the search string with a long list of possible links. Each link typically includes two or three lines of text extracted from each document, which means that screen space is sacrificed in the hopes that some of the information will be relevant enough to help the user decide which sites to access.

The Extent of the Markup of the Collection

Some digital collections consist of documents that have been tagged using a markup system such as those defined with SGML or XML. These kinds of collections are a special case, because they contain not only the information available to a reader of the text, but also information that is in some respects hidden from the reader by being contained in the tags, the attributes on the tags, and the values of the attributes. Depending on the complexity of the markup system that has been developed and applied, a collection of documents might have relatively simple information relating to formatting, or quite sophisticated semantic information in the form of hermeneutic interpretations of the material contained in the tags, or some level of encoding in between.

Although any level of encoding is potentially useful in developing a rich-prospect display, the more sophisticated levels of interpretive encoding are particularly interesting opportunities to make the hidden intelligence in the tags available for perusal and use by the people accessing the collection (we return to interpretive encoding in Chapter 5).

Form

There are several different strategies available to use in providing prospect. One method is to use the form of the visual material as an indication, not of the content, but of the type of the material that is being offered to the user. For example, in the desktop metaphor, there are standard icons that represent documents and folders, and variations of the icons are used to indicate whether a given document is an application or a data file that is associated with a particular application. It is possible to see the assembly of icons on the desktop or within a folder as a form of browsing interface.

There are two problems, however, with this approach. First, icons do need to be quite large, since they were originally intended to draw the user's attention to files on the desktop, rather than having been designed to work together as a complex display. Second, and more importantly, the icons do not provide a significant level of return on investment in visual terms. To see a thousand icons, each representing a data document, is to perceive a complex pattern composed of identical elements. This kind of display can provide, in fact, an instance of the sublime of repetition, where sheer numbers of identical or near-identical items can trigger an emotional response in the viewer. Unfortunately, however, all it conveys in informational terms is that there are many very similar data files available. In order for the files to be differentiated from each other, it is necessary to add textual labels (there are of course systems that also provide helpful previews of the contents of a file, such as an image, though the smaller the size of the icon, the less this is useful). If the icons are organised into groups, they become redundant once one is given per section, and the purpose of the display is therefore largely fulfilled by the content rather than by the form, even though the form is allocated a large portion of screen space.

Even in systems where the icons differ from each other in a significant degree, there are still details of display that can render the interface more or less useful. In the Data Mountain visual interface, for example (Czerwinski et al. 1999), web sites are shown as thumbnail images using a snapshot of the actual home page of the URL. Each image is therefore unique, but the interface allows a nontrivial amount of visual occlusion between images, rendering all but the front image difficult to interpret.

Another form-based display is the one used by the Alexandria Digital Library (http://clients.alexandria.ucsb.edu/globetrotter/), where geocentric information is made available to the users through the use of a visual footprint, which consists of an outline superimposed on the surface of a map. The contours of the outline in this case are significant, since the superimposition indicates the region of interest to the user. These visual footprints allow the user to query any region of the globe, independent of the name of the region, which simplifies the query in cases where the user may be uncertain of the spelling or where the designers of the system have not included all of the valid spellings (which often vary for geographic regions by dialect, language, and source). For example, the city known in the English-speaking world as Copenhagen is referred to by the people who live there as København. The difference in spelling – particularly in the initial consonant – means that an alphabetical listing of place names using the word "Copenhagen" might represent a barrier to København residents interested in finding out about their area.

Visual footprints also allow queries on regions which do not have names. For example, if a user of the system were to draw an irregular polygon around several cities, it is possible that the collective area indicated would not be known by a unique name. Similarly, a section chosen from the middle of a lake, ocean, or desert is unlikely to have its own name, yet the system of geo-information may contain relevant data concerning its climate, wildlife, topography or other features.

Based on the principle applied by the ADL, good candidate collections for queries and displays based on visual forms are those which have some pre-existing visual vocabulary that can be used as the basis for the system. In cases where the collection itself is naturally associated with visual materials, the use of visual access methods is in alignment with the underlying content domain. Other systems may also be able to effectively adapt visual forms through the use of metaphor, symbolism, and other sign systems which associate meaning with visual material (as opposed, for example, to text). For example, Dyens et al. (2008) described a system of information cartography that mapped semantic values onto a geographical landscape, providing the user with a sense of the relative scale and position of various concepts in a corpus on post-humanism.

In the case of ADL, for example, the map of the globe or the region under study is the pre-existing visual element that serves as the basis for the footprints, which are themselves a type of visual query on the system. The user of the ADL collection does not retrieve information by typing text: instead, the material is accessed by placing a bounded region onto a globe. An example of a related kind of pre-existing visual information is in the typical interface to a museum, where the visual basis for the query is a floorplan that allows visitors to quickly narrow their interest from a position of prospect on the entire building to the details of a particular room or area.

Content

Although systems that use form as the basis for prospect do exist, the most common method of providing meaning to the user is through displays based on content. The primary kind of content-based display uses text, which has the advantage of potentially conveying a maximum amount of meaning, but the disadvantage that it is only accessible to people who are literate in the language and share a common orthography (and in contexts where text labels can helpfully represent and differentiate items in a collection). It is also not uncommon for text itself to be wasted space in terms of the information it conveys, either because it is repeated unnecessarily or because it does not sufficiently differentiate the items it represents. Unnecessarily repeated text often appears as labels which are intended to structure the display and make the user aware of the kinds of data available. In cases where elements of the same kind are repeated, these labels quickly become redundant. Insufficiently differentiated text occurs in cases where a representation which is supposed to distinguish one item from another instead serves to indicate similarity. An example might be in a keyword listing where the same keyword has been applied to every item shown, and is used as a part of the display of each item, rather than appearing as a key to the whole page. European archival records of the soldiers killed in the First World War, for instance, will sometimes list the names next to a conventional military designation such as "killed in action," which can continue for page after page of entries until the reader is numbed, as perhaps they are intended to be, by the sheer repetition.

For displays where only a few items are shown, inefficient text is not necessarily a serious problem, although it can become a source of irritation over time rather than through repetition at one time. For displays intended to provide prospect, however, it seems clear that redundancies should be avoided wherever possible in order to maximise the effective use of the limited screen real estate.

It is also important to note that meaningful representation by content does not necessarily imply a textual representation. Collections of images, for instance, or video clips, might be better represented by thumbnail images than by textual labels. For example, the Photomesa interface (Bederson 2001) provides the user with a wall of thumbnail versions of photographs which are perhaps surprisingly accessible to browsing, given the complexity of their initial visual impact. The problem with visual representations is that they may need to be comparatively large in order to be distinguishable, which has implications for the design in terms of screen real estate. There are also limits to what a perceiver can tolerate in terms of visual complexity or simple overload. In some cases, such as the Mandala Browser, we have found that users are satisfied with simple colored dots, on the basis that they recognise that the position of the dots next to the magnets, combined with the association by color, conveys the central meaning of the system, and that each dot can also be used as a link to call up the underlying text.

Relationship

For a rich-prospect display to convey a maximum amount of meaning in a form that is readily understandable, one strategy is to emphasise relationships among the collection items rather than either the content or the form. Starfield displays (Ahlberg and Shneiderman 1994b) are one form of relationship display where form and content have been reduced, sometimes to a single pixel, in order to provide as simple a visual presentation as possible. The information conveyed in a starfield interface, as in our Mandala Browser, is therefore primarily in the form of relational positioning, with some selected document characteristics used to group individual collection items into larger aggregates.

The primary disadvantage of starfield interfaces is that in order to keep the size within reasonable bounds, the individual items are not meaningful in themselves. There are essentially two solutions to this problem – make the individual items meaningful, or else associate them in some accessible way with other kinds of representation that are meaningful, whether in the current window or in an associated one.

Facets

In a somewhat different context, the synthesis of various kinds of information is also at the heart of a form of classification system known as facet analytical theory. Originally formulated by Ranganathan in the 1930s, facet analysis is a relatively complex approach to knowledge representation governed by 3 planes, 46 canons, 13 postulates, and 22 principles, which have been subsequently modified and adapted by other researchers in the library sciences (Spiteri 1998). The three planes of facet analysis represent, respectively, the need to divide a subject area into its component parts, choose appropriate terminology, and create a notation that preserves the notion of the components. The components must be mutually exclusive, so that individual items in the collection can be uniquely represented by combining the terms (Broughton 1998).

It is possible to consider the simpler forms of our showcase browsers as facet browsers, since the buttons for grouping items do often meet the criteria of applying to each item in the collection and being mutually exclusive. However, it is also true that many of the grouping criteria rely on the existence of a "not" or null group, and that in some cases (such as presentation keywords in the Delegate

Browser, or colors of pills in the pill identification system) the resulting groups are not mutually exclusive. One of the results of our study of the pill identification system is that we needed to abandon the notion of mutual exclusivity, and instead duplicate images during the grouping process, so that a capsule with a yellow top and a blue bottom would appear in both the yellow and blue groups. The alternative strategy, of creating a separate group for multi-colored pills, resulted in a set of pill images that was much less useful for the task of identification.

Hybrids

People are capable of perceiving and using a wide variety of complex nested and sequential analog affordances, so there is no a priori reason for rejecting the possibility of creating complex digital affordances. The most powerful tools are also often the tools that are most flexible – that is, they provide the user with the greatest number of affordances, including the possibility of using the tool in ways that the designer did not anticipate. There is also an argument for designing tools that can follow users as their competencies grow and their demands for flexibility and power expand.

Hybrid forms of the meaningful display of items have the potential to open up additional affordances by combining the relevant features of each of the specialised forms. If content, form, and relationship can all be deployed strategically together in order to convey meaning, along with a range of tools to allow various opportunities to act on that meaning, it may be possible to expand the benefits to the user of the interface beyond the affordances available through a representation that relies on only one of these methods.

One of our current strategies for hybrid displays builds on an insight from Giacometti et al. (2008) that the organisation of the items should always contribute to the meaning of the display. That is, the way the items are organised should always make sense to the user. With this in mind, we are currently designing a system where the structure of the surface provides the relationship dimension, with items represented by form and content located in such a way as to add to the meaning. Conventional examples of this approach include the Cartesian X-Y coordinate system, maps, radar plots, and target diagrams. We are attempting to generalise from these examples to produce a system that can be flexibly adapted to different kinds of data.

Amount of Information on Display

No matter what kind of display is appropriate for a given user in a particular context, the question remains as to how much information is necessary or potentially useful. There is some need to manage the limited amount of available screen space, and independent of the screen space available, the cognitive demands of a rich-prospect form of display on the user are potentially quite high. A trade-off therefore exists between the choice to display as much information as possible, in the hopes that it will prove useful to someone, and the structuring of the information in such a way as to increase prospect.

Many of the current web search engines and document retrieval systems provide the user with a list of search results that scrolls vertically and consists of individual items that are approximately three lines each in length. An arbitrary display limit is usually set, with items over the limit either not available at all (for example, ACM) or else available in subsequent screens (for example, Google). This set of choices – to display the results in (1) some detail using (2) a vertical list of (3) limited length – all serve to reduce the amount of prospect available to the user. An alternative strategy with more prospect might create a structured display of very short representations, perhaps clustered around relevance rating, and numbering at least in the thousands, which would give the user as much as two orders of magnitude more information to work with. The presentation of so much information of course requires a variety of strategies to make it manageable rather than overwhelming, but visually structuring large amounts of information in useful ways is a challenge the visual communication design community has taken on for several generations, and many strategies are available.

there are tags of type A which can contain subtags of type B, which in turn can contain subtags of type A. Complete display of the tagsets would therefore require some indication of the places where recursion is possible.

Display of the tagging, on the other hand, needs to indicate the places where recursion has been applied. Further research is necessary to determine how often this has occurred in the Orlando documents, and also to understand whether the user would benefit from a display that indicates the precise location of each tag within the recursive hierarchy, or whether the display of sections of the hierarchy as a kind of local nesting of tags would be sufficiently informative.

In cases where hierarchy is less significant to the user, some of the options discussed below for providing prospect on the documents in the collection could also be applied to the problem of providing prospect on the tagset. In order of increasing prospect, these options include:

- picklists, where people can choose tags from a menu or other form of interactive list
- microtext picklists, which provide tags in tiny text, often with a fisheye effect to make the tags at the cursor location more legible
- walls of text, consisting of multiple columns filling a screen with tags
- panoramas, where people can pan back and forth over displays of tags that extend beyond the left and right edges of the screen

As with prospect on the contents, prospect on the tagset can be structured in ways that are more or less complex. It may also be useful in some cases to provide people with tools that can be used to manipulate the display of the tagset, either through sorting or subsetting or grouping the tags according to criteria relevant to the task at hand.

Should the Presentation of the Tagsets Keep them Distinct?

The design process for tagset displays in a rich-prospect interface should give attention to the unique aspects of the particular tagset. One question that arises in the Orlando example is whether or not it is useful to differentiate among the tagsets used by the project. These include writing, biography, events, topics, and bibliography. The display might, for instance, make the point that the different document types have each been tagged using a different tagset. On the other hand, the display might merge the tagsets into one larger meaningful representation, since there is considerable overlap, especially between the tagsets for the writing and biography documents (the tagsets for events and topics are considerably smaller, and the tagging correspondingly less complex). The various solutions will each result in a different user understanding of the collection, which implies that the interface designer needs to address this issue with the developers of the collection.

Chapter 5

Textual Markup for Digital Collections

Markup grammars such as Structured Generalised Markup Language (SGML) and eXtensible Markup Language (XML) are important because they can be used to define customised tagsets, making it possible for people to embed additional knowledge in the text, including interpretive material. The purpose of text tagging is to facilitate retrieval and representation through applying what is essentially a controlled vocabulary of tags. A collection with an interpretive level of tagging is one where information is included in the tags that is otherwise not available in the text. Examples include regularisation of people's names, and specifics of dates and locations that are only mentioned in general terms in the text (for instance, "yesterday" in a letter where the exact date can be ascertained). The presence of tagging in a collection provides an opportunity for designers to make the tagged material visible to the users of the collection, in ways that will provide greater prospect and all its related advantages.

While there is a variety of new potential affordances and perceptual opportunities provided by rich-prospect interfaces to digital collections, the degree of complexity increases when the principle of providing prospect is applied to interpretively tagged text collections. In order to provide rich prospect on any tagged collection, it is necessary to consider not only the display of the contents of the collection, but also the display of the tags, tag attributes, and the values contained in the attributes. Since one potential use of tagged text is to allow the user to extract relevant sections of documents, it may also be necessary to consider some means of providing prospect on segments of documents, rather than treating each document as a single entity.

Each of these components of the tagged collection may lend itself to more than one strategy for providing prospect. Although in most cases the tagset (or, alternatively, in SGML the document type definition and in XML the schema) is considered something to be used "under the hood," to make the markup more consistent and the retrieval algorithms more effective, there is also a case to be made in many situations for exposing the tagset to the user. That is, it may be useful in some instances to provide a rich-prospect form of display of the tagset itself, independent of the way in which it has been applied in the documents. Display of the tagset may provide perceptual features that give insight into the nature of the collection and how it has been understood by the people who developed it. It may also provide opportunities for action, by allowing the user to manipulate the display in various ways, or by using components from the display in the construction of queries on the collection. We have attempted a variety of approaches to exposing the tagset, including picklists to construct queries (Orlando's tag search; Mandala), filters after queries (Orlando's simple search), interactive choices of tags that immediately add or subtract information from the main display (Texttiles; the Dynamic TOC).

Rich prospect on the tagging of a collection, on the other hand, may turn out in many cases to be above the level of manageable size, simply by requiring the display of too many items. Strategies may therefore need to be adopted to provide other forms of prospect, involving logical subsets of the tagset, or the display of a subset based on the tagging as it has been applied in individual documents that have been opened for reading.

Examination of the tagset and tagging in the Orlando Project, for example, indicates that even the most straightforward approaches to providing some meaningful representation of every item in the collection can quickly result in a number of complexities. Orlando, published by Cambridge University Press, is an integrated history of women's writing in the British Isles, and, though it does not use the standardised TEI tagset, does make extensive use of tags that are common in many digital humanities projects. These include the <Name> tag and a tag for dated text, called <ChronStruct>. However, even a tag as seemingly straightforward as <Name> can prove complicated in practice. In Orlando, for example, not every name in the collection is the name of an author, and not every reference to an author who is represented in the collection appears as the text of a given <Name> tag – in some cases, the tagged text contains only an indirect or oblique reference to the person, and the contents of the <Name: standard> attribute are essential to anyone who wants to know who the person was. There are also anonymous authors, authors with names that are the same as other authors, and authors with pseudonyms. For people mentioned but not represented in the collection, there are those whose names appear in relation to only one author who is represented, those who appear in relation to multiple authors, and those who were important historical figures in their own right, involved in activities that may appear as part of the events database.

These details complicate the use of names as a form of meaningful representation, and need to be taken into consideration by the designer hoping to provide a rich-prospect display based on the <Name> tag and its attributes.

If the user is to have access to the tagsets, several design issues need to be addressed. The first two issues relate to the general questions "why?" and "how?" while the last two issues deal with questions of how the various components might interact with each other. The issues are:

- What might the user gain by having prospect on the tagsets?
- How might prospect on the tagsets be provided?
- Should the presentation of the tagsets keep them distinct?
- How could tagset prospect interact with collection prospect?

What Might the User Gain by Having Prospect on the Tagsets?

The original purpose for tagging a document with an SGML-defined threefold: so that the grammar of the markup can be enforced for consiste correctness; so that the markup can serve as a support tool for a retrieval alg and so that the markup can be used as a means of facilitating formatting. T the tagsets available to the users in any form is, therefore, to repurpose the to a new use or set of uses, which include making visible some of the orga principles of the collection, as well as the ways in which the designers tagsets understood the material being created. One potential benefit for the in gaining such an understanding is that it may serve as a form of education i content domain.

Depending on the tools that are provided, the user may also benefit from opportunity to use the tagset in formulating queries. In cases where the nat of the query is congruent with the tagset, knowing which tags are available c potentially help the user to refine the query to make the best use of the tagg material. If the system also provides the user with feedback as to the actual quer being formulated – possibly in a Structured Query Language (SQL) or a hierarchica query language like XPath – it may also be possible for sophisticated users to learn to formulate or modify queries using the appropriate syntax. Additional features such as a query formulation wizard, which walks the user in steps through the process, can assist in the process of growing familiar with query formulation through examining the tagset.

Knowledge of the tags, attributes, and attribute values that were used can also suggest, not only more accurate forms of previous queries, but also new queries that might otherwise not come to mind. In this context, the tags, attributes, and attribute values become visible cues to the kinds of information available in the collection.

How might Prospect on the Tagset be Provided?

Most tagsets are hierarchical (sometimes called the "Ordered Hierarchy of Conte Objects" or OHCO (DeRose et al. 1990), although some researchers have suggest that flat tagsets may in fact be more appropriate and useful for humanities mater (for example, Liu and Smith 2008). The position of a tag within the hierarchy n in some cases be significant enough that the user would benefit from knowing position. Options for creating a display that indicates hierarchical position inc the use of layering, clustering, and tree diagrams. However, because tree diag can quickly extend past the boundaries of a normal screen, they should be vis optimised where possible in order to save space and allow for greater prospe the whole.

In applying these concepts to our example Orlando project, a further diff arises from the fact that the tag definitions are, in some cases, recursive. T

The first solution has the advantage of keeping the use of the tagsets in constructing searching criteria clearly in line with the design of the collection. For example, if the user is looking specifically at Biography documents, then if the display does not distinguish among the tagsets, the situation may arise where searches are being performed on Biography documents using tags that do not occur in them. Maintaining an alignment between the form of the interface and the form of the collection is useful in helping the reader come to an understanding of the collection. However, in this case, the replication of some of the tags across the tagsets results in a degree of redundancy which might prove irritating or confusing to some people.

A more flexible solution might be, therefore, to have the display of the tagsets change automatically to accommodate the various kinds of searches. For someone interested in looking at the Biography documents, a toggle on the display used to constrain the search could also trigger a change in the display of the tagsets so that only the Biography tags are visible. If the person were interested in all kinds of documents, then the complete amalgamated tagset could be shown. The advantage of this strategy is that the options available conform to the current environment. The disadvantage is that the appearance and disappearance of interface options can be disorienting, and also tends to restrict the reader from easily coming to an understanding of the larger system and the tools it contains. A practical issue also arises with respect to the way in which picklist contents are toggled. Using a scripting language such as javascript, it is possible to change the contents of a picklist on the fly, without modifying anything else on the page. However, this approach violates an important web usability standard, in particular making screen reading more difficult for people who are visually impaired, since they may not be aware that a picklist they've already read has changed.

There is a third form of display that circumvents the problem of confronting the user with an interface where a choice in one area generates unexpected changes in other areas. Such a display would be one that constrains the search options and the representation of the tagset so that rather than invisibly linking them, the system would show them in parallel. In computing terms, the difference is between a modal solution, where the current activity limits the range of possible actions, and a non-modal one, where the user is not constrained by the environment of the current activity. The classic modal situation is the dialog box that appears and suspends access to anything else on the screen, requiring a response from the user before any other activity can proceed. In general, the computing community has recognised that modal situations should be avoided wherever possible, although modality in menu choices remains quite a common design feature.

How could Tagset Prospect Interact with Collection Prospect?

If both the collection's documents and the collection's tagsets are made available to the user through some form of rich-prospect display, the resulting material will usually be too complicated to fit, at a legible font size, onto a standard monitor screen.

However, if the material were to be presented as microtext, or represented with minimal visual elements such as colored dots, then it would be possible to provide simultaneous display of both the tagsets and the collection. If the two forms of display were allowed to interact, then the user would be able to associate documents in the collection with the tags they contain. If the attributes and attribute values were also made available, then the degree of complexity would increase, but so would the potential functionality. Finally, if the user can also provide search criteria, or make use of other features to sort, subset, and group the material, and have those features interact with all the other forms of display, the result is a rich-prospect interface on the entire collection, augmented by some tools that make use of the new opportunities for action provided by having some meaningful representation available. This kind of interface has the potential to allow people insight into the collection, and also to provide them with a variety of new affordances that assist in working with general areas of research interest.

The details of how best to display each kind of material, how to visually represent the interactions among the different kinds, and how to provide tools for generating the interactions are all significant decisions. For any given case, it is going to be necessary to investigate the user community in order to establish the extent to which these prospect-related strategies can work, and also to determine which visual formats are most conducive to people learning and using the system.

One possible strategy is to provide the various displays as separate windows or dialog boxes, which can be opened or closed by the user in much the same way that tool palettes are open or closed in programs related to digital image-making. Another solution may be to provide the user with a set of wizards that break the process into sequential steps. The various strategies are not mutually exclusive, but can coexist in the same interface.

Star Diagrams

In the Orlando project, we chose to use a selective representation of the tagset. Orlando contains biographical and writing histories of over a thousand women writers. Each document is extensively tagged using one of five project document type definitions, which total over 250 tags. In order to expose these tags to the reader, we created a set of topic map diagrams that each present a single focus. In Figure 5.1, for example, we show the "core" tags of the system, which are central to the interpretation of the material that was adopted by the domain experts who created the content.

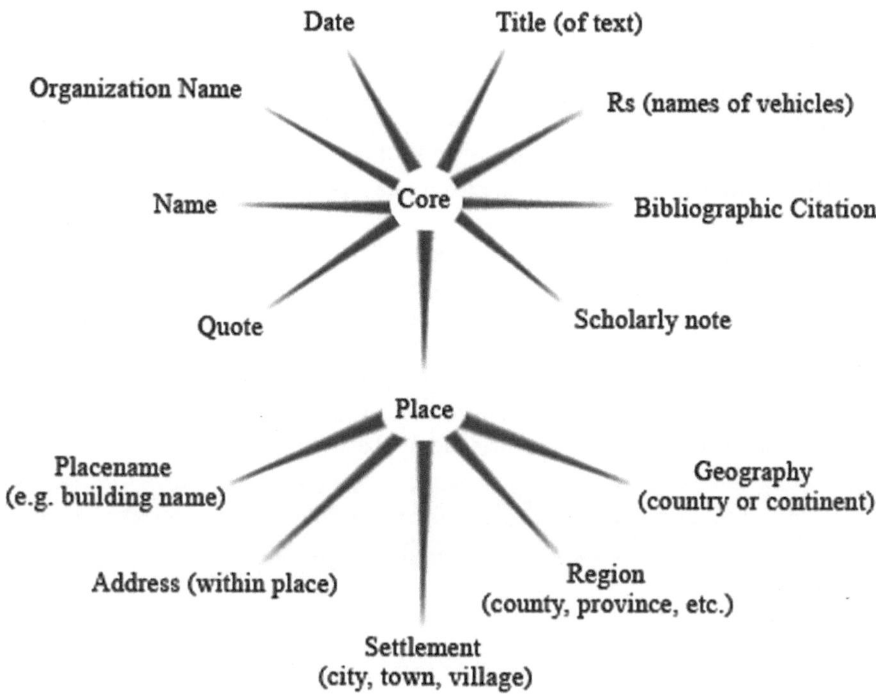

Figure 5.1 The Orlando core tags[1]

The core tag diagram is one of five diagrams that are available in the help system and on the page where people can construct tag-based queries. These represent a relatively small but highly significant portion of the document type definitions (DTDs). The language used in the diagrams is also a translation into English of the more technical-sounding (and concise) tag names; the same translation has been applied to the tags that appear in the picklists of the query pages.

Prospect on Connections

In an area related to tag display, we faced a particularly interesting challenge in the Orlando Six Degrees of Connection project, where the goal was to leverage the tagging of the biocritical documents about the more than 1,200 British women writers to help researchers look for connections between the women. In this case, a connection was defined as co-occurrence within either a woman's document, or

1 The Orlando core tags are shown here in a topic map. Including the second-level tags under <Place>, the diagram represents roughly 5% of the Orlando tags, but this is an important 5% because many of them appear in nearly every document in the system. Design by Stan Ruecker.

else within a single short section inside the document (the choice is available to the user). Connections between women can be constrained in any number of ways by the user, so that only those connections involving some organisational affiliation, for instance, can be selected. Nonetheless, there are roughly 8 million words in the Orlando textbase, and approximately 3 million instances of tagging (Brown et al. 2010), so to display a set of paths from one woman to another often involves dozens of scrolling pages of results.

We approached the problem from two different directions. In the first case (Figure 5.2), we provide a display of the scrolling list of paths, but place a small, interactive prospect panel above the list. The user can select the names in the tagcloud in the panel to filter the items on the results list underneath. In keeping with the rich-prospect browsing principles, each entry is also a link back to the original text passage, so that the entire display becomes a means of selecting accessing additional pieces of the Orlando textbase.

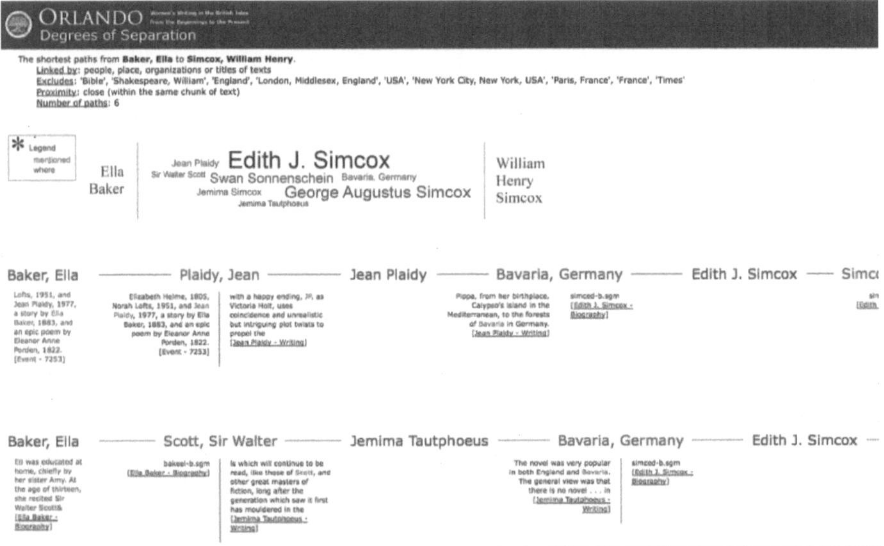

Figure 5.2 The Orlando six degrees prototype[2]

Another version of the Orlando six degrees prototype (Figure 5.3) shows an overview of all links in the system, organised chronologically with a date scrubber on a full prospect strip across the bottom and a main display that shows a kind of bar graph representing the number of links. Clicking one of the bars draws the associated names to that bar, somewhat like a swarm of bees converging on a flower.

2 The Orlando six degrees prototype includes a version where prospect on the role of other women in connecting two women is provided by an interactive tagcloud. Design by Milena Radzikowska.

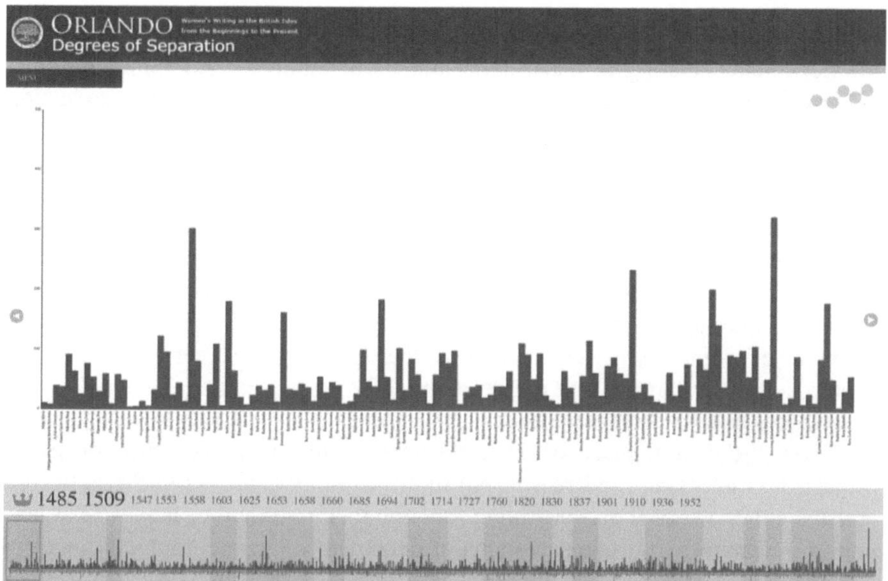

Figure 5.3 Orlando six degrees cityscape[3]

One of the difficulties with the cityscape design is that the names are listed both in a small font and rotated 90 degrees, making them difficult to read. An alternative vertical design has the names listed in normal orientation down the left side. The problem with that approach is that the list of names is even smaller, though perhaps a fisheye display that expands the current location of the mouse, like a magnifying glass, would help navigation in that case.

Names

> The users' interests will have to be brought into contact with our purposes and intentions, the story we want to tell, the emphases we wish to make, the misconceptions (some of a monumental nature) we wish to redress. (Butler 1998)

The names of people figure prominently in most digital collections, and in some cases they are central to the organisation of the material. For example, the primary organising scheme of the Orlando collection is biocritical, with supporting documentation that is historical. The user's focus may involve either of these perspectives, depending on whether the emphasis is on the individual author or the contextual events. It is also possible that the user may shift perspective

3 This cityscape version of the Orlando six degrees prototype provides an overview of all links in the system. Design by Milena Radzikowska.

in the course of a single use of the collection, first examining, for example, the documents relating to a particular author or authors, then following some historical thread from one of the documents out into the larger events collection, spending some time looking into the history, then perhaps returning to the author. The number of possible paths through the collection materials is open to the interests of the individual researcher. The central organising principle of the collection is nonetheless the biocritical material, since it is in the biography and writing documents that the Orlando project is making its principal contribution to literary scholarship. The events are not primarily intended to be new contributions to history, although some of the ones focusing on women's writing or the other activities of women may very well serve that function. In general, however, the events as they currently stand are designed to be contextualising material for the biographies and writing documents.

Given the central place of these document pairs in the organisation of the project, it is necessary and reasonable to allow the user access to the collection through either a search or a browsing function that gives author names as at least one of the meaningful representations of documents. The biography and writing documents were written with the intention that they be treated as texts in their entirety: the user would find an author of interest, call up the full texts of the biography and writing documents, and read through them.

Extending the Rich-Prospect Name Display

Finding a particular author by name can pose some significant challenges. First of all, not every author used a single name during her entire writing career, and some authors used many different names. Even the most common cases of authors with pen names can leave the reader in some doubt as to where to look for material: should someone looking for information on George Eliot, for instance, look under Eliot or under Mary Ann Evans?

As in most projects of this kind, Orlando includes a Standard attribute on the <Name> tag, so that taggers can specify a consistent name throughout the collection. The taggers identify standard names by consulting a Name Authority List for the project, which was developed by the project textbase manager based on the following set of authorities, in order:

i. The Orlando document archive catalog
ii. *The Feminist companion to literature in English: women writers from the Middle Ages to the present*: for women writers
iii. *The Oxford companion to English literature* (5th edn): for male writers
iv. *Dictionary of National Biography*: for British non-writers (except for those with peerage title)
v. British Library Catalogue online
vi. *Everyman's Encyclopedia /Encyclopedia Britannica*

vii. Library of Congress authority files
viii G.E. Cokayne, Complete Peerage
ix. The volume authors (Clements et al. 2006)

Standard names do not have to be attached just to pen names, however. They have also been used for identifying people where the actual text only gives an oblique reference. As a hypothetical example, the text might read "Nancy Mitford's sister was also a writer" and the <Name> tag on "sister" provides the standard name Jessica Mitford, to distinguish her from the three other Mitford sisters who were not writers.

In addition to the <Name> tag, there is also a <personName> tag, which is used at the beginning of each biocritical document to clearly identify the author under discussion. The definition of the Orlando <personName> tag provides for a number of possible subtags, which are listed in the project glossary as follows:

> PersonName is a Div1 content element. It has the following sub-elements to capture specific names:

- surname
- birthname
- professionalTitle
- indexed
- married
- nickname
- pseudonym
- religious
- royal
- selfConstructed
- styled
- titled

(Clements et al. 2006)

These details of tagging practice become significant for the design of an interface that makes the names visible to the user. If the designer wants the rich-prospect display to include not just a single authoritative name for each person, but rather all of the names used for that person throughout the collection, the list becomes fairly complicated. It might include the contents of the <personName> and <Name> tags, their attributes, and their subtags. The result might, therefore, include a list of non-unique identifiers such as "brother," "sister," "mother", and so on.

Avoiding the problem of identifying people by non-unique names is the purpose of using a name authority list in the first place. However, this solution does not accommodate two cases: the situation where a reader is interested in a common name shared by multiple people; and the case where the reader has a particular search target in mind, but has only a vague sense of who the person might be. As a hypothetical example, the user might be thinking "I would like to find a particular woman writer from the Renaissance. All I can remember is that she was the mother of another woman writer, and they both wrote plays." In order to allow for this kind of search, it might be useful to allow the user to see the full display of the contents of all name tags, perhaps including a few words on either side of the tag to provide context, as is done in concordances using the Key Word in Context (KWIC) visualisation. In any case, the display would include a number of non-unique identifiers.

The choice of whether or not it is appropriate to use a particular set of non-unique identifiers rests on how they have been tagged. There are three possible scenarios: they may prove to be too common in the collection to be useful for differentiating items; they may turn out to be too inconsistently applied to be of any real use; or, they may turn out to be both consistently applied and uncommon enough to be of value.

One class of those identifiers which may prove too common to be useful are those relating to families. For example, many of the women discussed in the collection are someone's mother or someone's sister. If the taggers have consistently attached a <Name> tag and standard attribute to uses of the words "mother" and "sister," there may simply be too many of them for the designation to be helpful in differentiating items (although the identifiers may, in this case, prove useful for grouping items). In fact, the tagging has not been applied to every instance of names, but instead to one instance in each logical unit of retrievable text.

In terms of those identifiers which are too inconsistently tagged to be useful, it may turn out to be the case that the taggers have marked with a <Name> tag some, but not many, of the instances of familial roles. If that were the case, then for the few that have been marked, there are two possible states: the identification might be significant, or it might be trivial. The choice of whether or not to draw on such identifiers as components in the interface name display would therefore need to be determined by looking at the actual implementation of the tagging across all the documents, in order to see if some logical system has been applied in the choice of when a familial role should receive a <Name> tag.

In the final class, the non-unique identifiers may prove to be both consistently applied and uncommon enough to be of value. For example, here is a fairly typical <Name> tag from the Orlando biography document of Henrietta Battier: "<NAME STANDARD="Russell, William, Lord">Lord Russell</NAME>" (Clements et al. 2006). As it happens, Lord William Russell lived in the late eighteenth century. But he is identified in the text that the reader sees as "Lord Russell," and William Russell is only one of several Lords Russell that have held the title over the generations. If the name display includes both the <Standard> attribute value and the contents of the tag, there will be both the unique standard name "Lord William Russell" and the non-unique name "Lord Russell." If another of the Lords Russell is mentioned in the collection somewhere, then the link specified by "Lord Russell" would need to point to the references to both people. However, being able to identify all the Lords Russell in the collection at one time may be useful to some researchers.

In summary, a display that results from using some massaged form of the text inside the <Name> and <personName> tags would show more entries than there are documents. That is, there would be a many-to-one relationship between document names and documents. This form of display might help facilitate retrieval by people who are unfamiliar with the variations of naming that might apply to someone they are interested in finding. It might also be useful for people who are looking for groups of names that fall into some recognisable class that would otherwise be difficult to identify.

Providing people with some means of switching the display between one-to-one and many-to-one representations would provide both affordances. For example, a user might be interested in finding all the women in the Orlando biocritical materials who held the title "Lady." For some of these writers, the title may be part of the standard designation. For others, it may appear in the text of a <Name> tag but would not necessarily form part of the standard designation. If the display could be expanded from the form where it shows a one-to-one relationship between document titles and contents to a form where it shows a many-to-one relationship, it might be possible to provide the user with some means to find and group the entries of both kinds. On the other hand, once the reader has identified particular people of interest, switching the display back to one-to-one would reduce the complexity at the point when it is no longer required.

In its optimum form, the system would provide the user with a means of changing the display among its three or four potential forms, with the default display being the one that shows one meaningful representation per document (or, in the case of Orlando, one meaningful representation per document pair). The choices would be:

- show standard author name only (one per document)
- show all possible forms of author names (likely more than one per document)
- show all possible author names and oblique references (perhaps several per document)
- show all possible author names and oblique references in context (concordance style)

A dialog of this kind could be designed to apply either to the entire display or to some pre-selected subset.

Dates

In addition to the names of people, most digital collections include date information, which can sometimes be very complex. The TEI P5 <date> tag definition (www.

tei-c.org/release/doc/tei-p5-doc/en/html/ref-date.html) is accordingly flexible, with 28 possible attributes. The potential affordances related to dates include searching, grouping, and arranging chronologically. In some cases, providing the user with the ability to extract and chronologically arrange materials is a central feature of the collection.

For example, the Orlando Project placed an emphasis on tagging material so that it could be arranged chronologically: "As perhaps the most vital tool for relating historical events and processes to each other, and to the over-arching narrative, we have chosen chronology" (Grundy et al. 2000). This decision has had far-reaching consequences, both for the tagset and for the tagging on the project, because in order to make chronologies available to the reader, it is necessary to attach dates wherever possible. The tags used in Orlando are <Date>, <DateRange>, and <DateStruct>. Dates are, however, only important insofar as they are associated with a block of text. The tag that creates this association in the Orlando Project is <ChronStruct>.

<ChronStruct> is in some senses a fundamental building block of the Orlando tagsets. It occurs in the events tagset as <ChronEvent>, but the purpose of the tags is similar in that both the <ChronStruct> and the <ChronEvent> hold together a date, some tagged text, and the bibliographical references associated with the text. To simplify the following discussion, the term <ChronStruct> will therefore be used to signify both tags.

As far as the user reading the collection contents is concerned, the <ChronStruct> itself is a container: it does not directly contain any text (direct child nodes of non-whitespace text). Instead, it contains subtags that contain text. It also contains attributes that are useful in displaying material that has been extracted from the collection to be displayed in chronologies.

The following <ChronStruct> occurs in the biography of Mary Somerville, a Scottish mathematician and scientist who lived from 1780 to 1872:

> <CHRONSTRUCT RELEVANCE="SELECTIVE" CHRONCOLUMN="BRITISHWOMENWRITERS" RESP="CJH"> <DATESTRUCT VALUE="1825–06-"> <SEASON> Summer</SEASON> <YEAR> 1825</YEAR> </DATESTRUCT> <CHRONPROSE> MS undertook her first scientific investigation: she designed and conducted a number of experiments to determine the effect of light on magnetism.</CHRONPROSE> <BIBCIT PLACEHOLDER="Patterson, Mary Fairfax, 213" DBREF="7510"> 213</BIBCIT> </CHRONSTRUCT> (Clements et al. 2006)

From the reader's perspective, the experiment occurred in the summer of 1825. From the perspective of the Value attribute on the <DateStruct>, the experiment occurred in June of 1825, which would allow the system to sort this <ChronStruct> to appear in a chronology at the beginning of the summer.

The following instructions to taggers emphasise the nature of <ChronStruct> as an extractable unit:

> Because chronStructs may be removed from the documents in which they were created and be placed alongside unrelated information, always make sure that you put enough information in a chronStruct such that it will make sense when read out of context. Make sure that any important names, dates, places, or orgNames are tagged inside a chronStruct. Also, do not use pronouns in a chronStruct unless their referent is also present. (Clements et al. 2006)

Dates and Chronologies

It is seldom a simple matter to provide accurate dates for every piece of significant information. Our example Orlando project materials cover centuries of women's writing and historical events. Some of this material could be associated with a single day that is part of the historical record, while in other cases the events might have taken place on a single day, but the recorded account does not provide an accurate indication of which day that might be. In other cases, the events span a range of time, the endpoints of which might be very precise (marked, for example, by the signing of a treaty or the publication of an article in a daily newspaper) or only approximate, or there may be a range that only contains a start date (for example, "By 1900 women accounted for twelve percent of the library staff in Britain whereas in America ninety-five percent of library staff were women" (Grundy et al. 2000)).

Each of the possible date configurations has implications for the way the system is going to construct and arrange chronologies. For example, if a <ChronStruct> specifies the month "May," the algorithm could sort that piece of text anywhere in the month – to the beginning, middle, or end. In the case of a month, the position is not particularly critical in terms of accuracy, but if the date specifies only a year, there is some considerable difference between the beginning and end of a year, and even more difference in the case of a decade or a century.

If the <ChronStruct> explicitly includes a date range, there is a similar problem of deciding how to position the material. The default solution is to use the earliest date in the range, but in cases where a number of other <ChronStructs> are also visible, the reader can lose track of the number of texts that should be understood as occurring during the same period. Chronological searches on Orlando currently sort in the following order:

- year-only dates
- year/month dates
- year/month/day dates

A given year may have few or many <ChronStructs>; 1621, for example, currently has 15 items in its full chronology, while 1921 has 70 year-only dates and 62 others that are either year/month or year/month/day – an order of magnitude difference (Grundy et al. 2000).

Complications involving date accuracy and format are, however, not the only complications in the Orlando tagset and its use of dates.

<Date: Certainty>

In addition to the accuracy with which a date or date range can be specified, there are also indications of how the user is to interpret the degree to which the date is reliable. Since much of the Orlando material is derived from historical sources, there is a range of certainty involved both in the original materials and in the reliability of the reporting. For example, someone remembering an event from 20 years past will usually be less accurate to the day than someone recording an event that happened only yesterday. Some sources are also more consistently reliable than others.

The tags relating to dates in the Orlando Project are therefore equipped with the attribute "Certainty," which provides the tagger with the facility to indicate the reliability of each date. In the case of <DateRange>, there are separate Certainty attributes for both the "From" and "To" parts of the equation. The predefined values of the Certainty attribute are: By, Cert (certain), C (circa), Roughly Dated, and After.

Displaying <Date: Certainty>

These values represent an interesting challenge in terms of interface design, since although they are all relevant attribute values for Certainty, they are not syntactically nor semantically in the same class with each other. The user who wishes to understand and use the Certainty attribute values is therefore required to make a different mental adjustment for each of them. Three of the values – Cert, C, and Roughly Dated – might be visualised as concentric circles around a point in time. Appropriate synonyms for these values might be, respectively: confident, approximate, and rough estimate. The other two values – By and After – might be visualised respectively as a line with an endpoint and a starting point with a line.

The Certainty attribute is important not only because it provides significant information about each date, but also because it provides an example of an attribute whose values could be used to structure the display through either grouping or subsetting the items.

Displaying Chronologies

Various strategies exist for displaying chronological material. Some of these have been developed for print and repurposed for electronic media, while others are primarily electronic both in origin and use. These strategies include:

- timelines
- timefields

- scattergrams
- sequential prospect
- rich prospect

Timelines

The standard technology for displaying chronological material is the historical timeline, where a directed horizontal line is used to indicate sequence in time, and individual events are indicated either through parallel lines that represent duration, or through perpendicular lines that represent punctive events. Either may be labelled with a brief descriptive text. Explanatory material, usually quite brief for reasons of conserving space, is also sometimes available, as are images that can serve to provide additional information and may also help to orient the viewer.

Timelines have a long history as a print technology, and their repurposing for digital displays can draw on the existing visual vocabulary. Additional factors come into play, however, since digital timelines can be generated by the user or automatically by the system, rather than exclusively by the designer. Issues of selection and preference and visual weight that would normally have been under the control of the designer therefore become available as options for the reader. In cases where the timelines can be stored as a form of interaction history, the reader also has the opportunity to communicate with subsequent readers. The use of interactive timelines to convey insights into chronological materials is one of the most exciting areas of possible future research on interaction histories in collections like Orlando.

Timelines are exciting in part because they are a form of visual narrative that is relatively accessible to everyone. Their primary constraints, especially when designed for use on a monitor, are their size and complexity. It is difficult to fit much information on a horizontal strip that will sit within the margins of a browser.

One solution is therefore to provide the user with a magnification strategy, so the timeline can be scaled, either through the addition or removal of secondary events, or else through physically changing the size of the display through some process of magnification or its reverse.

Timefields

Another recent development in the use of electronic timelines is their application to the display of temporal modeling, where individual perspectives are central to the concept of what constitutes the information on a timeline. As a consequence, the timeline needs to accommodate conflicting witnesses, and alternative outcomes need to be shown as modifications to the timeline (Drucker and Nowviskie 2003). In the Catastrophic Nowslider Demo, the user chooses points on a timeslider that represent the current state of information available to the heroine of a narrative. As the information point shifts, so does the temporal model.

Based on the temporal modeling project, we are currently in the process of creating the next generation of prototypes for people working with time-based material. Our current design, called Timefields, provides a space-time continuum for each person or group, where each sheet or field is composed of events that not only create the field, but also distort it in ways that can have echoes in other nearby fields. For example, an event for one person may have a duration of several months, while for another person the impact of that event is on a single moment in time. Different people may also not share the same perspective on the significance or impact of events, or even agree on the order or timing of events.

Scattergrams

Another means of providing prospect on a chronology is to create a plot of points, each of which represents a single entry or event in the chronology. The distribution of points along the horizontal axis indicates how many events occur in the collection at each time.

Like timelines, scattergrams can be used at various scales, with the display collapsing individual points into aggregate points as the timescale increases. Alternatively, the number of points can remain fixed but the vertical size of the scattergram can increase as the horizontal scale decreases, in order to accommodate increased stacking of the event points.

As a means of accessing a collection, a scattergram can be used to select subsets of events inside a range set by the user. The texts represented by the points can then be collected into a subsequent display for further refinement, perhaps through first changing their representation, as is done by Manovich (2009), into some form that is more meaningful than a point. Alternatively, the selected points can be used directly as a collection of items to expand for reading.

Scattergrams have an advantage over rich-prospect displays showing more elaborate representations of items, that they are relatively compact, and, as with rich-prospect displays, if the relationship is one-to-one between points and collection entries, the display can give the user some sense of the structure of the collection in terms of the amount of material available for each period in the chronology. However, scattergrams have the disadvantage that the points themselves are not intrinsically meaningful.

Some meaning can be applied to the individual points, primarily through color coding, since the single pixels are not amenable to differentiation by shape. However, if the scattergram is implemented in such a way that the user can magnify it, then there is the possibility of having the individual points expand into larger representations that could be meaningful, either through shape or labeling. As the scattergram has been magnified, it will become less compact, but will transform into what is essentially another rich-prospect display.

Sequential prospect

Having all of the items on display at one time inevitably requires the use of strategies to accommodate the limited screen real estate. A method that sidesteps this necessity is to have some form of sequential prospect, where the user is able to scan through a representation of the collection items by viewing them one at a time in quick succession. The coverflow displays created by Enright and del Strother, and used since 2006 on various Apple products, are one form of sequential prospect.

Another example is the range slider developed by Ahlberg and Shneiderman (1994a), which allows the user to move a horizontal thumb in order to view a lengthy list of entries. The technical obstacle to be overcome in the use of sequential prospect sliders is that for fairly large collections, the position of the thumb on the bar itself is not an appropriate means of setting the location in the collection, since the length of the bar would need to extend well beyond the sides of the screen. The suggested alternative approximates the position of the thumb but with a much finer level of granularity, by using the position of the mouse to determine which item to display. Since the mouse movement can be coupled fairly loosely to the thumb movement, even a fairly small slider can be used to traverse collections numbering in the tens of thousands of items.

In the case of a text collection like Orlando, such a device might be used to provide prospect on several different kinds of information. For instance, a pair of sliders might be used to display on one hand the list of tags in the tagset, and on the other hand a matched list of all texts found in the tag. An alternative pair of sliders could be used to show respectively all available tag attributes and their attribute values. A slider could also be used to display all of the names in the collection, all of the dates in the collection, or all of the documents in the collection.

Sequential prospect has the strong advantage of not requiring excessive amounts of screen space while still providing the user with some means of looking directly at collection contents, tagsets, and so on. If the sliders are also amenable to different kinds of sorting, then the user would have the opportunity to determine the order in which the items are going to appear. For example, the same slider might be used to show the names of the authors receiving biocritical treatment, first in alphabetical order, then in chronological order by date of birth. Additional indexical cues might be added in support of each kind of sorting, so that for example if the slider is horizontal and the name appears above it, then the letter of the alphabet or relevant date might simultaneously appear beneath the slider.

Rich prospect on chronologies

In order for an interface to have a rich-prospect form of display for chronological data, it is necessary to show some meaningful representation of every chronological item, either within the entire collection or within the current date range of interest. Chronological items are generally quite brief, consisting largely of single sentences or short paragraphs. One solution is therefore to provide chronological material as a complete listing of <ChronStruct> contents.

The disadvantage of using the entire entries is that even single sentences can quickly fill the available screen space, especially when it is necessary to provide additional line spacing between items to indicate that they are not part of the same entry. In order to take maximum advantage of the available screen area, it is therefore preferable to find some means of representing chronological events in an abbreviated form.

A basic strategy would be to represent the items in a chronology as dates. However, the meaning inherent in a date is only a small part of the event. In cases where the events occur simultaneously or in quick succession, the dates may either need to be refined to an unreasonable degree in order to distinguish the events, or else a single date may have to be used to access multiple events.

In order to provide more information about the events and to avoid the one-to-many relationship between interface items and chronological events, it would therefore be more useful to create a display representation that included both the date and a brief keyword, phrase, or title to label the event. If the keywords are not unique, then they would be useful in grouping or subsetting a larger display into sections related to various topics of potential interest to the reader. For example, the keyword "suffrage" might be associated with events in the Orlando Project relating to the securing of votes for women.

However, once the items marked "suffrage" are grouped or extracted as a subset, it is no longer useful to mark them with that non-unique keyword, because every item in the display would use the same word. For purposes of distinguishing between items in the same group, it would be useful to provide a second, unique keyword or phrase which could be used to replace or supplement the non-unique keyword and date. Since the point of creating the representation of items is to save screen space, substituting the unique keyword for the non-unique one may be the best option, with the non-unique keyword perhaps being moved to a position that indicates that it applies to the entire group or subset of representations.

The disadvantage of keywords is that they are labor-intensive to apply and maintain, since each event must be keyworded at both the unique and non-unique levels. The list of keywords also needs to be established in such a way that changes are kept to a minimum, since the addition of new keywords would require that someone review previously keyworded events in order to see if the new keyword also applies.

Attaching a keyword is also an act of interpretation that is analogous to the interpretation involved in attaching textual markup. One solution is therefore to apply as many keywords as possible. However, if the purpose of keywords is to simplify the display, then a long list of keywords is not going to be any more useful than a descriptive phrase might be, since both involve several words to describe a single event.

Since many of the events in the Orlando Project relate to historical activities of people or organisations, one possible strategy would be to use the existing tagging to generate descriptive text for representing the items. The representation would then consist of a date, the contents or standard attribute contents of one of the other core tags such as <name>, <place>, or <orgname> (which would be in most cases non-unique), and a tag selected from a list of potentially relevant ones. For example, one event might be described as date, name, and a tag relating to life stages: 1879, Annie Kenney, birth. Another event might be displayed as date, place, and a tag relating to historical activity: 18 June 1815, Waterloo, battle.

Using the existing tagging to generate representations has the advantage that it can be automated and does not rely on the maintenance of keyword lists and their application. However, there may be cases where the algorithms for selection are not going to result in meaningful text that genuinely represents the major contents of events. Further research in this area would be useful.

<ChronStruct: Relevance>

In order to provide an idea of how important an individual event was in the grand scheme of history, the <ChronStruct> tag includes an attribute for relevance. The relevance attribute has four possible values: Selective, Period, Decade, and Comprehensive. They are in increasing order of magnitude of results. The system is designed in such a way that searching for <ChronStruct: Relevance: Period> will actually return not just the Period items, but also the <ChronStruct> paragraphs that were marked with <ChronStruct: Relevance: Selective>. Similar treatment is given to each of the subsequent attribute values, so that searching, for example, for <ChronStruct: Relevance: Comprehensive> will return all <ChronStruct>s.

In addition to the relative scale, the semantics of the attribute values are also significant. The first value – Selective – is used to mark only those items which the project personnel consider essential to a basic chronology. The paragraphs describing landmark events in an author's life, such as birth, death, and major writing or publishing activities (such as first and last publication, or publication of the most famous works), are all marked with <ChronStruct: Relevance: Selective>. If the user searches the collection for a particular author and constrains the search for only the selective ChronStructs, the result will be a brief sketch of the highlights of the author's life and writing career, along with major contemporaneous world events.

The next value – Period – is used for material that might be appropriate for a standard undergraduate university course, as for example a course in Renaissance literature. Period also indicates material that falls within identifiable historical eras that are not necessarily equivalent to the ones usually applied to literary studies. For example, if a user were interested in writing activities during the War of the Roses, the Period attribute would be appropriate.

The third possible attribute value for <ChronStruct: Relevance> is Decade, which is used to locate details surrounding a particular historical event or relatively short span of time. For example, while a user interested in women's suffrage would likely want to search for Relevance: Period, a user interested in the first incarceration of suffragists such as Millicent Garrett Fawcett might prefer to search using Relevance: Decade.

The final possible value for <ChronStruct: Relevance> is Comprehensive, which is used to mark material that is significant in the biography or writing career of an author, but which is not necessarily of historical importance.

The <ChronStruct: Relevance> attribute and its four possible values are significant because they will constrain the results that the user can expect to obtain from a given date search. However, the details of how they have been defined and implemented represent a potential obstacle to the user, which is exacerbated by the fact there is no standard terminology available to indicate what the attribute values signify.

Displaying <ChronStruct: Relevance>

The attributes on <ChronStruct: Relevance> will determine the size of the set returned to the user by a chronology search; it is therefore necessary that the user be able to specify which of the four options are appropriate for a given search. Our default solution in the published interface has been to provide the user with a set of radio buttons, which are a standard GUI method of allowing mutually exclusive choices.

However, a radio button choice on a search screen constrains the user to one selection at a time, which indicates that the values are mutually exclusive. Since this is not the case, even though a set of radio buttons could be repurposed to provide the user with the correct result, the meaning of the selection tool is fundamentally misleading.

Another standard selection tool is the set of check boxes. Check boxes allow the user to have multiple simultaneous selections. In an interface that does not specify how the multiple choices are to be combined by the search engine, the selection is ambiguous. On the one hand, choosing more than one item might mean that they all need to be present in the result (a logical AND). On the other hand, choosing more than one item might mean that any one of them should be present, but that it is not necessarily for them all to be present (a logical OR). A third logical possibility is even more difficult to communicate – this is the logical XOR, or the case where one or the other but not both items should be present in the search results.

Check boxes also do not indicate to the user that the values themselves are additive: instead, they are assumed to be distinct from each other. The difference between a radio button and a check box is simply that the radio buttons only allow one choice at a time, while the check boxes allow multiple choices. The visual syntax of the two devices therefore indicates that the one has a constraint that the other does not have.

In the case of a selection mechanism for the interface to a search engine, another possibility would be to use a slider that moves between the anchors "selective" and "comprehensive." However, like radio buttons and check boxes, sliders have an enculturated semantics – in this case, one that suggests a continuum. Since the values available for <ChronStruct: Relevance> consist of four discrete possibilities, a slider sends the wrong message to the user.

It is possible, however, to develop prospect-related solutions for providing the user with the necessary functionality, without requiring that the user understand the <ChronStruct: Relevance> attribute values.

The key point to be made with respect to <ChronStruct: Relevance> is that the values are additive. In order for the interface to indicate to the user the proper relation between the values, it is therefore useful to consider alternatives that are also additive.

The <ChronStruct: Relevance> attribute values may therefore be a case where the existing interface options are not appropriate. What is required is that the user understand that selecting each of the available values in turn would generate an expanding set of results, with the fewest results occurring at "selective" and the most results at "comprehensive" (given that other search criteria remain constant).

One appropriate solution would therefore be to show the choices as a set of nested buttons, with "selective" in the center and "comprehensive" as the label on the largest button. Constraining the buttons so that the inner ones are automatically selected when the user chooses an outer one makes the choice clear, even when the choices are available only as part of a search interface.[4]

With an additive selection mechanism, the user will know that choosing <ChronStruct: Relevance: Period> will provide more results than choosing <ChronStruct: Relevance: Selective>, but there is no indication of how many results there may be in either case.

If, however, the interface involved is one where a rich-prospect version of the tagging in the collection is available, the display of an additive grouping of tags makes the understanding of the Relevance values intuitively available to the user. The names of the relevance attributes are not essential to the display.

<ChronStruct: ChronColumn>

Like Relevance, ChronColumn is an essential attribute for users of the Orlando Project interested in retrieving, viewing, and otherwise working with material arranged in chronological order. Also like Relevance, the ChronColumn attribute has four possible values, which in this case are: British Women's Writing; Writing Climate; Social Climate; and National International. However, unlike the additive attribute values for Relevance, the ChronColumn values are used to mark information that is mutually exclusive. That is, for example, a <ChronStruct: ChronColumn: British Women's Writing> is not a subset of a <ChronStruct: ChronColumn: Social Climate>: the attribute values are used to distinguish between different kinds of material:

---

4 It is interesting to note that this solution was developed independently by different members of the Orlando delivery team. However, in prototyping and user testing, it was found by the study participants to be too confusing – in part because the concept of an additive control of any kind is unfamiliar to most people.

- The majority of the ChronStructs in the collection are about British Women Writers.
- Writing Climate marks equivalent material for male writers and women writers who are not British. It also marks anything else related to the literary industry.
- Social Climate, on the other hand, is the attribute value used to signify information on topics of historical interest which are outside the bounds of the literary. Events dealing with science, law, fashion, and so on would all be marked with Social Climate.
- Finally, National International is the attribute value for events related to areas such as military or political history.

The following text, a ChronStruct from the writing document of Christabel Pankhurst, is an example of a passage that has been marked with the ChronColumn attribute "British Women's Writing."

> 15 October 1908 CP gave a speech at the St James's Hall titled The Militant Methods of the N.W.S.P.U., which was published verbatim by The Woman's Press the same year. (Clements et al. 2006)

Here is the identical passage, with all of its tags visible:

> <CHRONSTRUCT RESP="KDC" CHRONCOLUMN="BRITISHWOMENW RITERS" RELEVANCE="SELECTIVE"> <DATE> 15 October 1908</DATE> <CHRONPROSE> CP gave a speech at the <PLACE> <PLACENAME> St James's Hall</PLACENAME> <SETTLEMENT REG="London"> </ SETTLEMENT></PLACE>titled<TITLETITLETYPE="MONOGRAPHIC"> The Militant Methods of the <ORGNAME STANDARD="Women's Social and Political Union"> N.W.S.P.U.</ORGNAME> </TITLE>, which was published verbatim by The <ORGNAME> Woman's Press</ORGNAME> the same year.</ CHRONPROSE> <BIBCIT PLACEHOLDER="Pankhurst, Militant Methods 34" DBREF="7998"> 34</BIBCIT> <BIBCIT PLACEHOLDER="OCLC" DBREF="1709"> </BIBCIT> </CHRONSTRUCT> (Clements et al. 2006)

A user interested in working with an events chronology might wish to combine results from any of the four possible ChronColumn values, or select a single value as the focus of attention. The Project focus is emphasised by the default chronological sort, which puts British Women Writer events at the top of any list of events that share the same date.

Displaying <ChronStruct: ChronColumn>

In order to facilitate searching for any combination of ChronColumn values, the standard interface tool that is most appropriate is a set of checkboxes, so that the values can be mixed and matched. The default setting for the checkboxes could either be to return just the British Women Writer ChronStructs, or else all the ChronStructs, depending on the preference of the collection designers. Since checkboxes are familiar to GUI users in general, as long as the interface shows the set of checkboxes, the user is able to modify the selection before running the search.

From the perspective of prospect, indicating which of the four ChronColumn attribute values has been applied to each of the items showing in a display is somewhat problematic. There are two basic classes of solution. The first, which is the one that has been implemented in the published textbase, involves associating the individual meaningful representations of items with some characteristic that indicates the ChronColumn attribute value. The second involves organising the display in such a way that items with the same ChronColumn values are visually grouped together.

Attaching Visual Cues to Individual Items

In the first category, possible solutions include the use of icons or text. Either of these elements could be further differentiated through secondary visual attributes such as the application of color. In the case of fonts, morphological changes could also be applied, consisting either of different fonts or different styles of the same font (for example, bold, italic, oblique).

The chosen strategy was to use an iconic representation of each of the values, and attach the icon to each element in the display. The result is that, in some cases, there can be a considerable degree of repetition of the same icons, since there may be hundreds or even thousands of items on display, each of which shares the same ChronColumn value. Another potential problem with icons is that their meaning is not always simple to establish, especially in the case of relatively complicated terms such as the ChronColumn values.

If the choice were to use text labels, similar problems may arise in terms of repetition and possible misinterpretation of meaning. Text may also require more screen real estate than icons.

Color-coding also presents several difficulties. First of all, the use of four different colors could pose problems for some readers, who may find some of the colors less congenial than others. There is also the problem that color is not in itself intrinsically meaningful, so that the user who has difficulty in associating meaning with an icon or a text label may find color-coding even more difficult to interpret or remember. Since many people only have access to printing in black and white, there is the added logistical problem that printouts might not preserve the color distinction. Finally, there is the problem that some percentage of the population is going to have difficulty with any system that relies heavily on distinctions based on color, because they are not able to perceive the colors distinctly, or in some cases, at all. The principle of inclusive design suggests that these people should wherever possible not require specialised equipment or strategies, but should be accommodated in the original design.

Font and other morphological variations share many of the problems associated with color: fonts are not intrinsically meaningful, which adds an arbitrary memory demand on the user. A display using four fonts or font styles simultaneously may also be unattractive or difficult to read.

Grouping Items

Grouping the items according to ChronColumn, on the other hand, can be more or less effective depending on the details of how the groups are arranged. For example, if each ChronColumn value were to be assigned to a column in a 4-column table, the result would be a fairly clear indication of which texts belonged to which value. However, the resulting four columns would each consist of relatively small horizontal portions of a standard monitor, making reading difficult and potentially irritating, especially in cases where screen space was lost to one or two entries in one column when another column extended to dozens.

A possible solution to the screen allocation problem in a tabular display would be to make the columns readily collapsible and expandable, so the user could choose whether to view them in parallel or to view each of them in turn. If some indications were also available to suggest which column belonged to which value, and perhaps also to suggest how many items were in each column, the display using columns might be relatively simple and intuitive to use.

Chapter 6
The Design of New Interface Tools

One of the primary problems with any rich-prospect interface is that to show so much information at one time is to risk overwhelming the user. Designers working on interfaces based on rich prospect therefore have to pay special attention to strategies for eliminating the sense of being overwhelmed by the display. As discussed in previous chapters, the main strategies are to ensure that the individual items are represented in a meaningful way, that the tools for manipulating the organisation of those items are readily identified, and that the principle of organisation makes immediate sense.

Methods that aren't Rich Prospect: Hierarchies and Taxonomies

Categorising information according to meta-schema criteria, while not providing rich prospect, does provide partial prospect and has been widely implemented; meta-schema allows users who are familiar with the system to traverse the collection efficiently from the top of the hierarchy, where the categories are large, to lower down, where there are more details. Well-known schemas include the Library of Congress subject headings and the biological taxonomy of Linnaeus.

The problem with having the user traverse a hierarchy, indexing system, or other taxonomy is that the information is effectively hidden behind the meta-schema. For people who are not familiar with the taxonomy or who do not ascribe to the presuppositions under which it has been constructed, the system can become a barrier rather than a tool, especially since items can usually only occupy one position at a time in a hierarchy. An example is the problem faced by academics in the late twentieth century working in Queer studies, who were interested in the history of sexuality, and in particular the issues of construction of gender and the development of the concepts of gay and lesbian, and their expression in literature and culture. The standard library cataloguing systems did not include the keywords "gay," "lesbian," or "queer" and it was therefore necessary for scholars in this field to attempt to identify appropriate texts by formulating alternative queries using the keywords that were available.

An alternative to accessing information through a hierarchical taxonomy is the application of facet analytical theory, where the content domain is divided into logical categories that are mutually exclusive. These categories can then be synthetically joined to form composite representations of each item in a collection related to that domain (Maple 1995). Examples include Flamenco, from researchers at Berkeley, and the Blacklight system from the University of Virginia.

Several methods of addressing these problems have also been developed using automated indexing systems; latent semantic indexing is one such strategy where concepts are formed by analysing the relationships between documents and the terms they contain. Another solution is to attempt to profile documents by statistical methods. N-grams, for example, which are based on counts of fixed-length sub-strings in a document (such as trigrams that consist of three words), have sometimes been used as an entirely automated system of indexing documents without any need to address the semantics (Liu et al. 2000).

Algorithmic Processes

It is therefore possible to design a system where a prospect view allows people to get an overview of a document or documents, while the tools produce emergent patterns superimposed on that overview based on the results of algorithmic processes, rather than predefined metadata. Bubblelines and Knots are examples of this approach, and we have a third design, also by Carlos Fiorentino, which is intended for people exploring patterns of repetition (Ruecker et al. 2008). Called "dialR for Repetition" (Figure 6.1), the prototype represents the document as a volumetric space, occupied by semi-transparent sheets full of text.

The user navigates the text by scrolling the space backward and forward. The main functionality of the system, however, is provided by the radar screens, which are used to capture repeated phrases (n-grams) in the document. The user enters a search term, and the system provides a list of n-grams containing that search term. It also plots the repetitions as colored rectangles superimposed on the text on the transparent sheets. Clicking on any of these sections in the text calls them up in a reading panel on the right.

One of the features that is significant here is that the n-grams that result from the search can be more or less sophisticated, depending on the quality of the algorithms used under the hood. For example, can the system identify only those n-grams that are exact lexical matches, or is it possible to match lemmatised forms (where words such as *run* and *ran* are counted together)? Do the words need to be in the same order? Can the user ask for parts of speech instead of specific words, so that it is possible to look for patterns, for instance, that use multiple adjectives? Does the system allow for a slop factor where a defined number of words can intervene within matched forms?

Each of the radar screens is in a sense also a rich-prospect display, where the screen can be thought of as a coil of rolled-up paper consisting of the entire string of text, turned sideways on to the viewer. The location of the search results on the radar screen therefore correspond to their location in the text. Finally, there are as many radar screens created as there are search terms, which allows the user of the system to keep track of multiple topics at the same time. The radars and the text highlights are color coded to make the connection between them as clear as possible.

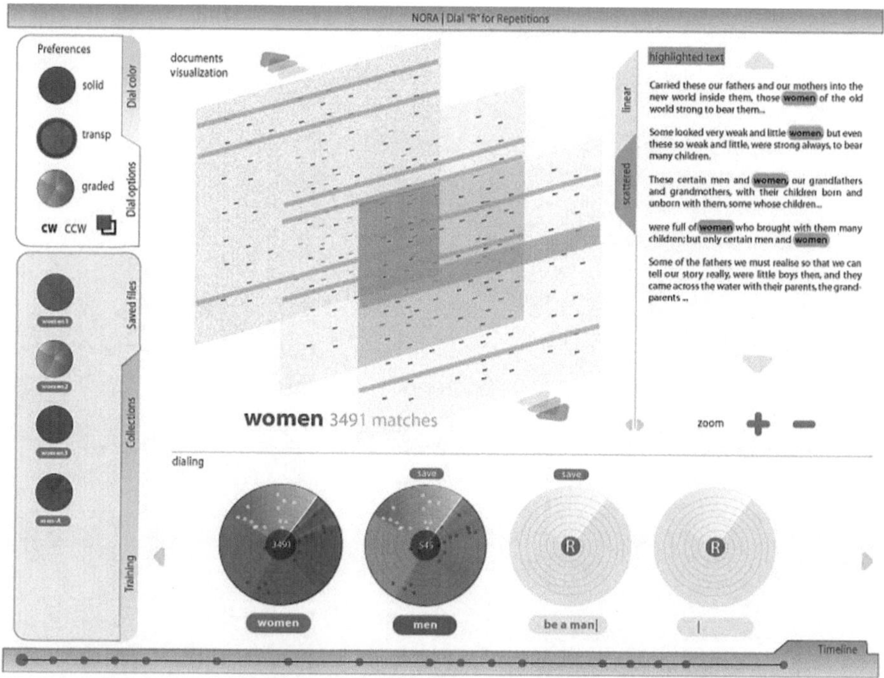

Figure 6.1 The dialR Prototype[1]

On the subject of automatically generated metadata, we took a somewhat interesting turn with the next project, which we called the Magic Circle (Figure 6.2).

Originally, we had been working with the problem of visually contextualising text analysis results for a single document within the collection that contained it. In particular, we were looking at the use of methods such as TF*IDF (a measure of how important a term is within a given document) or Dunning's Log Likelihood Ratio (a measure of how significant observed frequencies are between documents) to provide literary scholars with a quick snapshot of the characteristic vocabulary within one document against a background of similar documents. For example, a person might be interested in seeing what words appear at significantly lower or higher rates in *King Lear* as opposed to the other 10 Shakespearean tragedies.

With the Magic Circle, the score for a particular word in the single document (for example, Lear) could be placed in the center of a set of rings and wedges that presented scores for the same word within the background collection (for example, the other tragedies). We could then use the complexity of the rings and wedges to show different aspects of the collection, organising it, for instance, by size or date or author or whatever other collection-level metadata available.

1 The dialR Prototype displays the document not as a set of pages, but as a volume of space filled with semi-transparent sheets of text. Design by Carlos Fiorentino.

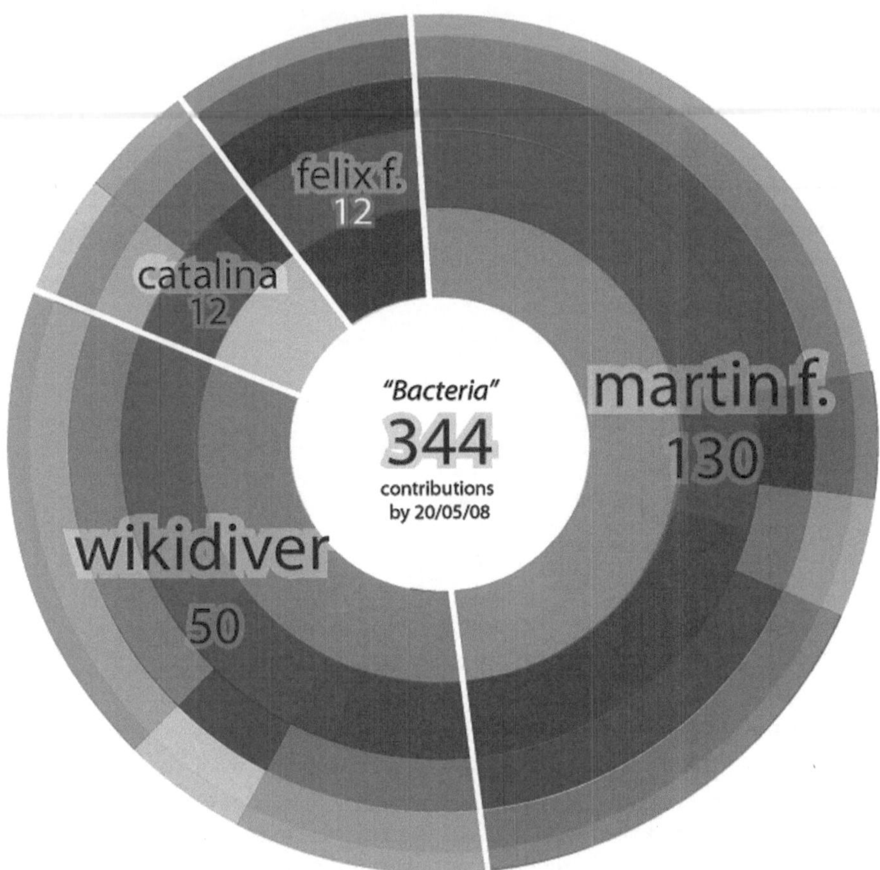

Figure 6.2 The Magic Circle[2]

As events transpired, however, we have yet to implement the Magic Circle in this context. Instead, we joined forces with another project (Stroulia and Arazy 2007) that was proposing authorship measures for wiki contributors. The idea is that authorship for wikis in general is more or less anonymous. It is possible to go and look at the revision history for any given page on a wiki, but that information is not foregrounded. However, in certain environments, such as for classroom assignments, or in business, or for research teams, it could conceivably be useful to know the relative contributions of different authors.

In this context, the Magic Circle becomes a visual measure of relative contribution, with the total score for contributions to a given page appearing in the middle, and the scores for individual authors placed on the wedges. The

2 The Magic Circle shows the relative contributions of wiki editors. Design by Carlos Fiorentino.

Figure 6.3 Sunword[3]

rings represent the different components of the score, with separate measures for additions, deletions, proofreading, structural changes, and changes to links.

However, for this particular transfer of the design, we have the unusual factor of wanting to avoid making it easy for people to "game" the system. That is, it should be obvious that the visualisation represents a combination of a total score for everyone, individual scores for each author, and the components of each author's score. The visualisation should not represent the algorithms so straightforwardly that people could easily raise their scores without actually making a significant contribution to the wiki. We did not, for instance, provide a link to the equations.

In our user study for this design (Arazy et al. 2010), we produced four variations, placed them next to the text of a wiki page, and printed them out. We used printed sketches because the prototype wasn't working yet at the time of the study. Then we recruited 10 participants – half from students who had used wikis for a classroom assignment, and half from people who had participated on research teams that use wikis. We were primarily interested in this study with the potential effects of having these kinds of visualisations present on the wiki page for anyone to see. We thought it might help motivate people to contribute, and that seemed to be how the participants responded to the sketches, although there were also several expressions of nervousness around the value of competition in what is after all essentially a collaborative working environment.

In the resulting prototype, we implemented a fifth design based on what we had learned, and we set it on a separate page rather than embedding it to the side

3 Sunword provides a summary overview of relative wiki contributions, as in the Magic Circle, only in this case none of the details are available. Design by Carlos Fiorentino.

of the working page. We also included the scores table so that people who were interested in studying the details of the algorithms had that information available.

One of the design alternatives to the Magic Circle, also by Carlos Fiorentino, is called Sunword (Figure 6.3).

Sunword provides what is essentially a tagcloud view of author names in the context of collaborative wiki work. The names are placed around a central number that is the aggregate score for the entire page, with the size of the names corresponding roughly to the relative contributions, which are shown as numbers placed beside each name.

We also have in this prototype a number of unexploited visual possibilities. The color-coding has not been used for anything, although it would be possible to use it to convey, for instance, which authors have contributed most recently, by having the colors fade with time. We have similarly made no particular use of the organisation around the perimeter, which could be set alphabetically, or by relative contribution, in which case the names would in some cases, where the scores were similar, form a lopsided circle, while in other cases, where the scores varied uniformly, we would end up with a spiral shape.

It is also possible, of course, for an existing hierarchy or classification system to be implemented as a visual component of an interface. A common strategy along these lines is to provide 26 links that each represents a letter of the English alphabet. For a collection where items are represented by author names, under each letter will be found the documents that were written by authors whose name begins with the letter. This approach has the advantage of subdividing the collection so that the user is not required to view lengthy lists. It has the disadvantage of providing no immediate prospect on the entire contents of the collection, so at a glance it is impossible to determine how many documents are available under each letter, or in fact whether there are any documents available at all. From the perspective of someone trying to use the collection, alphabetical lists provide only a single function. No one writes an article about authors whose last names start with the letter "M."

Large-Format Displays

One of the limitations in rich-prospect browsing is the amount of available screen real estate. An alternative to standard monitors is provided by large-format displays, which are becoming increasingly popular for the purpose of information dissemination, entertainment, or persuasion (Signindustry.com 2007). Commercial advertising (for example, Times Square), one form of a persuasive display, is the most common use of large-format displays (Dietz et al. 2004). In size and placement, large-format persuasive displays mimic traditional billboard advertisements; in content and multimedia use, they mimic television. Large-format displays are also used in a variety of ways in sports stadiums and even mega churches. In sport stadiums they display live action details, announcements, and shots of the viewing public. In mega churches they are used to support religious practice in ways similar to those used in the classroom: to display words to hymns and Bible verses, illustrate sermons, share announcements and video, and clarify material through PowerPoint slides (Wyche et al. 2007). These instances of large-format display are passive in nature and, for the most part, rely on viewing from a distance.

Large-format interactive displays have been used in a number of disciplines, for purposes as diverse as analysing intelligence reports (Booker et al. 2007), enhancing collaboration (Ni et al. 2006), and enriching informal shared spaces, such as foyers in university buildings, conferences centers, and cafés (Izadi et al. 2005), as well as physical library spaces (Grønbæk et al. 2006). Immersive imagery displays developed by Dietz and colleagues each contain an array of sensors that measure viewer proximity to parts of the screen and react accordingly, allowing for several simultaneous interactions (Dietz et al. 2004).

In addition to large-format displays, work has also been done on providing data on other interior surfaces. InfoGallery was developed and implemented as a Web-based infrastructure for enriching the physical library space with informative exhibits of digital library material and other relevant information such as RSS feeds (Grønbæk et al. 2006). Information is presented on a variety of surfaces in the library, including large-format cylindrical displays, ceilings, large flat panels, and floors. Some of the library displays enable interaction. For example, visitors can click or tap on a touch-sensitive surface to explore a piece of information in depth. Visitors can also drag a reference to this information to a Bluetooth phone or send it to an email address.

On the usability of large-format displays, Ni et al. (2006) studied the effects of display size and resolution on task performance in an information-rich virtual environment (IRVE). They found that users were most effective at performing IRVE search and comparison tasks on large-format, high-resolution displays. In addition, users working with large-format displays became less reliant on wayfinding aids in the IRVE to develop knowledge of the space they were navigating.

One of the goals of text visualisation is to represent meaningful features in the context of the entire document. However, one of the challenges that usually arises is how to overcome the constraints of limited display space, which forces the sequential traversal of these features. In representations that require scrolling, for instance, only the first few instances of the identified features are visible. One solution to this difficulty is to provide a microtext representation that fits into a single viewing field, but allows the user to navigate by zooming in toward the text in order to make it readable (Small 1996). Another strategy is to provide simultaneous document representations at different levels of granularity (Ruecker et al. 2005) so that the user can easily switch between an overview, a reading view, and specialised views that emphasise various kinds of information (such as word frequencies, collocations, or parts of speech).

In our "Novel as Slot Machine" project, we propose a wall-sized interface design that extends the notion of simultaneous document representation by providing the user with a set of complete microtext overviews of the document, one for every instance of repetition. This innovative design has three advantages for literary-pattern analysis that are not available in our other interface designs. First, the vast amount of available screen space eliminates concerns that would normally be introduced immediately about how much text can reasonably be shown and manipulated at one time. Second, the combination of the microtext columns and the reading slot means that the reader is working across multiple contexts that are each ready to hand and unambiguous in their relations. Third, a mechanism for selecting and displaying a pattern of repetitions, at random, provides an element of play and serendipity (Rockwell 2003).

The screen is divided into the following parts:

1. The display panel for viewing the entire novel in microtext together with all specified repetitions.
2. A right-hand control bar where the user can enter words or phrases to search for repeated forms, store results, and carry out other tasks.
3. A reading slot running horizontally across the middle of the screen which displays the paragraphs containing instances of the repeated word or phrase.
4. Tabs across the top to allow switching between different texts.

Upon launching the interface, users access the document for analysis by clicking on the "load" button and selecting the desired document. Once the entire text of the novel has been loaded into the first column, users cannot read it, because it is a microtext. What they can read is the text in the reading slot, which appears in a legible font size.

When users are ready, they can identify or search for a repetition in a number of different ways:

1. The first way is just like a slot machine: they push the "generate random repetition" button. This is a discovery tool: try one, see if you like it, and if not, then push the button again and see what you get.
2. The second way is by highlighting a piece of text that is of interest, which will cause a menu to slide up from the bottom of the slot giving the user the following options:
   - Run a default search.
   - Send the highlighted text and its context to a temporary storage area, or "suitcase".
   - Send just the highlighted text to "advanced search" for further customization.
   - Export that chunk into, for example, a .txt file.
3. The third way is to enter a search string, which will cause the system to identify all repetitions that contain that string.

To minimise walking back and forth between the text and the menu, the user can un-dock the menu and drag it closer to the text. Once a user runs a repetition search, the system generates one complete copy of the novel for every instance of the repetition, with a superimposed "reading slot" that contains the repeated word or phrase in its paragraph context. Each column is separated with a thick, white line; and each is numbered on the bottom. For every instance of the repetition, the system marks the spot of the repetition by making a tick on the left side, in the gutter. The user can also roll over any line of text that is not behind the slot, and see a customisable reading-view.

This interface will only be technically viable with the availability of low-cost high resolution wall-sized displays. Such displays have been the subject of experimentation by commercial developers of electronic paper (for example, Xerox, E-Ink, Phillips) and by theorists working with alternative forms of reading, such as the prototype reading wall, where users interact with a wall of text by physically sliding panels containing hyperlinks into position for more information (Back et al. 2001).

However, it also has to be recognised that providing all the data on a display the size of a domestic interior wall is not necessarily going to be sufficient to give the user a sense of prospect. The visual representation of the data needs to be designed in such a way that the minor features are seen as minor and the major features stand out. Human foveal saccades tend to cluster on areas of high contrast, such as edges between dark and light. Attention is drawn to these kinds of areas. Size matters. So does color. There is a wide range of techniques for the visual construction of information, from the use of a grid system for layout to the tendency for the eye to take directional cues from the shapes of objects. Optimum line lengths have also been studied, at least for printed text, where what is at issue is the point at which readers are still able to accurately monitor line starts to prevent reading errors caused by skipping lines or re-reading the current or previous ones.[4] In rich-prospect interfaces, these visual communication design techniques need to be applied so that the perceiver is able to make sense of the prospect quickly.

A related issue has to do with the limits on human visual acuity. The ISO standards for public signage suggest that there should be 12 mm of image height and 4.5 mm of text height for every meter of viewing distance. These standards are based on the Snellen chart used by optometrists to study vision. In order to survey the contents of a wall-sized display, it is necessary for the perceiver to stand at some remove. As the size of the display increases, the perceiver needs to stand further back in order to be able to survey all of it at once. Another ratio could therefore be calculated, comparing the size of the wall or other display with the amount of graphical or textual information it could contain at a size that is readable for a viewer able to survey all of it at once. It should be recognised, however, that it is not necessary to be able to read the text or resolve the images in

4 For print, the consensus seems to put that limit around 80–120 characters, but the estimates are sensitive to a wide range of factors.

order to pursue all the tasks. Manovich's cultural analytics projects, for example, often involve steps where the images are reduced to colored dots before being enlarged to recognisable sizes.

Persistence of Display

If the user is actively engaged with the rich-prospect interface, using various tools to reorganise or structure the meaningful representations of collection items, or subsetting or grouping them in some way, there is a question as to how the display should respond in terms of items that are not currently selected.

There are basically three possibilities. The first is that the material that is not within the current selection disappears from the screen, leaving the user with an intermediate result screen that only shows partial prospect. The second is that the unselected items remain visible, but the selected items are differentiated in some way, such as by color-coding, highlighting, or removal to a section of the screen distinct from the rest of the display. In our family of showcase browsers, we have often used removal to a strip of tiny images across the bottom of the screen. The third possibility is that the unselected items as individual items disappear, but the user is given a visual cue of their continued presence, such as an icon at the bottom of the screen that can be expanded to recall the rich prospect. Further research will be required to determine which of these strategies is best under which conditions, or whether they are equally useful. One means of evaluating them would be to create affordance strength vectors for each of the different interfaces, where the optimum form of display might be related to the subsequent task, such as adding items to the existing subset, changing the current selection in some way, or continuing to narrow the search by incremental grouping.

Priming

Human beings are able to locate and identify items more quickly if they have been primed to identify them by previous exposure, even if they do not have a conscious memory of having seen or heard the precue (Baars 1997, pp. 118–9, 170). The strategy of attempting to prime users with some form of fleeting image could prove useful to the interface design community, especially if the contents of the visual priming were related to the structure of the collection.

For example, in a rich-prospect interface that was organised in columns like a phone book, it might be possible to load the data in two steps, with the first increment showing only the column or section headings that provide the larger framework, and the second step filling in the data. Further research is necessary.

Ventral vs. Dorsal Stream Perception

Milner and Goodale (1995) suggest that there are two streams that are used for visually processing information in the human brain, and that one stream relates primarily to concept formation, while the other relates primarily to opportunities for action. If there are two distinct but interacting mechanisms, then it may be possible to design an interface in such a way as to facilitate either action or reflection, depending on the nature of the task. In addition to the possible implications for design, there are also implications for the study of interfaces and their affordances. For example, if dorsal perception (for action) is primarily tacit, while ventral perception is explicit (Michaels 2000, pp. 252–3), then it may happen that affordance strength vectors based on user reporting will be less accurate than affordance strength vectors based on evaluations by a third-party observer. Further research is necessary.

Mental Models

The mental model of the user in undertaking a task can have measurable effects on performance. In a study of wheel rotation responses, Guiard (1983) asked participants to control a cursor using a joystick, where the response direction was counter-intuitive: moving the joystick to the left moved the cursor to the right, and vice versa. One group was instructed in the mechanics of the response – namely, that the task was to control a cursor using a joystick – while the other group was told that the joystick was actually affixed to the underside of a steering wheel. The task for the two groups was identical, but the group with the steering wheel metaphor performed significantly better than the group who had not been provided with the metaphor.

Although metaphors are often considered as comparatively esoteric artifacts belonging primarily to the realm of literary expression, Lakoff (1980) makes the strong case that metaphoric thinking is in fact a widespread strategy and might correctly be understood as a fundamental part of human cognition. Drawing on examples from English diction and idiom, Lakoff demonstrates that metaphors structure a wide range of language, and by implication, thought. Metaphors are therefore a potentially powerful tool for the interface designer attempting to create intuitive electronic artifacts, although as Stubblefield (1998) points out, there is a necessary degree of caution required to ensure that the developers and users share a common understanding of the implications both of the metaphor itself, and of the consistency of its implementation in a particular system. In any fully developed system it is natural to expect that the metaphor will have been significantly stretched or modified.

The classic use of a metaphor to create a mental model for interface tasks is the computer desktop. However, the strategy of providing the user with a mental model for a task is amenable to extension into a wide variety of possible activities, including the use of rich-prospect browsing interfaces, where provision of a mental model appropriate to the interface, collection, or task might help to reduce the sense of visual overload.

Sequential vs. Spatial Prospect

Some previous researchers have suggested that a form of prospect is possible through a combination of an index and a sequential display. Ahlberg and Shneiderman (1994a), for example, presented the Alphaslider, which was a form of horizontal scrollbar with an internal index consisting of letters of the alphabet. The letters were spaced according to the number of documents in the collection, giving the user some limited sense of prospect. The primary strategy, however, was to have the titles of the items in the collection appear in rapid sequence in a display placed just above the slider. The items appear and disappear as the user moves the mouse, so it is possible to flash quickly through an alphabetical sequence. Novice users could locate a film title out of a collection of 10,000 titles in an average of 24 seconds, which compared favourably to menu selection systems containing an order of magnitude fewer entries.

Sequential display occurs in many systems that attempt to provide prospect in spite of limited screen space. Vertically scrolling windows and panoramas, for instance, both employ a form of sequential display, as do interfaces that use selective magnification as a tool. Ahlberg and Shneiderman (1994a) also mention the possibility of using the Times Square strategy of having text scroll past the user rather than having it appear in rapid sequence.

The question is whether the prospect provided by these means is adequate to create the various new affordances that are potentially available from more spatial forms. Further research is necessary.

Inter-Affordance Effects

In designing to provide new affordances, there is always the possibility that existing affordances will be affected in some significant way, and previous affordances will be reduced or lost as the new affordances are made available. In software development projects in general, unintended consequences of incremental changes can be guarded against in various ways, including modular design and the practice of retesting against a standard testbed that grows as the application expands.

Interaction Histories

In addition to providing prospect on a collection, it is also possible to provide a form of prospect related to interaction history, or the activities of previous users related either to individual documents in a collection or to the rich-prospect display as a whole.

Hill et al. (1992) present an interesting set of widgets designed to give prospect on the imaginary virtual wear and tear on digital documents caused by editing and reading. Their argument is that just as paper documents accrue thumbprints and coffee stains, which provide traces of previous use, so digital documents should visibly record handling. Based on interval sliders, the "edit wear" and "read wear" scroll bars show internal lines that correspond to areas of the document that have been edited or read. These marks allow users to see at a glance which areas of a document have received the most attention from previous editors and readers. In cases where discrete lines of marks are created to correspond to different periods, they also show which areas of the document have received attention most recently. The concept of graphically presenting edit or read wear could also be extended to entire collections of documents, as suggested in the case of web browsers by Wexelblat and Maes (1999).

Coordinating Multiple Views

Another natural extension of the idea of prospect in an interface is to provide multiple views that show the collection at different levels of granularity. These views are usually displayed simultaneously, but may also be shown consecutively. Baldonado et al. (2000) suggest eight rules to govern the development of interfaces that incorporate multiple views of either kind:

- **diversity**: multiple views are appropriate under the following conditions: when the collection has diverse attributes; allows for diverse models or levels of abstraction; or contains different genres. Multiple views can also help when the user profiles are diverse.
- **complementarity**: multiple views are useful for collections where different views can reveal patterns or disparities.
- **decomposition**: use multiple views to help the user divide and conquer complex data.
- **parsimony**: since multiple views add complexity for both the designer and the user, they should be used sparingly.
- **space/time resource optimisation**: there should be a return on investment for both the designers and the users.
- **self-evidence**: perceptual cues such as highlighting or coupling should be used to keep relationships between the views as clear as possible, although coupling needs to be judged against difficulty and speed, and should not be unidirectional.
- **consistency**: the interface for each view should use the same features in the same ways.
- **attention management**: the interface should use perceptual cues to help direct the user's attention appropriately.

In the case of rich-prospect interfaces, the allocation of time and space would need to be considered as a fairly central issue, since the rich-prospect display alone will require significant screen space, and any windows displayed at the same time will create an additional demand where the demand is already heavy.

Performance

System performance for rich-prospect interfaces is an ongoing issue. If the user needs to wait for the system to download a screen full of data before the process of looking for documents can even begin, frustration is going to result in many cases. As the internet matures, these performance issues may become less significant, provided that the nature of the collections does not also mature into forms that involve larger representations. It is currently within the constraints of the technology to download a screen full of text relatively quickly; to download a screen full of video thumbnails, however, would still pose a problem for most users.

Characteristics of Candidate Tasks

Although one of the advantages of a rich-prospect interface is that it should allow ready access to collection items even to people initially unfamiliar with the collection, the various features of such an interface and the tools that go with it do have a learning curve. User motivation to work with the rich-prospect interface will vary, however, depending on a number of factors related to the user and the task.

Just as some collections will be better candidates than others for the development of a rich-prospect interface, so some task characteristics, within the constraints of a particular user at a particular time, will be better suited to the use of such an interface. For example, users who have an understanding of the collection, and its significant features, that is congruent to the presuppositions of the designers will tend to find a rich-prospect interface more useful than users who do not share the same presuppositions.

Another user characteristic that might be useful is previous positive experiences in using rich-prospect interfaces, or conversely, previous negative experiences in using interfaces without some form of prospect. Such a statement, however, could be made about any form of technology. Unique to the rich-prospect approach is the need for the designer to assist users in considering screens full of information as an opportunity rather than a source of frustration or intimidation.

The degree to which the new opportunities for perception and action weigh against the potentially intimidating number of items in the display is going to be subject to a number of factors related to the nature of the material in the collection and the characteristics of the user. However, common analog artifacts such as maps, phone books, dictionaries, and encyclopedias lend support to the belief that, given the right conditions, people are able to manage large amounts of information.

Prospect as a Secondary Functionality

In addition to the projects where rich-prospect browsing was the primary focus, we have also produced designs and prototypes where the primary functionality we were interested in testing lay elsewhere, but we included some component that provided prospect. A good example is the Watching the Script (WtS) project (Figure 6.4), where we set out to provide students, actors, and directors with an online tool to help incorporate blocking information in reading plays (Sinclair et al. 2006).

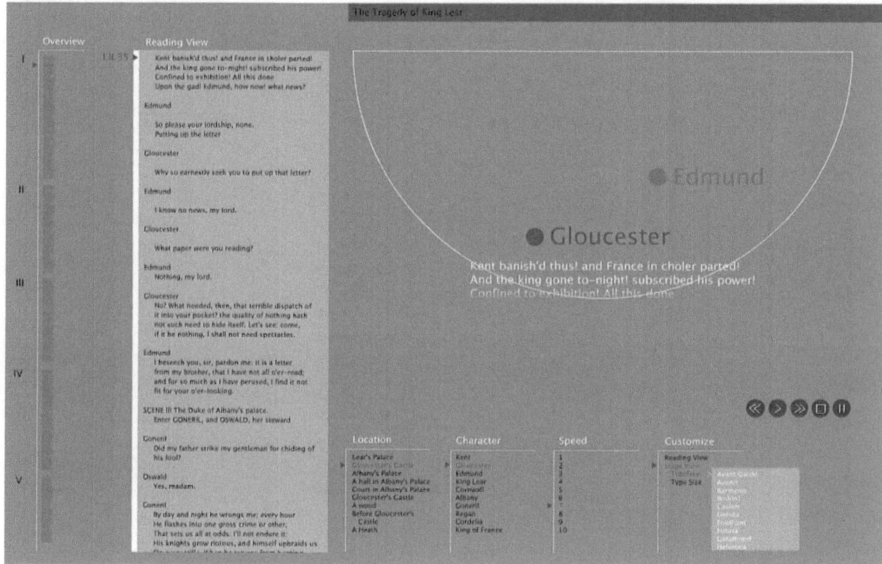

Figure 6.4 Watching the Script[5]

The main feature of WtS is the stylised stage, shown upper right, where colored dots appear and stand where the actors would appear and stand, and their speeches scroll out underneath them. We included a fairly wide set of affordances in the designs, including the ability to select the speeches by a single actor, or those occurring in a single location. The user can speed up or slow down the playback.

In addition, we provided both a more conventional reading view, on the left of the stage, and a prospect view of all speeches in the play, to the left of that. This microtext column also appears on the right side of the Mandala browser (Figure 4.1), allowing the Mandala user to step sequentially through a document even though the main purpose of the browser is to break up the document and treat it as a set of non-sequential chunks.

Although it isn't possible to put the entire text of a play into a column that will fit on a screen, and it often isn't possible to even have one line of pixels for every line in a play, a microtext column can still provide a number of affordances. For instance, it allows people to see at a glance the relative proportion of lines spoken in each Act.

5 Watching the Script was our first attempt to leverage the advantages of digital text for the benefit of people reading and working with plays. This system led subsequently to the Simulated Environment for Theater (SET) project, in 3D. Design by Sandra Gabriele.

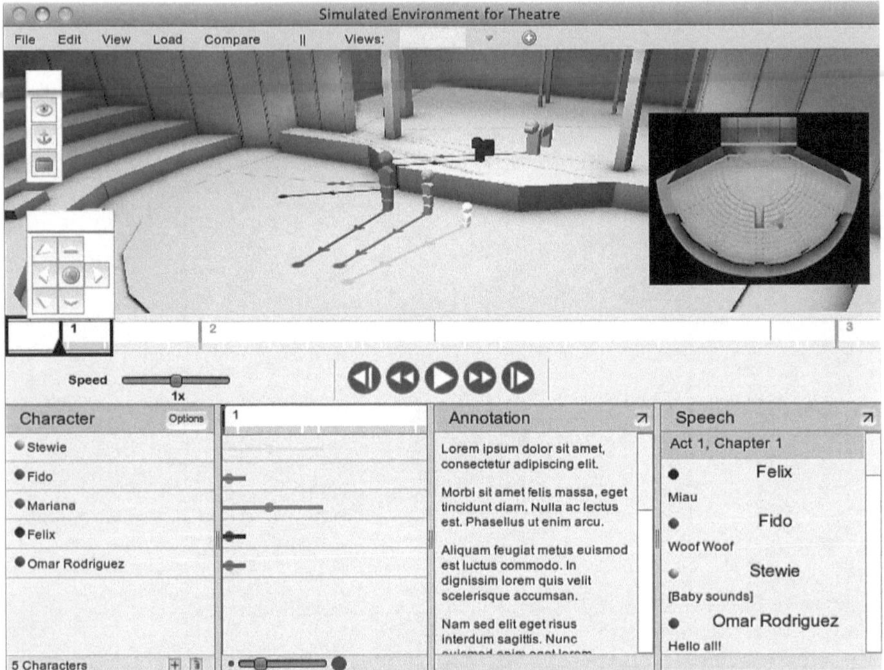

Figure 6.5 The Simulated Environment for Theater (SET)[6]

If the lines can be color-coded to match the characters (as is the case in Watching the Script), it also allows people to see the relative proportion of lines spoken by each character. For directors, the proximity of the lines of different characters can potentially help to plan double-casting, where a single actor plays more than one role. Adding a scrubber to the microtext column turns it into a navigation tool that works at a scale larger than speeding up or slowing down the playback on stage.

Yet, for all its many advantages, a microtext column is really a bonus feature in a prototype like Watching the Script. It would be perfectly reasonable to create a system of this kind without such a feature. However, once we began thinking about rich-prospect browsers and experimenting with their affordances, it seemed clear to us that a feature of this kind was worth including.

We have not included a microtext view, however, in the next phase of Watching the Script, which we call the Simulated Environment for Theatre (SET) (Figure 6.5). Led by Jennifer Roberts-Smith at the University of Waterloo, the SET project moves in a new direction, reducing the privileged position of the text in Watching

6 The Simulated Environment for Theater (SET) includes a view not only of the stage, but of the entire theater, allowing us to include perspectives from various points in the audience. In fact, the viewing angle moves around the entire space, as in a computer game. Design team led by Sandra Gabriele.

the Script to a more theatrical awareness of the stage as a location for action. The prospect view in SET is therefore more like the prospect in music software or film software, consisting of a timeline on which are superimposed a number of pieces of information about what is happening on stage (the user can zoom out on the timeline so that the entire play is visible, which does in fact produce a prospect view). The user can choose to replay the action at a pace set by a scrollbar, or can manually slide the scrubber across the entire timeline to see each phase of the action.

The choice of a timeline instead of a microtext script is indicative of the significance of the initial choice for a meaningful representation in rich-prospect browsing. The microtext column implies that a very important, perhaps the most important, aspect of a play is the dialogue (represented as text). The timeline, on the other hand, suggests that the action is central – the dialogue contributes to the action, but is not the focus.

Another prospect view that is included in both WtS and SET is the color-coded list of characters, which can be used in Director mode to help with the blocking task, and in Viewing mode to keep track of who is on stage and when they are speaking. An additional list in this case might consist of the names of the actors as well as the characters.

Prospect-Related Interface Tools

There is a variety of new opportunities for action that can be made available to users of digital collections through rich-prospect interfaces. These new affordances are based on the direct visible presence of information about the contents, structure, and other significant features of a collection, such as how it was understood by its developers, how it has been organised, and, in some cases, how it has been encoded with additional interpretive material that is not contained in the actual text. Although this visible information can make a significant difference in terms of user perception, by itself it is not sufficient to provide many new affordances. In order to be of greatest value, a rich-prospect interface needs to also provide a set of appropriate tools that can take advantage of the visible representation of the items in the collection and the other collection features. Some of these tools are also useful in contexts where the interface is not based on rich prospect, although the functioning from the user's perspective may vary significantly because of the differences between the two kinds of interface. The tools that are potentially useful in a rich-prospect context include the following, which we will develop in more detail below:

- zooming
- panning
- sorting
- selecting
- grouping

- renaming
- annotating
- opening
- structuring

Prospect-Related Interface Tools: Zooming

Since screen real estate can be an issue, magnification methods are one clear means of allowing the user to move from an overview to a detailed view at various levels of granularity. Strategies that involve zooming include fully collapsing the view through various stages ending in an icon or other representation (as in the collapsed window bar at the bottom of the screen in Windows environments); selective zooming through fisheyes (which warp the view to display more prominently the local items); and the use of three dimensional representations, where some objects recede in the virtual distance, while others advance.

Zooming that is accomplished through collapsing the view has the advantage that it requires a minimum amount of room on the screen in order to provide the user with a visual cue that something is present. It can be confusing, however, for users who are unfamiliar with the system and do not realise that the visual cues correspond to larger items. In its most extreme case, visual collapse of elements can result in them being hidden from the user altogether – typically these methods place the retrieval system under a menu or associate it with a keystroke or key sequence, which can be useful for a sophisticated user but disorienting for a novice. Adobe Photoshop, for example, allows the user to temporarily hide all the tool palettes by pushing the tab key. This feature allows a clear view of the image on the current working area, but requires that the user know the key combination that will bring the palettes back.

Selective zooming through fisheyes has the advantage that the items on display are constantly present to the user, which helps to prevent disorientation and provides a form of prospect (Bederson 2000). Fisheyes have the disadvantage, however, that they only allow expansion of a part of the display at a given time.

One way to avoid the possible disorientation caused by selectively collapsing the view is through a magnification strategy that changes the entire display. An example of this kind of zooming is in our SET project, where the user can expand the time scale by moving a slider that is associated with the stage view. This strategy has the advantage of allowing the system to animate the change rather than requiring a dramatic shift from one scale to another. It is still possible for the user to experience disorientation, since the expansion mechanism has to clearly maintain the current insertion point. If the view expands across multiple scales, however, from the largest overview to the closest detail, the insertion point cannot be clearly indicated, since what is a point at the least magnification becomes an area when expanded. One strategy might therefore be to allow the line indicating the insertion point to visually widen as the view expands. The ability to reset the insertion point size would then need to be added, to allow the user to see the minimal insertion line, regardless of the current scale.

Prospect-Related Interface Tools: Panning

Panning functions are often associated with zooming, since the user often requires some means of moving over or through the display. Panning can take various forms, including:

- implicit panning through positioning of the mouse (as in panoramas)
- specialised tools such as the repositioning hand that allows users to move the larger workspace within the viewing frame, and
- objects like the standard window scrollbars, with their directional arrows and thumb

All of these solutions are in some respects expressions of the limitations of the keyboard and mouse. There is a wide variety of other options that become available with alternative hardware, from touch screens, to video game controllers that allow complex navigation in three-dimensional environments, to steering wheels, joysticks, digital gloves, and positional trackers or sensors. Like the landscape metaphor itself, the hardware and software devices that simplify interaction in three virtual dimensions have so far found very limited implementation in the office or work environment, perhaps because they are so strongly associated with the discourse of digital games.

Prospect-Related Interface Tools: Sorting

If it is possible to make the representation of the individual items meaningful to the user, it is also possible to make the arrangement of the items meaningful. A common example might be where the display has been sorted so that the items are in alphabetical or chronological order. In those cases, the user is able to directly perceive the organising scheme, and can therefore use that knowledge to help in locating items where the approximate spelling is known but the exact spelling used by the system is uncertain, or where the spelling might be influenced for retrieval purposes by features which are often considered trivial by human beings, but represent potential difficulties for search engines – such as capitalisation and orthographic variation. Search engines typically fold case and perform lemmatisation and stemming to address the difficulties. Lemmas are words that have been inflected in some way to indicate conjugation (for verbs) or declension (for nouns), which results in words that are not of a form that is identical to the word being sought. For example, the user is looking for "chase" and the document has "chasing." Stemming is related to lemmatisation but consists of more simple truncation. The lemma of "chasing" is "chase" but the stem of "chasing" is "chas."

In addition to sorting the display alphabetically or chronologically, it is also possible to establish other sorting criteria which are potentially useful for particular users of a given collection. For example, in collections which consist of technical papers, it is sometimes useful to be able to see which papers have been most popular with previous readers. Citation-based text archives provide this function by indicating how often a given article has been cited by other articles in the collection (CiteSeer 2010). The number of citations is understood in these cases as an index to the significance of the article being cited. A rich-prospect interface to a citations-based collection might therefore sort the articles by number of citations. This is the approach we have taken in the design of the INKE Paper Drill (Figure 2.4).

A more specialised form of sorting might be provided in the case where an interaction history is available. If the system stores information on document access by user, it would be possible to give an individual heavy user of a collection a display sorted by frequency of previous use. In order to provide this kind of information, it is necessary to maintain user profiles by document over time, which has several implications for record-keeping in the system: should the user log in, or is it sufficient to have the system recognise the computer? If the latter, then what about cases of shared or public-access computers? If the former, where login is required, then the system is introducing an extra step between the user and the information, which may be in some cases a significant deterrent to using the system at all. Our current strategy, which is also emerging as an industry best practice, is to provide login at any point in the process, rather than requiring it at the beginning. This approach allows users to work with the system and take advantage of all the affordances that don't require logging in, and make the decision only at the point where the additional affordances (oftentimes simply saving the state of the interface) are perceive as warranting the further step.

An additional layer of complexity is added if the system is going to share an interaction history gained from one user of the system with other users. Amazon.com, for example, provides prospective book purchasers with information on related titles that have been of interest to other people who bought the current book. Since the company is a retailer, there are no serious implications to this sharing of anonymised information among users. However, in cases where the collection is an academic archive of primary materials, identifying connections among items is one of the professional activities performed by academics in the course of their research. To offer previous connections made by one academic to other users of the system might therefore introduce issues of academic privacy.

Another complex form of context is provided, not by a chronological sort per se, but rather by the choice of representation of the chronological sort. If the items in a chronology are used to create a timeline, it is possible to emphasise or de-emphasise individual items, create visual connections, and even generate what are essentially narratives or themes, through the visual presentation of the items. The visual representation therefore becomes a significant factor in the interpretation of the material. As Drucker (2009) puts it, each visual design carries along its own visual epistemology. As a result, each of the visual effects available to the designer needs to be carefully considered in the framework of the agendas to be served by a given collection.

Prospect-Related Interface Tools: Selecting

In order to work with any subset of the items shown in a rich-prospect interface, it is necessary for the user to be able to select individual items or subsets. A wide variety of selection mechanisms are part of the standard desktop environment, including:

- menus: usually visible across the top of the window
- picklists: called up by the menu items or by clicking on a selection box that expands
- check boxes: to allow multiple values in one field
- radio buttons: to provide the choices of mutually exclusive options in one field
- rollovers: it is possible to have elements react to the presence of the cursor
- clicking: it is normal to have elements respond to clicking with the cursor
- double-clicking: secondary behaviors can sometimes be triggered with two clicks in quick succession – selecting entire words or phrases in MS-Word is an example of this treatment being applied to use in selection
- right and left clicking: these can have different effects if two buttons are available and the software accommodates their use
- shift-clicking: allows the user to select multiple discontinuous items
- dragging a selection area: allows the user to select contiguous groups of items

In addition to these standard options, there have been research efforts to develop other strategies for object selection that work by modifying, extending, or supplementing the existing approaches. Baudisch (1998), for instance, describes the potential application of painting metaphors for item selection in cases where hundreds of items are involved, allowing for rapid and discontinuous selection of items. In its original formulation, the painting metaphor was intended for use with toggle maps, which are groups of check boxes, each of which has only one of two possible states – on or off. Baudisch also expands the idea for use in cases where multiple selection states are available to the user, by having the painting tool apply shades of gray that are incrementally darkened as the cursor is passed repeatedly over the area.

Prospect-Related Interface Tools: Grouping

A related but distinct area of visual presentation are those tools available to the user for grouping items together. A sorted list is not a set of groups because groups contain multiple subsets of items. In some cases it may be possible to determine in an a priori manner some of the ways in which items might be usefully grouped on behalf of the user. In other cases, it may be equally useful to provide the user some means of creating new groups of items. The two situations are also not mutually exclusive.

As with sorting, a priori grouping might be performed according to standard schemes such as the alphabetical or chronological, provided that the level of granularity still admits multiple items in each group. Particularly if the user has the ability to regroup what has been previously grouped or to control the collapse and expansion of the groups that have been defined, the affordances of prospect are not necessarily compromised and can in fact be supplemented.

One implementation of this idea is in the Scatter/Gather interface developed by Pirolli et al. (1996) where users are able to manipulate the items in a starfield display in order to create related groups. In this case, the groups might be organised according to any scheme that seems appropriate. For example, a user may be involved in sorting through web sites, and have one group for sites that have been visited and found interesting, another group for sites that have been visited and proven uninteresting, and a third group for sites yet to be visited. Another user may choose to create groups that represent sources of the sites, with commercial sites in one group, academic sites in another, and personal web pages in a third.

Special attention should be given to the visual format of groups, because it can have consequences both in terms of user perception and also in terms of the allocation of the limited screen real estate. Grouping can be indicated by physical connection (as in lines connecting related items); additional graphical elements (boxes or other shapes underlying related items); proximity; color-coding; and similarity of appearance in terms of form, texture, size, or any other visual attribute. Alignment on a grid can also be used to suggest grouping, as can placement onto a structured surface such as a target diagram. In general terms, it is better to resist adding new visual elements to a screen (such as boxes and arrows), but instead makes use of strategies that take advantage of layout or attributes assigned to existing visual elements.

Once the user focuses on a group, the question arises as to what should be done with the other groups. In a rich-prospect interface, it is preferable for items that fall outside the central group to still remain visible. This strategy has the advantage of not disrupting the prospect while at the same time allowing the user to focus attention on some part of the collection.

An example might be an interface that allows the user to view the material in alphabetical order, with some indication of the alphabet visible. In a dictionary or phone book, for example, there is not only the larger structure of the alphabet, but also the guide words in the header, which give a more precise indication of the range covered on each page. If a rich-prospect interface were to employ columns of alphabetised text, a similar use of column headers might be useful in terms of identifying subsets of the collection that are of particular interest. The difference between this approach and a conventional use of the alphabet for browsing is that the individual items remain visible rather than being hidden until a letter of the alphabet is selected.

In the interface design community, one tool that is sometimes applied to the problem of grouping is the interval slider, where a small horizontal or vertical bar represents the entire collection, and thumbs on the bar are positioned in order to select a subset or range of the total. On window sliders there is typically only a single thumb, since the goal is to specify the location of an insertion point. On subsetting sliders there are often two thumbs, which can be used to indicate the start and end points of the selection.

An alternative form of interval slider was developed by Eick (1994), who applied a painting metaphor in place of the thumbs. In Eick's model, sections of the bars are selected using a paint tool that can be applied to discontinuous portions, to create arbitrary selection groups for display. In a rich-prospect interface, a paint-based interval slider could be applied as a very flexible form of auxiliary selection device.

Prospect-Related Interface Tools: Renaming

One way of providing alternative browsing opportunities for the user without having to create multiple interfaces is to allow the user to select the meaningful representation of items from a list of options. This strategy is likely to be most effective in cases where there is a one-to-one correspondence between the various alternatives. For example, a collection of novels that provides alternative access by the names of the authors and the titles of the books has the disadvantage that one author might have written multiple titles in the collection. To allow the user to convert from a display of author names to a display of document titles is potentially disorienting, since the latter display will contain many more unique items than the former display. One solution to this problem would be to have both the author names and the titles listed together to form a meaningful representation that is a composite. Another possibility is to list the number of documents available for each author as a number placed next to the author's name, in which case the conversion to a display showing titles could derive from the numbers indicated. A third strategy would be to animate the conversion so that the transitions from author to title and back again are clearly shown. The fourth approach, which we used in Giacometti et al. (2008) for Texttiles, is to create more complex representations, with rectangles for groups, dots for items, text labels on the rectangles, and rollover dialog boxes for the information behind the dots.

Prospect-Related Interface Tools: Annotating

If the user is able to see the entire collection represented at once, and is able to sort and subset the material into various groups, it is also likely that some form of annotation would be helpful. At its basic level, this annotation function should allow the user to label the groups; at a slightly more sophisticated level, it should provide the ability to insert text, sound, images, or whatever the user desires at any point in the display, in order to help make sense of the whole. Within the context of a given collection and group of users, it may also be useful to consider having the annotations indicated by some form of visual cue, and to provide the users with the ability to switch them from visible to invisible.

There is also the possibility of the annotations of one user being persistent across sessions with the collection, which means that the system has to store not only the annotations, but also a user profile. Current strategies include having the user log in to a database or having the system automatically recognise the user's computer, which is not particularly helpful for users who do not always use the same computer. A hybrid approach is therefore to store a client certificate for the computer that provides the username, but still requires a password from anyone who wants to log in under that name.

Finally, there is the option of allowing the annotations of one user to be accessed by other users. Like interaction histories dealing with structure, interaction histories based on annotation have the potential to create new ways of understanding the material, independent of the discourse established by the original designers. Interaction histories also have their limitations – a primary one being that they are only as insightful as the people who create them. As with any kind of public system, such as bulletin boards, listservs, chat groups, and crowdsourced projects, it may therefore be helpful in some situations to have a human moderator involved, so that the system does not deteriorate rather than develop through use (though the opposite problem is probably more prevalent, where anticipated collaborations atrophy and cease).

Prospect-Related Interface Tools: Opening

Since the rich-prospect interface uses a simple representation of each item in the collection, there is the possibility that the user may wish to open the representation, either selectively for a subset of the collection or else for the entire display. The degree of expansion might be made available through a series of increments. Kaugars (1998) discusses a multi-scale text visualisation that has four increments: closed; thumbnail; semi-open; and fully open. A rich-prospect interface using this strategy might logically be positioned between the closed and thumbnail versions of display, in which case it could be designed to provide various levels of meaningful representation.

For example, a display might use a single word to represent each item in the collection, but each of these words or some set of them could be expanded under user control to replace the single words with a list of keywords or a phrase. Further expansion might replace the phrases with sentences or short abstracts; then the short abstracts could be replaced with full abstracts, and so on until the full documents are open. If the selection mechanism is provided in a way that is relatively intuitive and simple to use, a fluid change from one form to another could be made available, so that the incremental steps are not disorienting to the user. A further essential affordance would be to allow people to skip over intermediate steps.

Prospect-Related Interface Tools: Structuring

The structure of the display of the meaningful representations is a significant part of a rich-prospect interface. In addition to methods for visually associating some items with others, there is also the possibility of arranging the items within some larger structure that has been designed specifically to make examining the display easier and more useful.

One of the common structuring strategies for text items is to arrange them in columns rather than as a block of text. If the items are sorted alphabetically, they can also be marked with guides that indicate the first and last words in each column, or the range of the characters in the alphabet that the column represents. These elements perform a function similar to the page headers in a dictionary or the phone book, allowing the user to look through the display more quickly by scanning the headers than would be possible by looking only at the alphabetical list of items.

A related structuring strategy that applies to graphical objects as well as text is to arrange the display using a grid system. Grids have the advantage of allowing the designer to visually associate items through alignment, even in cases where the items might not be in immediate proximity on the screen. A typical example might be in the header or footer of a text document, where the author's name or article title might be flush left while the page number is flush right, but because these items occur on the same line, and are clearly outside the body text, the reader automatically associates them as both being part of the header or footer. Grid systems were widely employed by print designers for much of the past century, and have always been a basic feature of text layout programs. However, they are not yet strongly associated with the design of computer interfaces, perhaps in part because they have not been implemented as a standard component of web design applications. Unlike in the case of layout programs, interface design applications have not been derived from a tradition that includes the historical relationship between the technology of printing and the use of grid systems. In addition, it is possible to generalise the concept of the grid into other forms of structured surface, which provide an additional layer of useful information that lies beneath and informs the plotting of the items from the collection onto that surface.

Incorporation of Prior Affordances

A rich-prospect browsing interface may not be the interface of choice for every user on every occasion. Interfaces are by definition the mediating software between an application or a data collection and the person using the application or the collection. Different tasks therefore call for different kinds of interfaces.

This fact also holds true in the analog world, although the logistical difficulties and costs involved in making multiple physical interfaces available for most tools have often been prohibitive. Analog controls on a car, for instance, do not vary according to the intentions of the driver or the situation on the road.[7] Navigating in city traffic, driving hundreds of miles of straight highway on a clear summer day, and rolling down a twisted mountain trail in a blizzard all use essentially the same interface to the car, and the driver is required to adapt.

The constraints, however, are not so severe in the digital environment. There are no comparable physical reasons why there could not be different kinds of interfaces to electronic text collections depending on the different kinds of users or user needs. With such a strong cultural default in place for the analog world, there may be other reasons why alternative interfaces would not be acceptable to users. For one thing, there is the problem of having to identify and select among interfaces, unless the system does it automatically. If the system does not do it automatically, then the user has an extra step at the beginning of every task – namely, to identify the various options available and choose the appropriate one. It seems likely that the default interface would therefore be the one most frequently chosen. If the system does choose automatically, it may sometimes choose wrong or may initiate a change at an inopportune moment, potentially leaving the user feeling frustrated or helpless.

A third solution is therefore to make the functions available in search interfaces also available in browsing interfaces. To provide existing affordances by reapplying existing technologies in a new context does not seem like an unreasonable approach, and certainly to allow users to search a rich-prospect display by typing words into a keyhole search field does not compromise the new affordances of prospect. In fact, because the meaningful representation of every item in the collection is available for feedback, there are some increased opportunities made available. The same reasoning holds true for a variety of strategies used in search interfaces, including the use of indexes, keywords, and relevance ratings, just to name a few.

An example of a commercial interface that could be repurposed in this way is the one used by Amazon.com. The current Amazon interface includes limited prospect in the form of a tab system that allows users to focus the search within different product areas. The search function provides a list of results, each of which contains a variety of information, including standard fields such as bibliographical material and details of pricing and delivery, as well as related information of a less standard kind, such as sample pages, reader reviews, author statements, and a list of similar titles that might be of interest because they were part of purchase orders by other customers.

---

7 Digital information systems for cars have begun to provide some small variations in terms of feedback, including such features as proximity sensors and GPS navigation systems.

What Amazon does not currently offer is a system that allows the user to browse through a display of all the titles available. Since the number of possible products numbers in the millions, the entire collection is probably too large to be a good candidate for a rich-prospect interface. However, within a particular genre or subject area, there may be subsets of the entire collection that could be represented in some rich-prospect form. Whereas a single one of the current search results often extends beyond the length of a screen, in a rich-prospect interface, the individual items would be represented in a form short enough that a thousand or more of them might fit on the screen without the user having to scroll down to see the entire set. The designers of the system could then provide a variety of tools or enhancements for manipulating the display, which would depend in part on how the collection items have been identified and indexed within the underlying database.

Typeahead Searching

One of the possible enhancements to an existing search function is through typeahead, where the current search string as it is being created moves the insertion point on the display to match the text. The user of a search with a typeahead function therefore has live feedback on the success of the search even as it proceeds, as well as getting possible insights into available terms. If the color or some other visual feature of the found string is also changed by the interface, the user has a visual cue to identify the current position of the cursor. Typeahead functions have found commercial application in several document search systems, as well as some web browsers.

Typeahead searching, however, can only work on rich-prospect displays in cases where the search string belongs to the same category as the items being displayed for the meaningful representation of the collection. For example, if the collection is expressed as author names, and the user is searching by author, the system is providing appropriate feedback. However, if the rich-prospect interface is displaying authors and the user wishes to search by titles or keywords, the display is not helping the process. In this case, there are several alternatives. First, the system might respond by locating the appropriate title and highlighting the name of the author. The feedback would not match the input string, which is a serious problem. However, the user who has confidence in the system might nonetheless be able to understand that the items being highlighted or subsetted are those meeting the search criteria, even if the display is not the same. An alternative strategy is to have the system change the form of display to match the kind of search the user is performing. A combination of these strategies might be the most flexible solution, with the user able to specify the form of display independent of the form of the search, but with the system providing an optional prompt for cases where the search and display do not match. A third option is to have the browsing interface deactivated when the search string fails to correspond to the display, under the assumption that the user is not interested in watching the contents of the browsing interface, but simply intends to perform a straight search. Further research is necessary.

Where and When, Exactly? Prospect in Time and Space

A map is a prospect-based artifact. It provides in a portable form a part of what the view from a prominent viewpoint provides in a fixed form. In addition to being portable, it has the advantages that it can be tailored to emphasise particular information about the landscape, through various techniques that vary optical weight or tonality, as in the use of contrast, color, textual labels, and scale. Its primary disadvantages are similar to the disadvantages of prospect in general – namely, that the level of granularity of detail is not always sufficient to meet the intentions of the perceiver (or the map grows to be too large, eventually reaching the hypothetical one-to-one ratio described in fiction by Borges (1975).

There is, in maps as in the analog world, a natural trade-off between prospect and detail, which relates in the case of the map to the size and complexity of the printed artifact, and in the case of the analog world to the visibility of various details of the landscape from a given range and position. The kinds of information available from the prospect-based artifact and the situation of analog prospect may also differ, depending on the intentions of the creators of the map. As a general rule, maps are intended for wayfinding, which means that location cues are more significant than affordance cues. Different qualities of road surface are emphasised by thickness of line; rivers and other natural features are often color-coded and marked by contours and labels; landmarks are sometimes specified by name; the directions are spelled out; scale is indicated; and so on.

What is missing from a map are all the elements that are considered unimportant for wayfinding, or which are too detailed or otherwise problematic to be practical. Individual dwellings, for example, are usually not visible, and if they are visible they are not labelled. The purpose of the map is to direct the user to the correct block, after which the standard lot-numbering systems used for urban planning (at least in most North American cities) are expected to serve.

A perceiver in a position of prominence over a landscape may look at features such as potential sources of shelter, danger, food, or water, with the idea that some of these affordances may prove helpful. On the other hand, a person viewing a map may also be looking for sources of shelter, danger, food, or water, but will be seeing them primarily from the perspective of location, which is the main information the map can provide. Cues as to quality of the potential sources are not necessarily present in the prospect-based artifact.

On a standard road or city map, the information that has been selected is specifically intended to assist in wayfinding; further, the selected information is present in a standardised format, with conventional visual elements. An alternative prospect-based artifact is the aerial or satellite photograph, which often requires expert interpretation to distinguish the different component elements and what they signify. Aerial photographs contain a richness of visual detail that can paradoxically serve to obscure the prospect. Finally street-level views are even more specific, but have eliminated most of the prospect. It is for these reasons that systems like Google Maps provide the user with a choice of all three.

In addition to their default application in wayfinding, maps have been designed and used for a wide range of specialist purposes, including summarising political, economic, military, and climatic data, among others, sometimes in time series that indicate movements of people or resources over extended periods.

Virtual Datascapes

In the realm of interfaces onto collections of documents, the concept of a prospect-based artifact analogous to the map has been investigated in a number of ways. The most direct implementation is through the design of three-dimensional virtual landscapes, where digital elements are substituted for conventional landscape features. A document might be represented, for instance, by a structure that visually resembles a vertical block, which in its proportions resembles a featureless building. This metaphorical data building can be scaled according to the size of the document being represented. It can also be juxtaposed with other documents to create a cityscape of data buildings.

There are a number of difficulties that need to be addressed before this strategy can be widely adopted. First, it directly attempts to replace the desktop metaphor with a landscape metaphor, which brings with it the connotations of the computer game and what might be perceived as an inappropriate juxtaposition of the landscape with the office. Second, it is at one and the same time a form of visual overkill and visual impoverishment. A virtual landscape is a complex form of visual information, and that complexity is unnecessary, given the kinds of data that can be conveyed using the metaphor. Document size is a significant fact about a document, but from the perspective of the importance of the actual content of the document, it is not a very important fact. To scale data buildings according to the length of the documents they represent is to visually emphasise a comparatively trivial aspect of the collection. Building size, however, does not seem to provide an immediate analogy to any other document feature.

The virtual landscape is a form of visual impoverishment because although it resembles an aerial photograph (or perhaps an aerial video), the selective nature of the information makes it more like a map. Analog buildings have structural characteristics that are significant and interpretable. Digital buildings might have selected characteristics that provide additional information about the documents they represent. They might, for example, be color-coded. But the natural coupling between the appearance of buildings and their functions as human environments does not carry forward into the virtual world of datascapes. The mental models are not congruent in a way that is immediately obvious or fruitful.

Topic Maps

An alternative prospect-based artifact is the topic map, which is a form of entity-relationship (E-R) diagram. A topic map displays in a visual form the topics a document or collection contains and the relationships among the topics. The topic map has an advantage over the datascape in that the information it can represent is more significant than document size or document type – a topic map is an index to the significant content. In cases where the topics are linked to the documents they represent, a topic map also has the capacity of taking the user instantly to a desired destination.

In spite of their many admirable qualities, however, topic maps also have several limitations. First of all, from a visual perspective the form can contain features that are often unaesthetic and sometimes redundant. The information is usually composed of lines, boxes, and text. The boxes indicate entities and the lines indicate relationships among the entities. However, depending on the implementation, this system can be visually redundant along both these dimensions. The text items already indicate entities, and the Gestalt tendency to associate items in physical proximity with each other means that if related text items are juxtaposed, people will understand that they are related. As in the case of the datascape, the amount of visual emphasis given to relatively trivial or unnecessary information renders the standard E-R diagram less useful than it otherwise might be. If the redundant visual clutter is removed, then it is possible that additional meaningful information can be included in the form of numbers that indicate quantities of references or numbers of documents in the collection, and the text can be resized to cue the perceiver to relative numbers at a glance.

Leaving aside the question of its visual form, the topic map is also limited in terms of the kind of information it displays. A zoomable digital map intended for wayfinding in an analog city contains a variety of different kinds of relevant information. It has some lines that represent roads, others that represent regions, and still others for natural features, such as rivers or hills. It has a grid system of its own, usually overlaid on the grid system used by the city. It has an alphabetised index of street names. It has indicators of direction and scale. In comparison, the topic map onto a data collection shows *only* topics and their relationships (we say *only*, though of course representing relationships can be immensely informative). Forms augmented with numbers may also indicate how many documents of each kind are available in the collection. Versions with clickable entries may link to the actual documents, which is an extremely helpful feature, but only if the indexed topics are meaningful representations of the documents for a given user, and only if the number of documents is not overwhelming. If, for example, a single topic can be found in a thousand documents, a clickable topic map entry is not going to provide a very strong affordance.

In its strongest implementation, the topic map combines the advantages of a good index and keyword catalog, coupled with the dynamic opportunities for linking directly to the specified material that are made possible because the map leads to a digital collection. Topic maps are sufficiently useful that they have been adopted as an ISO standard, with an associated data standard and XML schema (Ontopia 2010). For the purposes of wayfinding within a document collection, however, there are more opportunities available.

Wayfinding

Norman Vinson (1999), with reference to work by Kevin Lynch (1960) and others, identifies five features that are often used by people for wayfinding in an analog environment, and suggests that analogous features might be useful in designing navigation strategies for the digital world. These features are paths, edges, districts, nodes, and landmarks. Most of these items are typically represented on maps. Paths are often shown as roads or public transit lines, and districts are often marked with outlines and text labels. Nodes are places where paths converge, which are visible on most maps. Some landmarks may be given, in the form of outlines and labels indicating prominent buildings or statues. Similar to nodes, edges – the boundary conditions between different kinds of landscape features – are often indicated but are not given particular emphasis.

In the world of digital collections, the concept of paths was introduced roughly 50 years before the invention of HTML. Bush (1945) suggested that a method might be developed to help over-taxed post-war scientists stay current in their literature, whereby specialists in what he called "trail blazing" would be able to create and store associated materials, in much the way an anthologiser compiles physical items:

> When the user is building a trail, he names it, inserts the name in his code book, and taps it out on his keyboard. Before him are the two items to be joined, projected onto adjacent viewing positions. Thereafter, at any time, when one of these items is in view, the other can be instantly recalled merely by tapping a button below the corresponding code space. Moreover, when numerous items have been thus joined together to form a trail, they can be reviewed in turn, rapidly or slowly, by deflecting a lever like that used for turning the pages of a book. It is exactly as though the physical items had been gathered together from widely separated sources and bound together to form a new book. It is more than this, for any item can be joined into numerous trails.

There are any number of hypertext or hypermedia authoring systems that resemble Bush's memex (though the concept of recorded trails that could be consulted by other users is absent in all major web browsers). Researchers at Brown University, for example, have developed a series of such tools, including:

- the Hypertext Editing System (HES) (1968)
- the File Retrieval and Editing System (FRESS) (1969)
- Intermedia (1985)
- Storyspace (1992)

These tools varied from one another in terms of technical implementation and range of features, but shared the capability of allowing the user to construct hyperlinked sets of information. Storyspace, for example, contained a menu item called Roadmap, which displayed a local map of paths.

Bush's ideas have also been implemented by Shipman et al. (2000) in a system designed for use in high school classrooms. Users are able to create an organising metastructure that combines existing web pages and annotations. This metastructure can be stored for subsequent use by other people, although there are issues related to copyright and the volatility of web materials which still remain to be addressed. If the system stores the pages, it not only infringes on copyright, but the pages may also become outdated. If the system does not store the pages, they may change, disappear, or move to a new server or URL, rendering the pathways that include them obsolete.

Bush's hypothetical memex and the Walden's Paths system of Shipman et al. allow users to create conceptual pathways through an electronic collection. They are not, however, particularly visual implementations of the idea of paths. Bush did not elaborate on interface ideas for the memex, and the published screen shots of Walden's Paths suggest that the web browser is the visual model adopted by the designers, with many boxes of text overlaid on each other.

An alternative display that does attempt to provide a visual implementation is the one described by Roussinov et al. (1999). Their map is intended to visually represent documents as clusters of color-coded and labelled icons on a grid. The user can open any of the items shown, and also has the ability to modify the map in various ways (for example, by rating the items shown for relevance, or removing irrelevant items altogether).

Digital versions of Vinson's other landscape features (edges, districts, nodes, and landmarks) are somewhat more difficult to identify within the desktop model, although they are fairly common in computer games and datascapes.

Panoramas

Interface panoramas are horizontally scrolling display fields that have typically been implemented based on 360 degrees, or an entire circle, of view. Many early implementations were designed for the purpose of displaying interior or exterior spaces by stitching together photographs; the technology has subsequently been extended to display other kinds of data as well. Panoramas are now used as interface tools showing a wide range of data, from network traffic to galleries of student art. By making individual items within the panorama clickable, the designer has the opportunity to make the view into an access tool, whether to more panoramas, larger format images, or any other kind of data files associated with the links.

Panoramas can be any height, and the contents typically scroll left or right at a speed determined by the current offset of the cursor off the center line. In some versions the panorama may also scroll vertically based on cursor offset up or down from the top or bottom of the pane containing the panorama; other versions have the panorama expand from a thin to thick display pane based on the vertical offset; still others have no vertical effects whatsoever. Earlier versions involving photos that had been amalgamated, as for example with QuickTime Virtual Reality (QTVR) often had an inadvertent fisheye lens effect which distorted the view and emphasised its artificiality. Panoramas created with alternative technologies, such as authoring platforms like Director or Flash, seldom show this kind of distortion.

In any case, as a strategy for providing prospect, the panorama has several advantages over the standard vertically scrolling window. First, it is controlled with cursor position rather than with a specialised device such as a scrollbar with arrows and a thumb. The effect of cursor position is arguably easier to identify and learn to use than a scrollbar, although it may be frustrating in cases where the response is sufficiently slow to create a time lag for the user, which might tend to decouple the stimulus from its feedback. The second advantage of the panorama is that it forms a complete circle, which means the user does not have to reverse the scrolling effect in order to arrive back at the beginning of the display. This continuous visual loop allows the user to pan around the entire view in either direction, at a speed that is under direct control, which quickly provides an overview of the entire display. Finally, panoramas are horizontal, which means looking at a panorama can be understood as analogous to obtaining prospect on a horizon. Although the interface is limited by the interactions of the mouse, the metaphor at work is that the user is standing at the center of a prominence and can look around at everything.

In combination, these three factors – ease of use; continuous looping under user control; and resemblance to an analog panorama – make interface panoramas a strong candidate technology for providing prospect. On the negative side of the scale are the features that sometimes make the panorama difficult to use, because it has several functions active at the same time. For instance, since cursor displacement off center determines both direction and speed, if someone wants to click an object that is visible on either of the sides of the panorama, the object will appear to run away from the cursor. People can learn to get around this problem by always moving items to be selected to the center of the panorama, where positioning the cursor will simultaneously stop the motion and allow for clicking. However, the more static quality of normal window pane movements, where the user is accustomed to seeing motionless contents unless one of the dedicated sliding tools is being employed, have created an enculturated expectation that objects will not skitter away when approached. Another design solution is therefore to add horizontal scroll bars or some other dedicated tool to control the scrolling of the panorama, which essentially converts it into a very wide scrolling window with the additional feature of wrapping back to the beginning rather than stopping at each end.

Depth of Field

In the analog world, prospect necessarily involves some depth of field. To have a view from a window onto a grove of deciduous trees is an experience involving prospect. To have a view from a window onto the trunk of a tree growing directly beside the building is to have an experience of thwarted prospect. One of the differences is depth of field. Landscape painting similarly attempts to suggest depth of field through a variety of techniques involving factors such as focal length, scale, perspective, foreground and background cues, occlusion of distant objects by closer ones, atmospheric effects such as color change or blurring, and so on.

In the digital environment, some depth cues are common while others are seldom seen. Occlusion, for instance, is a default behavior of windows, where the currently active window is intended to sit in front of any others that are open. Icons, however, are a bit more complex. Under the protocols for "drag and drop," the user is often able to trigger an application icon by placing a data icon on top of it. Folder icons, on the other hand, have the default behavior of ingesting other icons of any kind that are placed on them. The ingested icons disappear from view until the folder icon is opened. Under some conditions, it is also possible for one icon to simply occlude another, as can sometimes happen when folder contents that have been displayed as a list are subsequently displayed as a set of icons. From the user's perspective, these icon behaviors are sufficiently unrelated to depth cues that it is more realistic to discuss them as characteristics of icons rather than as metaphoric treatments of a virtual third dimension.

Some experimental designs, however, have attempted to make use of three dimensionality as a means of providing prospect without sacrificing too much screen space. An example is the kind of interface where items appear to advance and recede, either as individual objects or as parts of a larger rotating whole (such as Apple's Time Machine for browsing incremental backups of files). In general, however, the desktop and the application window are usually treated as flat surfaces. By implementing interfaces in three apparent dimensions, the developer has the opportunity to take advantage of a much larger display environment. However, there is the risk of creating too literal an interpretation of the landscape metaphor. A limited solution might therefore rely primarily on size changes that do not include perspectival narrowing, coupled with occlusion – provided that the occlusion is not implemented to such a degree as to eliminate prospect.

Chapter 7
Conclusions

This book has had several purposes. First, we hoped to introduce the principles of rich-prospect browsing to a wider audience of people working with digital cultural collections, with the hope that they would begin to implement these ideas in their own collections. Second, we wanted to show why we feel that this set of principles represents a useful way of looking at the design of browsing tools – namely, that we feel it has some theoretical grounding in the concepts of prospect and affordances, and that our various experiments have helped to examine and refine the principles. Third, we believed it might be possible to add to the ideas of prospect and affordances, by considering them in the light of the various tools we've built and the experiments we've run on them. Although there are some obvious limitations to what is possible with a rich-prospect design, there are limitations to what is possible with every kind of design. The decision that people need to make is therefore best informed by suggesting to them what the trade-offs are in choosing one approach over another. In the case of rich-prospect interfaces, the benefits are that the combination of meaningful representation of items with emergent tools for manipulating the display potentially results in an intuitive way for users to understand an entire collection and how its designers conceived of it. People are also able to see information that can remind them of things they've forgotten, or suggest to them things that they never knew. They can be reassured about what is included in a collection and what is not there. In some forms of rich prospect, the patterns that the interface generates can be used for critical tasks such as algorithmic criticism (textual analysis) or cultural analytics (studying large-scale cultural phenomena using digital artifacts). The difficulties arise in choosing an appropriate meaningful representation and in working with the available screen real estate and processing power.

The Purposes of an Interface

Having considered many of the details that go into the development of rich-prospect interfaces, and looked at some examples, this might be an opportune moment to revisit the question of what purpose interfaces serve. The answers, of course, are highly imbricated with the underlying data and algorithms that produce the substance represented by the interface. But leaving aside these nonetheless salient details, it is still possible to outline several higher-level conceptual reasons for the existence of an interface.

First, some interface, however rudimentary, is necessary between people and computers. Otherwise their interactions will be minimal, unproductive and unpredictable. The history of computing can be seen as running in parallel with the history of interface development, with batch processing at the beginning and highly nuanced communicative interactions more recently, not only between people and computers, but between people as mediated by computers. Some would contest this simplification, feeling that batch processing, especially of the type practiced by the big iron high-performance computing shops, is well and thriving. Be that as it may, the computer as a part of human life has grown in parallel with the accessibility of its interfaces with people. The goal of creating a human-language interface remains largely elusive, so we have opted instead for graphical interfaces. As many digital humanists are aware, a command-line interface can accomplish almost everything that a graphical interface can accomplish, and do it in most cases more quickly and easily. It is also true the affordances of web browser search fields are growing to resemble command lines. However, command-line interfaces are largely seen by the public as ancient technology, appropriate only for specialists (those who know the vocabulary needed to invoke commands with the properly expressed parameters). So it is not unreasonable to say that computer interfaces exist in large part to make computing accessible.

By extension, they also exist to make computing attractive. They are a means of increasing, not necessarily the affordances of computers, but rather their affordance strength. From the perspective of people who are creating a digital collection, it is therefore not unreasonable to think of the interface as a form of public relations or marketing (Terras 2010). Online materials and their uses compete for mindshare with a large number of other human activities, many of which will be attractive. It is therefore a kind of professional responsibility to make a conscientious effort to compete successfully.

One strategy is to pay as much attention as possible to the aesthetic function. Another is to increase the affordances of the collection through the provision of enhanced or standardised metadata, allowing collections to be used together. A third approach is to provide people with tools, such as interactive visualisations, that help make the material more useful because there are more things to do with it. A promising direction is Lev Manovich's cultural analytics (2009), which combines vast numbers of visual images with spreadsheets of metadata about the images, on large-scale displays that allow researchers to dynamically organise material in looking for interesting patterns. A perhaps more generalised formulation of a similar concept is Stephen Ramsay's algorithmic criticism (2003), where the computer is used to generate patterns that can be interrogated using the hermeneutic or interpretive skills of humanists trained to work with smaller datasets or other kinds of patterns. Our own interface that shows the most promise as a tool for this kind of interpretive analysis is the Mandala Browser.

Interfaces and Visualisations

A visualisation is a visual pattern that emerges from information and that is presented through some interface. Some visualisations are static, such as bar graphs and pie charts, and exist to represent and communicate conclusions. Having crunched the numbers, a static visualisation shows the result. Intrinsic in most forms of static visualisation is the conversion of some phenomenon into numbers that can then be rendered in visual form. Alternatively, it is possible to use existing visual elements to create patterns, as we've attempted to do in Piotr Michura's repetition loops, where the words themselves become the basis for the pattern being displayed.

For interfaces that have implemented the advice of Shneiderman et al. (1992) on the principle of direct manipulation, we can say that there is a sense in which the data are the visualisation, and the visualisation is the interface. That is, people will be able to interact with the information in front of them with a minimal degree of mediation from other interface gadgets such as buttons and menus and checkboxes and sliders. In practice, this approach to design is not always possible, although there are some excellent examples, such as the use of text for links. Our "designs for decision support" also use information displays as interactive elements, so that sensitivity thresholds, for instance, can be adjusted by moving a line on the face of a gear. In the showcase browsers, we have various kinds of information that function as interactive elements. The images on the home page are all links to more information. The buttons that group them or that toggle additional information off and on are also all generated from the collection metadata. Finally, the detail pages can serve as editing tools, so that people with the right authorisation to the system can log in and change whatever is visible.

Rich-prospect browsing interfaces can therefore be considered as a form of information visualisation. Most interfaces, however, are not visualisations per se, serving instead to provide access to information.

Prospect and Affordances

Gibson suggests that people are able to directly perceive opportunities for action in the environment. Appleton's idea is that people have a predilection for being able to obtain prospect on a landscape. If both theories are correct, then people who are able to obtain prospect should also be able to directly perceive at least some of the opportunities for action that prospect makes available, although it is also understood that perception and adoption of affordances in general require some degree of prior learning.

There are also differences to be considered between various kinds of opportunity for action. Some actions are sequential, as for example when a person leaves home to go out and buy a newspaper. Some actions are nested, as when someone grasps and turns a doorknob in order to open the door. Most actions need to be learned, as does the ability to perceive that they are possible, and there are significant differences in learning based on culture, interpersonal factors, and individual characteristics of the learner such as capacity, previous experience, and so on. The literature on affordances includes discussion and debate of over a dozen such topic areas, ranging from the ontological status of affordances to the nuances of intention in use, all within the context of either the natural environment or the built one, where the creation of new affordances is part of the reflexive cycle of affordance and perception that is intrinsic to human culture and development.

Situated within this larger framework, the creation and learning of new opportunities for action in the digital environment does not mark a dramatic change in human behavior. If some of these affordances relate to existing perceptual predilections in people, then those affordances should have the advantage of being built on strengths that have been long established.

Applying Rich Prospect to Computer Interfaces

Functions that are already available through interfaces with no prospect can also be available in interfaces with rich prospect. These functions include various forms of searching, either through simple text string comparisons or else through more sophisticated information retrieval algorithms that involve stemming, indexing, semantic clustering, and so on.

In addition, rich-prospect interfaces make possible several new opportunities for action. The new affordances discussed in this book include those for manipulating the rich-prospect display of meaningful representations of content items through zooming, panning, sorting, selecting, grouping, subsetting, renaming, annotating, opening, and structuring the items. Various technologies have been designed over the years by researchers and developers interested in facilitating each of these functions, although not always with respect to interfaces that could be strictly called rich prospect. The review of this literature on visualisation technologies yields strategies ranging from fisheye menus, which can be used to scan over areas of microtext (Bederson 2000), to the PhotoFinder toolkit, which provides the user with a wall of tiny photos and related utilities, as the interface to a digital photo archive (Shneiderman et al. 2002).

There are also several perceptual features that do not represent opportunities for action per se, but which are nonetheless of potential significance to users. The perceptual features that have been discussed in this book in terms of rich-prospect interfaces are those that permit direct insight into contents, structure, context, features, limitations, connections, trends, anomalies, navigation, reminders, reassurance, and a reduced sense of helplessness.

Applying Rich Prospect to Interpretively Tagged Text Collections

While there are a variety of new potential affordances and perceptual opportunities provided by rich-prospect interfaces to digital collections, the degree of complexity increases when prospect is applied to interpretively tagged text collections. A collection with an interpretive level of tagging is one where information is included in the tags that is otherwise not available in the text that the tags are marking.

In order to provide rich prospect on a tagged collection, it is necessary to consider not only the display of the contents of the collection, but also the display of the tags, tag attributes, and the values contained in the attributes. Since one potential use of tagged text is to allow the user to extract relevant sections of documents, it may also be necessary to consider some means of providing prospect on segments of documents, rather than treating each document as a single entity.

Each of these components of the interpretively tagged text collection may lend itself to more than one strategy for providing prospect. It may be useful in some instances, for example, to provide a rich-prospect form of display of the tagset itself, independent of the way in which it has been applied in the documents. Display of the tagset may provide perceptual features that give insight into the nature of the collection and how it has been understood by the people who developed it. It may also provide opportunities for action, by allowing the user to manipulate the display in various ways, or by using components from the display in the construction of queries on the collection.

Rich prospect on the tagging of a collection, on the other hand, may turn out in many cases to be above the level of manageable size, simply by requiring the display of too many items. Strategies may therefore be needed to provide other forms of prospect, involving subsets of the collection, extracted portions of multiple documents, or the display of the tagging as it has been applied in individual documents that have been opened for reading.

The design process for rich-prospect interfaces necessarily involves some mandatory activities, including the need to establish some appropriate means of representing every item in the collection and to determine in what ways the contents or tagging of the collection lend themselves to the provision of various methods for manipulating the display through sorting, grouping, subsetting and so on. It is also useful to establish which of the potential new affordances are of particular significance for a given set of users of a collection, whether through applying the factors in the affordance strength vector or through some other means.

In addition, it should be noted that not all collections are going to be amenable to rich-prospect display, since some may contain too many items, or the items may not be homogeneous enough for there to be a single means of representing them. In these latter cases it may be possible to identify more complex forms of representation that combine tags, attributes, or contents.

Evaluating New Affordances

The primary difficulty in the evaluation of new affordances is to avoid committing a category error: to keep from comparing apples and oranges, in the sense that a new affordance usually cannot be compared to an old one. By definition, new affordances are opportunities for action that were not previously available. In order to study an interface that offers new affordances, it is therefore useful to first determine whether the new affordances are of interest or potential benefit to the users of a particular collection. It is then necessary to determine the degree to which the new affordances are valuable as they have been implemented in the interface.

In this context, we have developed an affordance strength vector space containing factors that have been singled out as being potentially relevant in the discussion of the relative merits of various affordances. Each of the factors deals with the relation between the person and the object in a particular environment. By associating numeric ratings with the different factors, it is possible to arrive at an affordance strength vector value. By asking users to discuss each of the factors in the vector space, it is also possible to discover details that could not be captured by a simple numerical rating. Our affordance strength model has the following components: tacit capacity, situated potential (including awareness and environmental support), tendency (including motivation, preference, and habit), ability, and agential support.

What We Have Come to Believe to this Point

Research is an ongoing endeavour, and conclusions can be subject to revision. However, we have come to the following conclusions so far:

- People are not intimidated by thousands of items on the screen, provided that the items seem to adhere to some organising principle.
- As a corollary to the previous point: randomness makes people nervous.
- Controls need to look like controls (standard controls or recognisable metaphors) or they can easily be missed.
- Information doesn't need to be persistently visible in order for it to be useful in grouping.
- People should be able to mark the representations (such as images) in a rich-prospect browser.
- Given a flattened set of metadata, people will use each item roughly equally in grouping images.
- Interface vocabulary is less important than interface design in communicating how to use an interface.
- The rich-prospect browser does not need to be the central feature of the design – it is possible to strengthen other designs with some rich-prospect component.

- Although the contents of digital collections can have a pedagogical value, an online interface itself is not a good method of educating people.
- Realities of implementing designs (constraints of time, limitations of technologies, available programmers, and so on) can require some compromises but there is still clear value in designing from a strong conceptual framework.

Future Research

There are many areas where further research will be useful. We summarise a few here.

1. We would do well to study the implicit associations relating to the aesthetic function. Possible secondary measures include:
    - the willingness to engage in sustained use of the visualisation even without a clear agenda
    - the willingness to spend time troubleshooting
    - under-reporting of perceived estimates of time
2. The strategy of attempting to prime users with some form of fleeting image could prove useful to the interface design community, especially if the contents of the visual priming were related to the structure of the collection.
3. What can we learn about handling unselected items from a rich-prospect display? Should the material:
    - Disappear from the screen?
    - Remain visible but be de-emphasised somehow, and if so, is it better to use resizing, color-coding, or removal to another part of the screen, or a combination of the three?
    - Be aggregated into an icon that can be expanded?
4. How does sequential prospect compare to spatial prospect in providing each of the various related affordances?
5. What is the best method of highlighting search results when the search string is not currently displayed in the rich-prospect display?
    - Highlight the results even without the search term appearing.
    - Change the meaningful representation to match the category of the search term.
    - Allow the user to specify the form of display independent of the form of the search, but with the system providing an optional prompt for cases where the search and display do not match.
    - Have the browsing interface deactivated when the search string fails to correspond to the display, under the assumption that the user is not interested in watching the contents of the browsing interface, but simply intends to perform a straight search.

Design is a fundamental component of our process of developing prototype tools, especially for digital humanists. Although for us design is a research area in its own right, we also believe that the time and effort needed to design interfaces are a sound investment, one that seems undervalued in many academic projects. Design is a way of gaining the trust of users by expressing that their experience deserves attention; it also conveys the message that an attempt has been made to understand and model the domain of application. We have presented several of our projects, most of which have some form of prospect. The projects range from very real-world, intuitive and practical interfaces to more conceptual, unusual and experimental interfaces. In all cases we have been interested in how our knowledge of visual information design can inform development to produce interesting and useful tools for accessing and studying digital cultural heritage.

References

Ahlberg, C. and Shneiderman, B. (1994a). "The Alphaslider: a compact and rapid selector." *Conference Proceedings on Human factors in Computing Systems: celebrating interdependence*, pp. 365–71.

Ahlberg C. and Shneiderman, B. (1994b). "Visual information seeking: Tight coupling of dynamic query filters with starfield displays." In *Proc. Conference on Human Factors in Computing Systems* (CHI 94), ACM Press, 1994, pp. 313–17.

Albright, K.S. (2004). "Environmental Scanning: Radar for Success." *Information Management Journal. 38*(3), 38–45.

Appleton, J. (1975). *The experience of landscape*. London: John Wiley & Sons.

Arazy O., Stroulia, E., Ruecker, S., Arias, C., Fiorentino, C., Ganev, V., and Yau, T. (2010). "Recognizing Contributions in Wikis: Authorship Categories, Algorithms, and Visualizations." *Journal of the American Society for Information Science and Technology (JASIST). 61*(6), 1166–79.

Baars, B.J. (1997). *In the Theatre of Consciousness: The Workspace of the Mind.* NY and Oxford: Oxford University Press.

Back, M., Gold, R., Balsamo, A., Chow, M., Gorbet, M.G., Harrison, S.R., MacDonald, D., and Minneman, S.L. (2001). "Designing Innovative Reading Experiences for a Museum Exhibition." *IEEE Computer. 34*(1), 80–87.

Baldonado, M.Q.W., Woodruff, A, and Kuchinksy, A. (2000). "Guidelines for Using Multiple Views in Information Visualization." *Proceedings of the Working Conference on Advanced Visual Interfaces*, pp. 110–19. http://doi.acm.org/10.1145/345513.345271

Bardzell, J. (2009). Interaction criticism and aesthetics. In *Proceedings of the 27th international Conference on Human Factors in Computing Systems* (Boston, MA, USA, April 04–09, 2009). CHI '09. ACM, New York, NY, 2357–66. http://doi.acm.org.login.ezproxy.library.ualberta.ca/10.1145/1518701.1519063.

Baudisch, P. (1998). "Don't click, paint! Using toggle maps to manipulate sets of toggle switches." In *Proceedings of the 11th Annual ACM Symposium on User interface Software and Technology* (San Francisco, California, United States, November 01–04, 1998). UIST '98. ACM. NY, 65–66. DOI= http://doi.acm.org.login.ezproxy.library.ualberta.ca/10.1145/288392.288574.

Bederson, B.B. (2001). "PhotoMesa: a zoomable image browser using quantum treemaps and bubblemaps." *Proceedings of the 14th annual ACM symposium on User interface software and technology*, pp. 71–80. http://doi.acm.org/10.1145/502348.502359

Bederson, B.B. (2000). "Fisheye menus." *Proceedings of the 13th annual ACM symposium on user interface software and technology*, pp. 217–25. http://doi.acm.org/10.1145/354401.354782

Bertelsen, O.W. and Pold, S. (2004). "Criticism as an approach to interface aesthetics." *Proceedings of NordiCHI'2004*. Tampere, Finland, pp. 23–32.

Bingham, G.P. (2000). "Events (like objects) are things, can have affordance properties, and can be perceived." *Ecological Psychology*. *12*(1), 29–36.

Booker, J., Buennemeyer, T., Sabri, A., and North, C. (2007). "High-Resolution Displays Enhancing Geo-Temporal Data Visualizations." In *Proceedings of the 45th Annual Southeast Regional Conference*, Winston-Salem, NC, March 23–24, 2007. New York: ACM Press: 443–48.

Booth, W.C., Colomb, G.G., and Williams, J.M. (2008). *The Craft of Research*. 3rd Edn. University of Chicago Press.

Borges, J.L. (1975). "On Rigor in Science" in *A Universal History of Infamy*. Trans. Norman Thomas de Giovanni. London: Penguin Books. Video and Spanish soundtrack at: http://boingboing.net/2009/05/20/a-map-the-size-of-th.html

Boschker, M.S.J., Bakker, F.C., and Michaels, C.F. (2002). "Memory for the functional characteristics of climbing walls: Perceiving affordances." *Journal of Motor Behavior*. *34*(1), 25–36.

Broughton, V. (1998). "The revision process in UDC: An examination of the systematic auxiliary of 'Point-of-View' using facet analytical methods." Paper given at the IFLA General Conference Amsterdam. http://www.ifla.org/IV/ifla64/103-158e.htm

Brown, S., Antoniuk, J., Bauer, M., Berberich, J., Radzikowska, M., Ruecker, S., and Yung, T. (2010). "How Do You Visualize a Million Links?" Paper presented at the Digital Humanities 2010 conference. King's College London, July 7–11, 2010.

Bush, V. (1945). "As we may think." *The Atlantic Monthly*. *176*(1), 101–8. http://www.theatlantic.com/unbound/flashbks/computer/bushf.htm

Butler, T. (1998). "Eluding the Chains of Technology: Computer Systems for Orlando." In Hockey, S., Butler, T., Brown, S., and Fisher, S. *The Orlando Project: Humanities Computing in Conversation with Literary History*. ACH Session. http://xml.coverpages.org/hockeyACH97.html

Carroll, N. (2001). *Beyond Aesthetics: Philosophical Essays*. Cambridge University Press.

Chemero, A. (2001). "What we perceive when we perceive affordances: Commentary on Michaels (2000) "Information, perception, and action."" *Ecological Psychology*. *13*(2), 111–16.

Chow, R. and Ruecker, S. (2006). "Transferability – A Wonder on the Ground of Design Research." *Proceedings of Wonderground*. Lisbon, Portugal. November 1–5, 2006.

CiteSeer. (2010). NEC Research Institute. http://citeseer.nj.nec.com/

Clement, T., Steger, S., Unsworth, J., and Uszkalo, K. (2008). "How Not to Read a Million Books." Rutgers Seminar in *The History of the Book*. http://www3.isrl.illinois.edu/~unsworth/hownot2read.html

Clements, P., Brown, S., Grundy, I. (2006). *The Orlando Project: A History of Women's Writing in the British Isles from the Beginnings to the Present*. Cambridge University Press.

Cooper, A. (1998). *The Inmates are Running the Asylum: Why High Tech Products Drive Us Crazy and How to Restore the Sanity*. Indianapolis: SAMS.

Cyr, D. (2010). "Website Design and Trust Across Cultures." *Proceedings of the annual conference on Cultural Attitudes Toward Technology and Education (CATAC 2010)*. Vancouver, BC: University of British Columbia, June 15–18, 2010, pp. 135–49.

Czerwinski, M., Dumais, S., Robertson, G., Dziadosz, S., Tiernan, S., and van Dantzich, M. (1999). "Visualizing implicit queries for information management and retrieval." *Proceedings of the CHI 99 conference on Human factors in computing systems: the CHI is the limit*, pp. 560–67. http://doi.acm.org/10.1145/302979.303158

DeRose, S.J., Durand, D.G, Mylonas, E., and Renear, A.H. (1990). "What Is Text, Really?" *Journal of Computing in Higher Education. 1*(2), 3–26.

Dietz, P., Raskar, R., Booth, S., van Vaar, J., Wittenburg, K., and Knep, B. (2004). "Multi-Projectors and Implicit Interaction in Persuasive Public Displays." In *Proceedings of the Working Conference on Advanced Visual Interfaces, Gallipoli, Italy, May 25–28, 2004*. New York: ACM Press: 209–217.

Dillon, A. (2001). "Beyond usability: process, outcome and affect in human-computer interactions." *Canadian Journal of Library and Information Science, 26*(4), 57–69. Available at: http://www.ischool.utexas.edu/~adillon/publications.html

Djajadiningrat, J.P., Gaver, W.W., and Fres, J.W. (2000). "Interaction relabelling and extreme characters: methods for exploring aesthetic interactions." In *Proceedings of the 3rd Conference on Designing interactive Systems: Processes, Practices, Methods, and Techniques* (New York City, New York, United States, August 17–19, 2000). D. Boyarski and W.A. Kellogg (eds). DIS '00. ACM, New York, NY, 66–71. DOI= http://doi.acm.org.login.ezproxy.library.ualberta.ca/10.1145/347642.347664.

Drucker, J. (2009). *SpecLab: digital aesthetics and projects in speculative computing*. University of Chicago Press.

Drucker, J. and Nowviskie, B. (2003). *The Temporal Modelling Project*. http://www2.iath.virginia.edu/time/time.html

Dublin Core. (2010). Dublin Core Metadata Initiative. http://dublincore.org/documents/dces/

Dufrenne, M. (1973). *The phenomenology of aesthetic experience*. Evanston, Illinois: Northwestern University Press.

Dyens, O., Forest, D., Mondou, P, Cools, V., and Johnston, D. (2008). "Information visualization and text mining: application to a corpus on posthumanism."

Paper presented at the Digital Humanities 2008 conference. Oulu, Finland. June 25–29, 2008.

Eick, S.G. (1994). "Data Visualization Sliders." *Proceedings of the 7th annual ACM symposium on User interface software and technology*, pp. 119–20. http://doi.acm.org/10.1145/192426.192472.

Ellis, R.R., Flanagan, J.R. and Lederman, S.J. (1999). "The influence of visual illusions on grasp position." *Experimental Brain Research. 125*. 109–114.

Fishwick, P.A. (ed). (2006). *Aesthetic Computing*. Cambridge: MIT Press.

Fishwick, P.A., Diehl, S., Prophet, J., and Lowgren, J. (2005). "Perspectives in aesthetic computing." *Leonardo. 38*(2), 47–53.

Fleming, J. (1998). *Web Navigation: Designing the User Experience*. Sebastopol, CA: O'Reilly and Associates, Inc.

Frascara, J. (ed.). (2006). *Designing Effective Communications: Creating Contexts for Clarity and Meaning*. NY: Allworth Press.

Frascara, J. (1999). In conversation. University of Alberta, Edmonton.

Frascara, J. (1997). *User-centred Graphic Design*. London: Taylor and Francis.

Freisner, T. (2010). "History of SWOT Analysis." Chichester: Marketing Teacher, Ltd. http://www.marketingteacher.com/swot/history-of-swot.html

Galey, A. and Ruecker, S. (2010). "How a Prototype Argues." *Literary and Linguistic Computing. 25*(3).

Gaver, W. (1996). "Situating Action II: Affordances for Interaction: The Social Is Material for Design." *Ecological Psychology 8*(2), 111–29. Lawrence Erlbaum Associates, Inc.

Gaver, W., Bowers, J., Boucher, A., Law, A., Pennington, S., and Villar, N. (2006). "The history tablecloth: illuminating domestic activity." In *Proceedings of the 6th Conference on Designing interactive Systems* (University Park, PA, USA, June 26–28, 2006). DIS '06. ACM, NY, 199–208. DOI= http://doi.acm.org.login.ezproxy.library.ualberta.ca/10.1145/1142405.1142437.

Gaver, W., Dunne, T., and Pacenti, E. (1999). "Cultural Probes." *Interactions. 6*(1), 21–29.

Giacometti, A., Ruecker, S., Craig, I., Derksen, G., and Radzikowska, M. (2008). "Introducing the Ripper Interface for Text Collections." Paper presented at the Canadian Symposium on Text Analysis (CaSTA) Conference: New Directions in Text Analysis. A Joint Humanities Computing, Computer Science Conference at University of Saskatchewan, Saskatoon, October 16–18, 2008.

Gibson, E.J. (2000). "Where is the information for affordances?" *Ecological Psychology. 12*(1), 53–56.

Gibson, J.J. (1979). *The Ecological Approach to Visual Perception*. Boston: Houghton-Mifflin.

Gibson, J.J. (1979u). A Study in the Psychology of Decorative Art. In *The Purple Perils*. Unpublished manuscript. http://www.ksu.edu/psych/farris/gibson/files/decorative.html

Given, L., Sadler, B., Ruecker, S., and Ruskin, A. (2005). "Similarity Clustering as a Design Principle for Digital Collections: Creating Usable Interfaces for Seniors." Paper presented at the conference of the American Society for Information Science and Technology (ASIS&T) 2005. Charlotte, North Carolina. Oct 28–Nov 2, 2005.

Given, L., Ruecker, S., Simpson, H., Sadler, B., and Ruskin, A. (2007). "Inclusive Interface Design for Seniors: Exploring the Health Information-Seeking Context." *JASIST*. *58*(11), 1610–17.

Grønbæk, K., Rohde, A., Sundararajah, B., and Bech-Petersen, S. (2006). "InfoGallery: Informative Art Services for Physical Library Spaces." In *Proceedings of the 6th ACM/IEEE-CS Joint Conference on Digital Libraries, Chapel Hill, NC, June 11– 15, 2006*. New York: ACM Press: 21–30.

Grundy, I., Clements, P., Brown, S., Butler, T., Cameron, R., Coulombe, G., Fisher, S., and Wood, J. (2000). Dates and ChronStructs: Dynamic Chronology in the Orlando Project. *Literary and Linguistic Computing*. *15*(3), (2000), 265–89.

Guiard, Y. (1983). "The lateral coding of rotation: A study of the Simon effect with wheel-rotation responses." *Journal of Motor Behavior*, 15, 331–42.

Hallnäs, L. and Redström, J. (2002). "From use to presence. On the expressions and aesthetics of everyday computational things." *ACM Transactions on Computer-Human Interaction (ToCHI)*. *9*(2), 106–124.

Hecht, H. (2000). "Are events and affordances commensurate terms?" *Ecological Psychology*. *12*(1), 57–63.

Helmer-Poggenpohl, S. (1999). "Design Moves: Approximating a desired future with users." *Conference proceedings on Design and the Social Sciences: Making Connections*. Edmonton, Alberta, Canada. Sept. 30 – Oct. 3, 1999.

Hill, L.L., Carver, L., Larsgaard, M., Dolin, R., Frew, T.R., and Rae, M.A. (2000). "Alexandria digital library: user evaluation studies and system design." *Journal of the American Society for Information Science*. *51*(3), 246–59.

Hill, W.C., Hollan, J.D., Wroblewski, D., and McCandless, T. (1992). "Edit Wear and Read Wear." Conference proceedings on Human factors in computing systems, pp. 3–9. http://doi.acm.org/10.1145/142750.142751

Hockey, S. (2000). *Electronic Texts in the Humanities*. Oxford University Press.

Höge, H. (1990). "Ecological perception and aesthetics: pictures are affordance-free." In Klaus Landwehr (ed.). *Ecological Perception Research, Visual Communication, and Aesthetics*. NY: Springer-Verlag.

Hommel, B. (1993). "Inverting the Simon effect by intention: determinants of direction and extent of effects of irrelevant spatial information." *Psychological Research*. *55*, 270–79.

Hoyer, K.F. (2000). In conversation. Calgary, Alberta.

Hutchby, I. (2003) "Affordances and the Analysis of Technologically Mediated Interaction." *Sociology*. *37*(3), 581–89.

Hutchby, I. (2001) "Technologies, Texts and Affordances." *Sociology*. *35*(2), 441–56.

Izadi, S., Fitzpatrick, G., Rodden, T., Harry, Yvonne, and Siân. (2005). "The Iterative Design and Study of a Large Display for Shared and Sociable Spaces." In *Proceedings of the 2005 Conference on Designing For User Experience,*

San Francisco, CA, November 03–05, 2005. ACM International Conference Proceeding Series, vol. 135. New York: ACM Press: 2–19.

Jennings, M. (2000). "Theory and Models for Creating Engaging and Immersive Ecommerce Websites." *Proceedings of SIGCPR, Evanston, Illinois*. NY: ACM Press, 77–85.

Jordan, P. (2003). Workshop on personas and scenarios. Include 2003. Helen Hamlyn Research Institute, Royal College of Art, London, England. March 25–8, 2003.

Jordan, P. (2000). *Designing Pleasurable Products: An Introduction to the New Human Factors*. London: Taylor and Francis.

Karvonen, K. (2000). "The beauty of simplicity." *Proceedings on the 2000 conference on Universal Usability*.

Kaugars, K. (1998). "Integrated multi scale text retrieval visualization." *Proceedings of the conference on CHI 98 summary: human factors in computing systems*, pp. 307–8. http://doi.acm.org/10.1145/286498.286782

Khaslavsky, J. and Shedroff, N. (1999). "Understanding the Seductive Experience." *Communications of the ACM*. *42*(5), 45–49.

Koffka, K. (1935). *Principles of Gestalt Psychology*. NY: Harcourt, Brace, and World, Inc.

Kotchoubey, B. (2000). "About hens and eggs – perception and action, ecology and neuroscience: a reply to Michaels (2000)." *Ecological Psychology*. *13*(2), 123–33.

Kurosu, M. and Kashimura, K. (1995). "Apparent Usability vs. Inherent Usability: Experimental analysis on the determinants of the apparent usability." *CHI-95 Mosaic of Creativity*. NY: ACM Press, 292–93.

Lakoff, G. (1980). *Metaphors we live by*. The University of Chicago Press.

Lim, L. (2010). "Impacts of Culture on Web Usability." *Proceedings of the annual conference on Cultural Attitudes Toward Technology and Education (CATAC 2010)*. Vancouver, BC: University of British Columbia. June 15–18, 2010, pp. 124–34.

Lintern, G. (2000). "An affordance-based perspective on human-machine interface design." *Ecological Psychology*. *12*(1), 65–9.

Liu, Y., and Smith, J. (2008). "A Relational Database Model for Text Encoding." [2008, rept. 2008]. *Digital Studies / Le Champ NuméRique, 0*(0.12). http://www.digitalstudies.org/ojs/index.php/digital_studies/article/view/133/182

Liu, Y.H., Dantzig, P., Sachs, M., Corey, J.T., Hinnebusch, M.T., Damashek, M., and Cohen, J. (2000). Visualizing document classification: A search aid for the digital library. *Journal of the American Society for Information Science*. *51*(3), 216–227. http://www3.interscience.wiley.com/cgi-bin/issuetoc?ID=69501275

Livingstone, M. (2002). *Vision and Art: the Biology of Seeing*. NY: Harry N. Abrams, Inc.

Luis, S.-M., and Dyson, M.C. (2008). "The effect of violating visual conventions of a website on user performance and disorientation. How bad can it be?" *Proceedings of SIGDOC'08*, Sept. 22–24, 2008, Lisbon, Portugal, pp. 47–54.

Lynch, K. (1960). *The Image of the City*. Cambridge: MIT Press.

Manovich, L. (2009). "Cultural Analytics." Plenary address presented at the Digital Humanities 2009 conference. University of Maryland. June 22–25, 2009.

Maple, A. (1995). *Faceted Access: A Review of the Literature*. Presented at the Music Library Association Annual Meeting. http://library.music.indiana.edu/tech_s/mla/facacc.rev Marshall, C.C. and Brush, A.J. (2004). "Exploring the Relationship between Personal and Public Annotations." In *Proceedings of the ACM/IEEE Joint Conference on Digital Libraries (JCDL04), Tucson, Arizona, June 7–11, 2004*, pp. 349–57.

Mauss, M. (1935, 1973). "Techniques of the body." In Roy Bailey et al. (eds). *Economy and Society*. London: Routledge and Kegan Paul.

McCarty, W. (1991). "Finding Implicit Patterns in Ovid's Metamorphoses with TACT." *CCH Working Papers*. v1. http://www.kcl.ac.uk/humanities/cch/chwp/mccarty/index.html

Mehta, P., Stafford, A., Bouchard, M., Ruecker, S., Anvik, K., Rossello, X., and Shiri, A. (2009). "Four Ways of Making Sense: Designing and Implementing Searchling, a Visual Thesaurus-Enhanced Interface for Multilingual Digital Libraries." *Proceedings of the Chicago Colloquium on Digital Humanities and Computer Science*. *1*(1).

Meredith-Lobay, M. (2009). *A Contextual Landscape Study of the Early Christian Churches of Argyll: the persistence of memory*. British Archaeological Reports, Brit. Ser. No. 488.

Metadata Encoding and Transmission Standard. (2010). Library of Congress. http://www.loc.gov/standards/mets/

Michaels, C.F. (2000). "Information, perception, and action: what should ecological psychologists learn from Milner and Goodale (1995)?" *Ecological Psychology*. *12*(3), 241–58.

Milic, L. (1967). "Winged Words: Varieties of Computer Application to Literature." *Computers and the Humanities*. 2(1).

Milner, A.D. and Goodale, M.A. (1995). *The Visual Brain in Action*. Oxford University Press.

Mitchell, T.C. (1993). *Redefining Designing: From form to experience*. New York: Van Nostrand Reinhold.

Moretti, F. (2005). *Graphs, Maps, Trees: Abstract Models for a Literary History*. London: Verso.

Munro, T. (1956). *Toward Science in Aesthetics: Selected Essays*. NY: Liberal Arts Press.

Nakamura, J. and Csikszentmihalyi, M. (2002). "The concept of flow." In C.R. Snyder and S.J. Lopez (eds), *Handbook of positive psychology*. Oxford, UK: Oxford University Press, pp. 89–105.

Nelson, T. (1980). *Literary Machines: The report on, and of, Project Xanadu concerning word processing, electronic publishing, hypertext, thinkertoys, tomorrow's intellectual revolution, and certain other topics including knowledge, education and freedom*. Sausalito, California: Mindful Press.

Nelson, T., Johnson, T., Strong, M. and Rudakewich, G. (2001). "Perception of tree canopy." *Journal of Environmental Psychology. 21*(3), 315–24.

Ni, Tao, Bowman, D.A, and Jian Chen. (2006). "Increased Display Size and Resolution Improve Task Performance in Information-Rich Virtual Environments." In *Proceedings of Graphics Interface 2006, Quebec, Canada, June 07–09, 2006*. ACM International Conference Proceeding Series, vol. 137. New York: ACM Press: 139–46.

Ngo, D.C.L., Teo, L.S., and Byrne, J.G. (2002). "Evaluating Interface Esthetics." *Knowledge and Information Systems. 4*, 46–79.

Norman, D.A. (1993). *Things That Make Us Smart: Defending Human Attributes in the Age of the Machine*. Reading, Massachusetts: Addison-Wesley Publishing Company.

Norman, D.A. (1990). *The Design of Everyday Things*. NY: Doubleday.

Ontopia. (2010). *Ontopia: Solutions for Managing Knowledge and Information.* http://www.ontopia.net/section.jsp?id=specifications

Paredes-Olea, M., Ruecker, S., Fiorentino, C., and Forbes, F. (2008). "Using an Affordance Strength Approach to Study the Possible Redeployment of Designs for Decision Support Visualization." Paper presented at the 9th Advances in Qualitative Methods Conference 2008. Banff, Canada. October 8–11, 2008.

Petersen, M.G., Iverson, O., Krogh, P. and Ludvigsen, M. (2004). "Aesthetic interaction: a pragmatist's aesthetics of interactive systems." *Proceedings of Designing Interactive Systems*. NY: ACM Press, 269–76.

Pickering, J. (2000). "On the proper treatment of affordance: formality or mutuality?" *Ecological Psychology. 12*(1), 71–77.

Pirolli, P., Schank, P., Hearst, M., and Diehl, C. (1996). "Scatter / Gather Browsing Communicates the Topic Structure of a Very Large Text Collection." Proceedings of the SIGCHI conference on Human factors in computing systems: common ground, pp. 213–220. http://doi.acm.org/10.1145/238386.238489

Potter, R. (1991). "Statistical Analysis of Literature: A Retrospective on *Computers and the Humanities*, 1966–1990." *Computers and the Humanities*. (25)6.

Pujol, M. (2001). "Design as a social practice." Public lecture. Trans. Jorge Frascara. Edmonton: Department of Art and Design, University of Alberta.

Pye, D. (1978). *The nature and aesthetics of design*. NY: Van Nostrand Reinhold.

Ramsay, S. (2003). "Toward an Algorithmic Criticism." *Literary and Linguistic Computing. 18*(2), 167–74.

Renear, A. (2004). "Text Encoding." In *A Companion to Digital Humanities*, (eds) Susan Schreibman, Ray Siemens, John Unsworth. Oxford: Blackwell. http://www.digitalhumanities.org/companion/

Rockwell, G. (2003). "Serious Play at Hand: Is Gaming Serious Research in the Humanities?" *Text Technology*, 2.

Roussinov, D., Tolle, K., Ramsey, M., McQuaid, M., and Chen, H. (1999). "Visualizing Internet search results with adaptive self-organizing maps." *Proceedings of the 22nd annual international ACM SIGIR conference on*

Research and development in information retrieval. p. 336. http://doi.acm.org/10.1145/312624.312773.

Ruecker, S., Homich, E., and Sinclair, S. (2005). "Multi-level Document Visualization." *Visible Language*, *39*(1), 33–42.

Ruecker, S., Lewcio, M., Plouffe, M., and Wynne, M. (2006). "I never forget a face: a rich-prospect image browser for conferences." Paper presented at the Society for Digital Humanities (SDH/SEMI) conference. York University, Toronto. May 29–31, 2006.

Ruecker, S., Radzikowska, M., Michura, P., Fiorentino, C., and Clement, T. (2008). "Visualizing Repetition in Text." Reassembling the Disassembled Book: Symposium of the Congress of the Humanities and Social Sciences, University of Saskatchewan, May 2007. Brent Nelson (ed.), Special Issue of *CH Working Papers*. August 2008.

Ruecker, S., Radzikowska, M., and Sinclair, S. (2009). "Designing Data Mining Droplets: New Interface Objects for the Humanities Scholar." *Digital Humanities Quarterly*. *3*(3).

Ruecker, S. and Liepert, S. (2006). "Taking Mendeleyev's Correspondence Course: Interface Design Lessons from the Periodic Table of the Elements." *Information Design Journal and Document Design*. *14*(3), 236–45.

Ruecker, S. and Liepert, S. (2004). "Strategies for Creating Rich Prospect in Interfaces." Paper presented at the Joint International Conference of the Association for Literary and Linguistic Computing (ALLC) and the Association for Computers and the Humanities (ACH). Göteborg, Sweden. June 11–16, 2004.

Sanders, J.T. (1997). "An ontology of affordances." *Ecological Psychology*. *9*(1), 97–112.

Shipman III, F.M., Furuta, R., Brenner, D., Chung, C.C., and Hsieh, H.W. (2000). "Guided paths through Web-based collections: Design, experiences, and adaptations." *Journal of the American Society for Information Science*. *51*(3), 260–72. http://www3.interscience.wiley.com/cgi-bin/issuetoc?ID=69501275

Shiri, A., Ruecker, S., Fiorentino, C., Stafford, A., Bouchard, M., and Bieber, M. "Designing a Semantically Rich Visual Interface for Cultural Digital libraries Using the UNESCO Multilingual Thesaurus." Paper presented at Cultural Attitudes Toward Technology and Education. Vancouver, BC: University of British Columbia. June 15–18, 2010.

Shneiderman, B., Kang, H., Kules, B., Plaisant, C., Rose, A., and Rucheir, R. (2002). PhotoFinder Project. http://www.cs.umd.edu/hcil/photolib/

Shneiderman, B., Williamson, C. and Ahlberg, C. (1992). "Dynamic Queries: Database Searching by Direct Manipulation." *Proceedings of the SIGCHI conference on human factors in computing systems*, pp. 669–70. http://doi.acm.org/10.1145/142750.143082. [Accessed: March 10, 2006.]

Sinclair, S. and Ruecker, S. (2006). "The Digital Play Book: An Environment for Interacting with Play Scripts." *Canadian Theatre Review*. *127*, 38–41.

Sinclair, S., Ruecker, S., Gabriele, S., and Sapp, A. (2006). "Digital Scripts on a Virtual Stage: The Design of New Online Tools for Drama Students." *Proceedings of the Fifth IASTED International Conference on Web-Based Education (WBE 2006)*. (Ed.) V. Uskov. ACTA Press. Puerto Vallarta, Mexico. Jan 23–25, 2006, pp. 155–59.

Sless, D. (2004). "Designing Public Documents." *Information Design Journal + Document Design. 12*(1), 24–35.

Sless, D. and Wiseman, R. (1997). *Writing about medicines for people*. 2nd Edn. Melbourne: Communication Research Institute of Australia.

Small, D. (1996). "Navigating Large Bodies of Text", *IBM Systems Journal. 35*, 3–4.

Spamnet. (2010). http://www.cloudmark.com/en/company/about-us.html

Spiteri, L. (1998). "A Simplified Model for Facet Analysis." *Canadian Journal of Information and Library Science. 23*, 1–30. Reprinted at http://aifia.org/pg/a_simplified_model_for_facet_analysis.php

Springer, M., Dulabahn, B., Michel, P., Natanson, B., Reser, D., Woodward, D., and Zinkham, H. (2008). "For the Common Good: The Library of Congress Flickr Pilot Project." Library of Congress. http://www.loc.gov/rr/print/flickr_report_final.pdf.

Stafford, A., Shiri, A., Ruecker, S., Bouchard, M., Mehta P., Anvik, K., and Rossello, X. (2008). "Searchling: User-Centered Evaluation of a Visual Thesaurus-Enhanced Interface for Multilingual Digital Libraries." In *Research and Advanced Technology for Digital Libraries*. Lecture Notes in Computer Science. Heidelberg: Springer Berlin, pp. 117–21.

Strawson, P.F. (1959). *Individuals*. London: Methuen.

Stroulia, E. and Arazy, O. (2007). "Wiki User Contribution." *IBM CASCON 2007*. Toronto, Ontario.

Stubblefield, W.A. (1998). "Patterns of Change in Design Metaphor: A Case Study." *Conference proceedings on Human factors in computing systems*. Los Angeles, CA, USA, pp. 73–80. http://www.acm.org/pubs/citations/proceedings/chi/274644/p73-stubblefield/

Taylor, R., Boulanger, P., and Olivier, P. (2009). "Creating dream.Medusa to Encourage Dialogue in Performance." In *Proceedings of the 10th international Symposium on Smart Graphics* (Salamanca, Spain, May 28–30, 2009). A. Butz, B. Fisher, M. Christie, A. Krüger, P. Olivier, and R. Therón (eds). *Lecture Notes In Computer Science*, vol. 5531. Springer-Verlag, Berlin, Heidelberg, pp. 275–78. DOI= http://dx.doi.org.login.ezproxy.library.ualberta.ca/10.1007/978–3-642–02115–2_24.

Terras, M. (2010). "Present, Not Voting: Digital Humanities in the Panopticon." Closing Plenary lecture, Digital Humanities 2010. University College London, July 2010. Plenary text available, recording available at www.arts-humanities.net.

Tractinsky, N. (1997). "Aesthetics and apparent usability: empirically assessing cultural and methodological issues." *Proceedings of CHI'97*. NY: ACM Press, 115–22.

Tufte, E.R. (1990). *Envisioning Information*. Cheshire, Connecticut: Graphics Press LLC.

Turvey, M.T. and Shaw, R.S. (1979). "The primacy of perceiving: An ecological reformulation of perception for understanding memory." In L.G. Nilsson (ed.), *Perspectives on memory research*. Hillsdale, NJ: Erlbaum.

Udsen, L.E. and Jørgensen, A.H. (2005). "The aesthetic turn: unravelling recent aesthetic approaches to human-computer interaction." *Digital Creativity*. *16*(4), 205–16.

Ullman, S. (1980). "Against direct perception." *Behavioral and Brain Sciences*. *3*, 373–81.

Unsworth, J. (2005). "New methods for humanities research." 2005 Lyman Award Lecture. Available at: http://www3.isrl.uiuc.edu/~unsworth/lyman.htm.

Van der Kamp, J., Savelsbergh, G.J.P. and Rosengren, K.S. (2001). "The separation of action and perception and the issue of affordances." *Ecological Psychology*. *2*(427), 167–72.

Van Leeuwen, C. and Stins, J. (1994). "Perceivable information or – the happy marriage between ecological psychology and gestalt." *Philosophical Psychology*. *2*(772), 267–85.

Vicente, K.J. (2002). "Ecological Interface Design: Progress and Challenges." *Human Factors*. *44*(1), 62–78. http://web2.infotrac-custom.com/pdfserve/get_item/1/Sf006d5w4 _1/SB389_01.pdf

Vinson, N.G. (1999). "Design guidelines for landmarks to support navigation in virtual environments." *Proceedings of the CHI 99 conference on human factors in computing systems: the CHI is the limit*. http://www.acm.org/pubs/citations/proceedings/chi/302979/p278–vinson/

Vygotsky, L.S. (1978). *Mind in society: the development of higher psychological processes*. Cambridge, MA: Harvard University Press.

Warren, W.H., Jr. (1984). "Perceiving affordances: visual guidance of stair climbing." *Journal of Experimental Psychology*. *10*(5), 683–703.

Wexelblat, A. and Maes, P. (1999). "Footprints: History-Rich Tools for Information Foraging." *Proceedings of the CHI 99 conference on Human factors in computing systems: the CHI is the limit*. Pittsburgh, PA USA, pp. 270–277. http://doi.acm.org/10.1145/302979.303060

Winograd, T. and Flores, F. (1986). *Understanding computers and cognition: a new foundation for design*. Norwood, NJ: Ablex Pub. Corp.

Wyche, S.P., Medynskiy, E., and Grinter, R.E. (2007). "Exploring Large Displays in American Megachurches." Work-in-progress, Extended Abstracts, Proc. ACM SIGCHI Conf. on Human Factors in Computing Systems (CHI '07), San Jose, CA, pp. 2771–76.

Index